The Impossible Dream 1967 Red Sox: Birth of Red Sox Nation

About The Author

Herb Crehan, a recognized authority on Boston baseball history and the publisher of *www.bostonbaseballhistory.com*, is in his 21st season as a contributing writer for the Boston Red Sox. He has written well over 125 feature articles for the team's official program. Crehan speaks extensively on Boston baseball history, including appearances at the National Baseball Hall of Fame in Cooperstown, NY, WBZ radio, NPR's "All Things Considered," *Forbes*.com, and numerous Society of Baseball Research (SABR) meetings.

Books by Herb Crehan

LIGHTNING IN A BOTTLE: The Sox of '67, Branden Publications, Boston, MA—1992

Red Sox Heroes of Yesteryear, Rounder Books, Cambridge, MA—2005

Books as a Contributing Author

Boston Red Sox-100 Years—The Official Retrospective, The Sporting News, St. Louis, MO—2001

The Yankees vs. Red Sox Reader, Carroll & Graf Publishers, New York, NY—2005

'75 The Red Sox Team That Saved Baseball, Rounder Books, Cambridge, MA—2005

The 1967 Impossible Dream Red Sox, Rounder Books, Cambridge, MA—2007

Red Sox Baseball in the Days of Ike and Elvis, American Society of Baseball Research, Phoenix, AZ—2012

Magazine Articles

Boston Baseball (1992-1995)

Red Sox Magazine (1996-present)

SABR: The Baseball Research Journal

Website—*bostonbaseballhistory.com* (Jan 2013), Publisher

To John

an all-star fan

The Impossible Dream
1967 Red Sox: Birth of
Red Sox Nation

Herb Crehan

Herb Crehan

SUMMER
GAME
BOOKS

ISBN: 978-1-938545-68-9 (pbk)
ISBN: 978-1-938545-69-6 (ebook)

Portions of this book were published in 1992 by Branden Books under the title *Lightning in a Bottle.*

For permission requests, and for information regarding bulk purchases or additional distribution, write to the publisher at

info@summergamebooks.com

or to

Summer Game Books
Attn: Walter Friedman
PO Box 818
South Orange, NJ 07079

All photographs in the book used with the permission of the Boston Red Sox.

Dedication

This book is dedicated to James W. Ryan who was my mentor and dear friend. If it hadn't been for Jim's help with LIGHTNING IN A BOTTLE: The Sox of '67, *I would never have written a single word for publication.*

H.F.C.

Acknowledgments

I am an average Red Sox fan sitting out in section 10 enjoying the game that I love. Dick Johnson, curator of the Sports Museum of New England once referred to me as "everyfan," and I consider that the ultimate compliment. Because I am not a baseball writer by profession and I have no training in the field, I am especially indebted to many people.

First and foremost I want to thank my wife, the Lovely Janet Salsman, who has proofread and improved everything I have ever written. I want to thank the Red Sox organization and especially Debbie Matson who is a great editor and an even better person, the late Dick Bresciani, Pam (Ganley) Nenn, and Gordon Edes.

It is essential to thank the members of 1967 Boston Red Sox and their extended family that have given generously of their time: Mike Andrews, Gary Bell, Dennis Bennett, Bucky Brandon, Billy & Richie Conigliaro, Bobby Doerr, Russ Gibson, Ken Harrelson, Dalton Jones, Jim Lonborg, Dan Osinski, Rico Petrocelli, Billy Rohr, Mike Ryan, Jose Santiago, George Scott, Reggie Smith, Lee Stange, Gary Waslewski, Dick Williams, Jose Tartabull, George Thomas, and Carl Yastrzemski.

Each player interview was different and all of the memories were unique, but every player emphasized how much they loved the Boston fans. And I owe a special thank you to Jim Lonborg for writing the foreword to this book.

I also want to thank Walt Friedman, publisher of *Summer Game Books*, for his help in bringing this book to fruition and for his commitment to publishing baseball books.

Over the years many people have been helpful and encouraging and that would include Dick Johnson of the Sports Museum of New England, Saul Wisnia, Bill Nowlin, Kevin McNamara, and all of my colleagues at the Boston and Rhode Island chapters of SABR. If I have forgotten anyone that deserves to be acknowledged here please accept my apologies and heartfelt thanks.

It is important that I acknowledge and thank my daughters Kerry Crehan Dunnell and Alison Crehan Feeney, my son and namesake Herb3, my grandson Jackson Dunnell, my granddaughter Moira Feeney, and my sister Ann Crehan Curley for their love and support.

Finally, to any of you who taken the time to tell me you enjoyed my writing, thanks so very much. You are the reason I write about baseball.

Contents

1967 AL Cy Young Award winner Jim Lonborg.

Foreword

by Jim Lonborg

How is it possible that 50 years have passed since Rich Rollins of the Twins popped up to Rico Petrocelli, and the Red Sox completed an Impossible Dream season to go on to the World Series against the St. Louis Cardinals?

I still remember—

- Yaz chasing down a deep fly ball in Yankee Stadium in April to save Billy Rohr's near no-hitter in his first major league start;

- A mob of thousands of fans meeting us at Logan Airport in July after coming home with a ten-game winning streak;

- The ghastly sound of Jack Hamilton's high, inside pitch hitting Tony Conigliaro in the head;

- Jose Tartabull throwing out Ken Berry in late August at Comiskey Park in Chicago with a great catch and tag by Elston Howard at home plate;

- The joy filling Fenway Park as the fans celebrated our pennant-winning victory over the Twins on the last day of the 1967 season;

- And most especially, the tears of happiness streaming down the face of our owner, Tom Yawkey, as I handed him the game-winning baseball hours after the fans had left Fenway Park to celebrate the great Red Sox victory.

Herb Crehan's retrospective on the 1967 Impossible Dream season will help you to remember all of these moments and many, many more. Enjoy!

James R. Lonborg
Scituate, MA
July, 2016

The Impossible Dream
1967 Red Sox: Birth of
Red Sox Nation

Prologue

A Brief History of the Boston Red Sox

In the beginning, Boston was a baseball powerhouse. From 1871 to 1918, Boston was the undisputed baseball (or "base ball" as it was frequently spelled then) capital of the world. The Boston Red Stockings were so successful in the National Association, finishing first four times between 1871 and 1875, that this first professional baseball league disbanded after the 1875 season for lack of competition!

The Boston Red Stockings–known as the Beaneaters from 1883 to 1906–were the dominant franchise of the newly-formed National league during the first 25 years of that league. Between 1876 and 1900, the Red Stockings/Beaneaters finished in first place eight times, more than any other city in the National League.

When the upstart American League was founded in 1901, the Boston Americans were a charter franchise. The Americans looked to the Beaneaters as their first source for talent, and most of their Catholic players, led by third baseman Jimmy Collins, signed with the new club.

The Americans had a new ballpark, the Huntington Avenue Grounds, their tickets were 50 cents compared to the Beaneaters' $1.00, and they had recruited a number of Boston's favorite players. It is no surprise then, that the Americans outdrew the Beaneaters by 3-to-1 over the next five years.

The Americans' popularity grew in 1903, when they defeated the National League's Pittsburgh Pirates five-games-to-three in the

1

first World Series ever played. By 1911, the Americans, who had been renamed the "Red Sox" in 1908, were so popular that they had outgrown the 10,000 fan capacity of the Huntington Avenue Grounds and construction began on a new stadium in the nearby Fenway section of Boston.

This state-of-the-art ballpark had a capacity of 24,000 when it was opened on April 20, 1912, with a game against the New York Highlanders—who were renamed the "Yankees" the following season. Naming the park was easy for owner John I. Taylor of the *Boston Globe family*. "It's in the Fenway section isn't it?" Taylor exclaimed. "Then call it Fenway Park," he ordered.

The 1912 season was a banner year for the Red Sox. The team won 105 games—still the highest win total in franchise history—and captured the American League pennant. More than 8,000 seats along the third base line towards the leftfield wall and in the right field bleachers were added to Fenway for the World Series, bringing the capacity to 32,000. The Red Sox defeated John McGraw's New York Giants four-games-to-three to complete a memorable season.

While the Red Sox were winning the hearts and minds of Boston baseball fans, the original Boston baseball team, the Beaneaters, rechristened the "Braves" in 1912, were toiling along in relative obscurity. Burdened by an antiquated stadium, South End Grounds III, and a second-division club, the Braves were outdrawn by the Red Sox by a wide margin. In 1912, the Red Sox drew an average of 7,800 fans per game at Fenway Park, while the Braves attracted fewer than 1,600 per game to the South End Grounds.

But all of this changed unexpectedly, albeit briefly, in 1914. On the fourth of July in 1914, the Braves were mired in eighth and last place in the National League. With a record of 26-40, 15 games out of first place another desultory season seemed on tap for the hapless Braves.

But then the Braves won nine out of twelve games and moved up to seventh place. Led by the pitching of Dick Rudolph and the infield play of Rabbit Maranville, the Braves won 17 of the next 20 games and leapfrogged into fourth place, 6.5 games out of first on August 8th.

When the Braves returned from a long road trip on September 6, they were tied for first place and they were the toast of the town in Boston. The Braves played the remainder of their home games at Fenway

Park beginning with a morning-afternoon doubleheader on Labor Day. The morning game drew 35,000 fans and the afternoon game attracted 39,134, for a combined record Boston attendance of over 74,000 fans in one day.

In total, the Braves won 70 of their last 89 games to finish first, 10.5 games ahead of the New York Giants. The Braves added to their legend by sweeping the heavily-favored Philadelphia Athletics in four games to win the World Championship. The 1914 Boston Braves have been known as the "Miracle Braves" for over 100 years.

The Braves' owners topped off the 1914 World Championship by constructing a new ballpark in the Allston section of Boston about one mile from Fenway Park. Braves Field opened on August 18, 1915, before more than 40,000 fans who watched the Braves defeat the St. Louis Cardinals by a score of 3-1. *Baseball Magazine* described the new park as "The World's Greatest Baseball Park." Boston was now the only American city with two new state-of-the-art ballparks.

Since the Braves grabbed all the attention in 1914, little was noted of the Red Sox acquisition of a nineteen year-old left-handed pitcher name George Herman "Babe" Ruth. Ruth had been purchased from the Baltimore Orioles of the International League that season and Babe pitched in two games for the Red Sox before being sent to Providence, RI, in the International League for more seasoning.

In 1915 the Babe was ready for the major leagues and his 18 wins for the Red Sox helped Boston to the American League pennant. Led by the outstanding outfield of Tris Speaker, Harry Hooper and Duffy Lewis, the Red Sox defeated the Philadelphia Phillies in five games for the club's third World Championship.

In 1916, the Red Sox won the American League pennant again and the pitching staff was led by Babe Ruth's 23 victories. The Red Sox defeated the Brooklyn Dodgers in five games for their third World Championship in the five seasons 1912 to 1916.

The 1918 season was shortened in deference to World War I, and the Red Sox won their sixth American League pennant in the 18 years of the league's existence with 75 wins in 126 games. Boston defeated the Chicago Cubs four-games-to-two with Babe Ruth the winning pitcher in Games One and Four.

The 1918 World Champion Boston Red Sox.

Between the 1916 and 1918 World Series, the Babe had put together a stretch of twenty-nine and two-thirds consecutive innings of shutout baseball. This scoreless streak would remain the World Series record until broken by the Yankees' Whitey Ford in 1961.

When the 1918 World Series came to an end, the Red Sox had won all five of their World Series appearances. And after dominating the National League in the nineteenth century, the 1914 Miracle Braves had added another Boston World Championship. At this point there was no disputing Boston as the world's baseball hub.

In 1919, Babe Ruth played mainly in the outfield and he shocked the baseball world with a record-setting 29 home runs. Despite this display of power, the Red Sox fell to fifth place and never really contended for the league lead.

On January 20, 1920, Red Sox owner Harry Frazee sold Babe Ruth to the New York Yankees for $125,000. Long-time Red Sox fans chuckle at the notion of a curse by the Bambino because the Sultan of Swat was delighted to perform on the larger stage of New York City. Boston was a provincial city where plays tried out for Broadway. New York City was Broadway.

At the time of the sale, the prevailing theme of the Boston newspapers was, "Good riddance to the big dope. He was a lot more trouble than he was worth."

While Ruth's departure was by far the most egregious transaction, Frazee gradually dismantled his entire World Championship team over several years. Outstanding players like Harry Hooper, Everett Scott, and Herb Pennock, among others were either sold or traded, generally to the Yankees.

Now if this book was about the highlights of the Red Sox in the 1920s and early 1930s, the reader would be at the Index by this point. The team's lowlights would take a little longer to digest, but even they were deadly predictable. The high point of this era probably occurred when Harry Frazee sold the club in 1923.

By the time of the sale, the damage to the Red Sox had already occurred. From 1920 to 1932, the Boston franchise was to finish in fifth place twice, in seventh place twice, and in eighth place (last place in those days) nine times. In that period, nine managers tried their hand at the helm, but the talent just wasn't there for any of them to succeed.

In 1932, when the Depression began to wrap its tentacles tightly around the nation's economy, only 182,000 (fool) hardy fans found their way to Fenway Park. Sadly by this time, the lovely, cozy park was beginning to deteriorate.

Bob Quinn, the new owner of the Red Sox, by all accounts had good intentions but little more money than Frazee. Times were so bad that in 1926, when the wooden bleachers in the left field corner burned to the level of the playing field, Quinn simply had his grounds-keepers rope off that section.

Just when the Red Sox's fortunes appeared to be at their darkest, a newly-minted New York City millionaire dug into his very deep pockets and came up with the right sum to purchase the Boston franchise from Quinn. The new owner was Thomas Austin Yawkey. It was February 1933 and the start of a new era: the unforgettable Yawkey Years.

No single man in Red Sox history was to have a greater effect on the team than Yawkey. He was to personally own the club for forty-four seasons. Following his death in 1976, his widow, Jean Yawkey, was the principal stockholder until her passing in 1992. And the Yawkey interest continued on though the Yawkey foundation until the sale of the team in 2002.

Yawkey had not picked up the Boston franchise to preside over its further decline. With a deep and opened purse, he acquired Lefty Grove, one of the premier lefthanded pitchers of the time.

In 1934, Yawkey plunked down the unheard of sum of $250,000 to obtain the services of Joe Cronin, the player-manager of the Washington Senators. (Cronin would become the manager the Boston Red Sox from 1935 to 1947 and then he move up to general manager of the club. Later he would become president of the American League.) The very next year, Yawkey shelled out another $150,000 for Jimmy Foxx, the Athletics' great home run hitter.

After laying out close to $1,000,000 on these and other deals, Yawkey had the personal satisfaction of seeing his troops begin to edge up in the standings. Miracle of miracles, in both 1938 and 1939 the Red Sox fought and clawed their way through their schedule to finish second behind the Yankees.

While Yawkey's millions made the Red Sox relevant again, their neighbors, the Boston Braves, were largely ignored by fans. From 1920 through 1939, the "Tribe" finished in the second division 17 times and in most years averaged fewer than 5,000 fans per game.

Recognizing that spending money on older veteran players could only take the team so far, Yawkey invested money in scouting minor leaguers and signing the best prospects available. In 1936 Yawkey had sent general manager Eddie Collins to scout the San Diego Padres in the Pacific Coast League. Collins signed Bobby Doerr, who would go on to become the greatest second baseman in Red Sox history.

But Collins liked another 17-year-old hitter even more than Doerr. This young slugger was named Theodore Samuel Williams. The Padres gave Collins an option to sign Williams at a later date and Collins signed him for the Red Sox after his 18th birthday in August, 1936.

Bobby Doerr joined the Red Sox in 1937 and Ted Williams joined him for the 1939 season. At the end of the 1939 season the Red Sox acquired a fleet center fielder named Dominic DiMaggio from the San Diego Seals and Dom broke in with the Red Sox in 1940.

And in 1940 the Red Sox acquired a young shortstop from Portland, OR, named John Paveskovich. Paveskovich would come to be known as Johnny Pesky and he became the team's starting shortstop in 1942. These four players would form the nucleus of the Boston Red Sox from 1942 to 1951.

The 1941 Red Sox finished second to the Yankees, a full 17 games behind, as Ted Williams batted .406 to become the last major league .400 hitter. In 1942 the team again finished second to the Yankees but cut the margin to eight games.

All four All-Star Red Sox players saw action during World War II, and spring training in 1946 at Sarasota, Florida, was a homecoming. Johnny Pesky told me, "We had all made it back. A lot of people didn't. We were together again, and we were playing baseball."

Not only did the 1946 Red Sox live to play ball again but they represented their best team since the 1918 Boston Red Sox. The pitching staff was anchored by Dave "Boo" Ferris who won 25 games and Tex Hughson who was a 20-game winner. Veteran Rudy York at first base added power to go with Williams, Doerr, DiMaggio and Pesky.

The Teammates: Williams, DiMaggio, Doerr, and Pesky.

The 1946 Red Sox won 41 of their first 50 games, clinched the American League pennant on September 13, and ended the season with 104 victories. The Red Sox were heavily favored over the St. Louis Cardinals in the World Series but Enos Slaughter's mad-dash for home in Game Seven clinched the World Championship for the Cards.

The 1947 Red Sox finished a disappointing third, far out of the race, but the 1948 club stayed in the hunt all season and tied the Cleveland Indians for first place in the American League. All of Boston had baseball fever because the Braves had won the National League pennant and the stage was set for a subway Series. Unfortunately, Red Sox manager Joe McCarthy played a hunch and started journeyman pitcher Denny Galehouse in the one-game playoff with the Indians, and the Red Sox lost 8-3.

If possible, the 1949 season broke more Red Sox fans' hearts than 1948. The Red Sox held a one game lead in the American League when they headed to New York for the final two games of the season. The Yankees won both games and advanced to the World Series and the Red Sox went home for the winter.

The 1950 Red Sox won 94 games, batted over .300 as a team, and still finished third in the American League, four games behind the first place Yankees. The 1951 Red Sox represented the last hurrah for Bobby Doerr, Ted Williams, Dom DiMaggio, and Johnny Pesky. But the team could only manage 87 victories and finished in third place in the American League.

Bobby Doerr developed a bad back during the 1951 season and he retired before the 1952 season at the young age of 33. Looking back at all the Red Sox close calls during his career, Bobby Doerr told me, "If we only had one more solid pitcher those years I think we would have been in the World Series several times. We never had enough pitching."

Johnny Pesky, who was traded to the Detroit Tigers in June 1952, echoed Doerr's comments about pitching. But he added, "Give the Yankees some credit. They had a very good team and it was tough to beat them."

Ted Williams played in just six games in 1952 before he left for active duty with the Marines in the Korean War. Dom DiMaggio was the only player left from the four west coast All-Stars and he finished out the 1952 season with the sixth place Red Sox. But Dom retired abruptly at the beginning of the 1953 season when new manager Lou Boudreau relegated him to the bench, replacing him in center field with the immortal Tommy Umphlett.

As the sun was setting on the Red Sox pennant chances, the Boston Braves were making plans to leave Boston. The team went to spring training in 1953 as the Boston Braves and when spring training ended they were the Milwaukee Braves. Boston's days as a two-team city had come to an end after 52 years.

Ted Williams returned from active service with the Marines in July 1953 and appeared in 37 games that season. Boudreau's "youth movement" produced a fourth place finish, which became the norm for four seasons.

While the Red Sox were never in the pennant race during the 1950's, their outfield of Ted Williams in left field, Jimmy Piersall in center field, and Jackie Jensen in right field was among the best in franchise history.

The mercurial Piersall was a fan favorite after overcoming a nervous breakdown to become an All-Star player.

The 1950s were a tempestuous time for Ted Williams. He missed the company of Pesky and DiMaggio and especially the calming influence of Bobby Doerr. At various times Ted made an obscene gesture at Boston fans, spit in the direction of the Fenway Park press box, and in a fit of anger, had a bat sail into the seats by the Boston dugout, hitting Joe Cronin's housekeeper in the forehead.

The Red Sox improved to third place in 1957, and Ted Williams hit .388 at age 38. His average fell to .328 the following year but that was good enough to win the American League batting title as the Sox held on to third place. At age 39, Williams was the oldest player to win a league batting title.

In 1959, the Red Sox became the 16th and last major league team to add an African American player when shortstop Pumpsie Green joined the club in July. The team's reputation for a lack of sensitivity on racial matters would haunt the Red Sox for decades to come.

That season Ted Williams hit only .254 and owner Tom Yawkey urged him to retire before he damaged his legacy. Stubborn to the end, Williams insisted on playing in 1960 at age 41. Ted defied the odds and the Gods, batting .316 in his final season. And he homered in last major league at-bat for good measure!

Despite the mediocrity of the Red Sox teams of the 1950's, attendance at Fenway Park remained strong. On average, the club drew in excess of a million fans per year and attendance exceeded the American League average in eight of the ten years. This was partly due to wishful thinking for a contending team, a little bit because of the departure of the Braves, but mostly because Bostonians and New Englanders love baseball.

Ted Williams' retirement left a tremendous void in the Boston baseball scene. For all, or parts of four decades, Ted had dominated the Boston sports pages. No professional athlete, including Babe Ruth during his time with the Red Sox, had captured fans' attention the way that Ted had.

No one would ever replace Ted Williams but it fell to 21 year-old rookie Carl Michael Yastrzemski to take Ted's position in left field. The son of a potato farmer from Long Island, Yaz had signed with the Red Sox in 1958 after one year at Notre Dame, and he spent two seasons in the Red Sox minor league system where he batted well over .300 both years.

Yaz was five inches shorter than Williams and thirty or so pounds lighter and any way you looked at it he suffered in comparison to Ted. Yaz had been gifted with an athlete's eyehand coordination and balance; Williams had borrowed God's own swing and improved upon it. Williams was lithe and natural; Yaz was compact and choppy.

It was not of his making but Yaz immediately had to deal with a media pack determined to fill the Williams' void and eager to do it under the glare of TV lights. While he shared intensity, a work ethic, and a total dedication to the game with Williams, Yaz had a far more difficult struggle in the beginning of his career.

At one point early on, an SOS was dispatched to Williams who generously returned to tutor his heir apparent. Ted scrutinized Yaz's batting style, provided him with a few hitting tips, urged one and all to be patient with the budding star and returned without a backward glance to his favorite pastime: salmon fishing. Yaz progressed to .296 in 1962 and earned his initial batting crown in 1963 with an average of .321.

Other than watching Yaz developing into an All Star there was little reason to follow the Red Sox from 1961 to 1963. The 1961 Red Sox finished sixth, 33 games behind the first-place Yankees and attendance at Fenway fell to 850,000. Things deteriorated further in 1962, as the team fell to eighth place in the American League and attendance dropped to 733,000.

In 1963, Boston-favorite Johnny Pesky was named to manage the Red Sox and the team stayed within 10 games of first place through late July. A contending team boosted attendance to 943,000 but when no moves were made at the July 31st trading deadline the club went into free-fall, ending up in seventh place.

As in past years, the gradual emergence of future stars produced by the minor league system served to provide the fans with some bright spots through some overcast years. Local boy Tony Conigliaro burst upon the Red Sox scene as a 19-year-old rookie in 1964, taking the town by storm with a batting average of .290 and twenty-four home runs.

Rico Petrocelli, making his debut in 1965, quickly laid claim to the "shortstop of the future" role. Pitcher Jim Lonborg joined the club that same year, and while his freshman record of 9-17 was disappointing, there was no question about the promise of the righty's arm and his native intelligence. Rico told me later, "Guys like me, Lonnie [Jim Lonborg] and Dalton [Jones] had no business playing in the big leagues at that point. But there was no one else and it served us well later."

In 1966, two additional future stars appeared in Boston flannels. George Scott displayed a golden touch around first base and contributed twenty-seven home runs to the cause. Joe Foy showed himself to be a steady third baseman as a rookie, chipping in with fifteen home runs and sixty-three RBI.

In that same year, Jose Santiago and John Wyatt were acquired from Kansas City to give additional strength to the starting pitching rotation and bullpen, respectively. The acquisition of Lee Stange from Cleveland during the 1966 season provided further stability to a struggling corps of starting pitchers.

As the 1966 season drew to a close, there was some reason for optimism about the future. It was mostly based on the fact that a nucleus of regulars was beginning to take shape as a team, and further top prospects were on the way to Boston from the Toronto farm club. It could be said that the team had bottomed out in 1966 and now was headed for much higher rungs on the league's ladder of success.

During the off-season the Red Sox hired 37-year-old Dick Williams, who had managed their Toronto farm team to consecutive Calder Cup championships, to manage the team in 1967. In his introductory press conference, Williams made it clear that he expected his team to improve and to play hard.

There was, however, no getting around the fact that the Red Sox had finished ninth in 1966, twenty-six games out of first place. Moreover, fans were staying away in droves and Fenway Park was beginning to look a little ragged around the edges. And with each passing season owner Tom Yawkey seemed to be a little later coming north from his South Carolina winter home.

Opening Day at Fenway Park is close to a state holiday. Fans that rarely appear during the balance of the season make it a point to be seen at Fenway on Opening Day. And 1967 marked the 97th consecutive year of professional baseball in Boston, more than any other city in the US. History is very important in Boston.

Many Red Sox fans in 1967 were third generation Boston baseball fans, and they had heard tales of Red Sox glory from their fathers and grandfathers. But for fans under the age of 25, the Red Sox in the World Series was the stuff of old newsreels.

On Opening Day the morning edition of *The Boston Globe* reminded fans that all they had to do to get the score of the Red Sox game was to call Avenue 2-2400 anytime between 1:30 pm and 1:30 am. Directly below was an ad from the Red Sox pointing out that "**Being there is <u>twice</u> the fun**," and reminding fans that there are still plenty of tickets available.

Boston sports fans were more interested in reading the story of the Boston Celtics loss to the Philadelphia 76ers by a score of 140-116. The loss eliminated the Celtics from the playoffs and snapped their string of eight straight World Championships.

No one was surprised when the April opener was postponed by a blast of artic air. Weather in Boston in April is very unpredictable. And only 8,234 fans appeared for the re-scheduled opener on April 12. Jim Lonborg pitched well for the home team and Red Sox fans went home happy after a 5-4 Boston win over the Chicago White Sox.

But if there was anyone in that "crowd" or even in the Red Sox dugout who thought the team would end up in the 1967 World Series, I have yet to meet him or her. Who knew, or even imagined, that the 1967 Boston Red Sox would catch lightning in a bottle!

Chapter 1

The Foundation of a Dream

March, 1967, Winter Haven, Florida

It was the bittersweet year of 1967, a half century ago in a time and place hardly remembered. A seemingly endless winter had given way to a cruel April. Americans were becoming grimly aware that the war in Vietnam was evolving inexorably into a national nightmare. Few then, however, could begin to comprehend the true cost.

Happily, on the home front, the baseball season was about to get underway with all its hype and fanfare and lofty dreams of glory to be played out on manicured diamonds across the breadth of the land. As always, the national pastime would serve as a nationwide panacea to shield the citizens from unpleasantness. In most minds, the boys of summer promptly took precedence over the boys of battle.

But in Boston, as on so many recent Opening Days, there was little joy, less to shout about and lots of lethargy. It is hard for fans under the age of 55 to appreciate the depth of cynicism surrounding the 1967 Red Sox. It had been 21 years since the team's last appearance in a World Series and the Red Sox hadn't finished in the first division since 1958.

When the Boston Red Sox spring training camp opened in Winter Haven, Florida, in late-February 1967, nobody was talking about an American League pennant or humming Broadway show tunes in the team's honor. The 1966 Red Sox had finished in ninth place and the team had lost a total of 190 games over the past two seasons. Las Vegas oddsmaker Jimmy "The Greek" Snyder thought so little of the team's chances that he rated them as 100-1 underdogs in the 1967 American League pennant race.

Baseball has always been the number one passion among New England sports fans. But in 1966 the Red Sox had averaged only about 10,000 fans per game, and in 1965 attendance at Fenway Park had totaled just 652,201.

New England sports fans followed stories from the Red Sox training camp as a harbinger of spring, but they were more excited about the Boston Celtics who were trying to extend their streak of eight straight World Championships, and the Boston Bruins who featured a rookie defenseman by the name of Bobby Orr.

But Red Sox rookie manager, Dick Williams, didn't share in the apathy surrounding the 1967 Red Sox. "I thought we would be a pretty decent team," Williams told me in a 2006 interview prior to his induction to the Red Sox Hall of Fame. Williams, who passed away in 2011 at the age of 82, quickly added, "I never thought for a minute that we would end up winning the American League pennant and playing in the seventh game of the World Series, but I knew we had some good young talent."

Dick Williams had played for thirteen seasons in the major leagues and finished his career with the Red Sox in 1964. As a younger player, Williams was a highly regarded prospect who broke in with the powerful Brooklyn Dodgers in 1951. The following season he suffered a three-way shoulder separation that turned a potential All-Star into a well-traveled big league jack-of-all-trades overnight.

Reflecting on his 1952 injury, Williams offered, "I had to become a smarter player. I spent a lot of time studying strategy and human nature. That injury put me on track to becoming a manager."

After his 1964 season with the team, Red Sox Farm Director Neal Mahoney offered Williams a job as a player/coach for the Red Sox Triple-A farm team in Seattle. When the Seattle franchise was moved to Toronto prior to the 1965 season, Williams was named to manage the club. He led Toronto to back-to-back championship seasons, and in October 1966 he was named to manage the Boston Red Sox. The 37-year-old Williams became the youngest manager in the American League.

At the press conference announcing his appointment, Williams promised Boston fans "a hustling team." He declined to predict where the team would finish but he did promise improvement. And he left no doubt about who was in charge.

Asked if the 1967 Red Sox would have a team captain, he responded, "No, I'm the only Chief. The players are the Indians." When writers reminded Williams that Carl Yastrzemski was the incumbent captain, he answered, "We won't have one next year."

Enterprising young *Boston Globe* reporter Will McDonough made a beeline to the Yastrzemski residence in Lynnfield, Massachusetts, for a reaction. If he expected Yaz to be upset by his "demotion," McDonough must have been disappointed.

"Happy is not the right word," Yaz responded. "Relieved is a better word," he continued. "To be honest, I never wanted to be captain. Now that I'm not, I feel like a weight has been taken off my shoulders."

Asked if he remembered being nervous just before camp opened, Dick Williams answered, "I wouldn't say I was nervous, because I knew I could do the job. But I was certainly apprehensive." The rookie big league manager added, "I had never run a big league camp before. I had run two spring camps for Toronto but that's the minor leagues and it's different.

"I was fortunate that I had a great coaching staff," Williams emphasized. "They were a big help organizing the camp. Eddie ["Pop"] Popowski had been in the organization for many years and he had managed most of our players in the minors.

"Bobby Doerr was just great and he had the respect of everyone," Williams continued, referring to the Hall of Fame second baseman. "And Al Lakeman had been on the staff the year before so he gave us some continuity. But Sal Maglie's [pitching coach] wife was critically ill so he couldn't be there when the camp opened."

Williams shook his head when he considered the number of coaches, instructors and the sophisticated equipment on hand at spring training in the 21st century. "I'm happy for the managers and all the resources they have today. But in 1967 it was just me and my three coaches, and four when Sal was able to get down there.

"Ted Williams was supposed to help out with the hitters but he was more interested in talking to the pitchers about throwing the slider,"

Dick Williams chuckled. "Dom DiMaggio came down after the camp had opened and he did help us with the outfielders."

Dick Williams was determined to stress fundamentals with his 1967 Red Sox team. He firmly believed that attention to detail made a big difference over a 162 game season.

"I grew up in baseball with the Brooklyn Dodgers system and we were grounded in baseball fundamentals from the beginning. We used to talk about doing things the Branch Rickey [legendary Dodgers general manager and Baseball Hall of Fame member] way, 'the Dodger way.' I wanted to make sure that our players knew how to play the game the right way.

"We spent the first two and one-half days of spring training in 1967 working with the whole team on fundamentals. We started out with the on-deck circle and worked our way around the infield. I was amazed that most of our players didn't know what the double line down the first base line meant," Williams marveled.

"We stopped going over the fundamentals when we finished with third base. With Carl Yastrzemski in left field and Tony Conigliaro in right, I figured the outfield was pretty well taken care of."

When Dick Williams addressed his twenty-four pitchers and four catchers on the first day of spring training, he made it clear that things would be different at the 1967 camp. Williams emphasized that workouts would be tightly organized and that drills would be scheduled down to the minute. But apparently pitchers Dennis Bennett and Bob Sadowski didn't get the message. The two roommates arrived twenty-five minutes late on the third day of camp, and then blamed the hotel switchboard operator for not placing their wake-up call.

"I was furious," Williams recalled. "But I knew how to solve it. I went into my office and called the switchboard operator at the Holiday Inn [Red Sox spring training headquarters]. I told her to call all the players at 7 AM every morning. Since workouts began at 10 [AM], I knew everyone would be on time. Then I called the two of them [Bennett and Sadowski] into my office and told them, 'This will not happen again!'"

Dick Williams declined to discuss the Bennett-Sadowski incident at his daily press conference, but he did tell reporters that he planned to let rookie Tony Horton battle incumbent George Scott for the regular first base position. He added that he would try Scott in the outfield and other infield positions during the spring. As spring training went on, Williams and Scott would spar on a number of issues, including where George would play and his on-going battle to get down to a reasonable playing weight.

"George didn't like my moving him around the field that spring," Dick Williams remembered clearly. "What he didn't realize was that I considered him to be one of our best athletes and I knew he could play almost anywhere. Horton could only play first base and we needed to see what he could do. I was pretty sure that the Boomer [Scott] would be our everyday first baseman, but the spring is when you work those things out," he emphasized.

Dick Williams was determined to use every minute in spring training camp productively. With that in mind, he set up volleyball net in foul territory down the leftfield line so the pitchers could get in some additional conditioning work.

"If the pitchers weren't throwing or running I wanted them to be active playing volleyball. Usually pitchers stand around in the outfield going through the motions of shagging fly balls. But mostly they just stood around talking, which didn't do them any good."

Pitcher Jose Santiago, who would go on to win twelve games for the 1967 Red Sox, remembers the volleyball games fondly. "Playing volleyball if we weren't working on our pitching was a lot of fun. It was boring standing around in the outfield watching the hitters bat. Like most of the guys, I had played other sports and I thought volleyball helped get us in shape," Jose remembered.

"That was Dick Williams for you," catcher Russ Gibson remarked, "always thinking. Even if no one had ever tried it before, Dick wasn't afraid to do something different." Gibson knew Williams better than most of the players. Russ had been the starting catcher, and a player-coach, under Dick Williams in Toronto in 1965 and 1966.

Another Williams' innovation was the use of videotape to help players to correct their flaws. "We may have been the first team to use videotape. If not, we were one of the first," Williams said. "And I have

AL Manager of the Year, Dick Williams.

to credit Dick O'Connell [Red Sox general manager] for getting me everything I needed to do my job. If I needed something Dick made sure I got it.

"When I played for the Red Sox [1963-1964], Johnny Pesky was the manager. He was a good manager and a terrific guy. But his general manager [Mike "Pinky" Higgins] didn't back him up; help him to do his job. I was very fortunate to have Dick O'Connell. He helped me any way he could," Williams declared emphatically.

In addition to dealing with eight-straight losing seasons, the Red Sox were battling their reputation as a racist organization. They had to live with the fact that they were the last major league team to add an African-American player and the team was finding it difficult to change their image.

While there is no evidence to suggest that longtime owner Tom Yawkey was personally a racist, he was unenlightened in his stewardship of the club. And he did show very poor judgment in his selection of general managers over the years.

Mike "Pinky" Higgins, who was a Yawkey drinking buddy and an avowed racist, had managed the team from 1955 through 1959, when Yawkey fired him in July 1959. Then Yawkey turned around and inexplicably rehired him as manager in June 1960 and then promoted Higgins to the post of Executive VP of Baseball in 1963.

When Higgins was fired in September 1965, he was replaced by O'Connell who had been with the Red Sox organization since 1946. O'Connell showed that he was color-blind through his transactions before and during the 1967 season. When he was hired as general manager of the Red Sox he told the media, "I don't care what color a player is as long as he can play. If he is any good I want to sign him."

Dick Williams acknowledged that he had a unique advantage when it came to evaluating his 1967 team: he had either played with or managed most of the players. "I had managed Joe Foy, Reggie Smith, Mike Andrews, Gibby [Russ Gibson], and others at Toronto. And I had played with guys like Yaz and Dalton Jones. I roomed with Tony Conigliaro's suitcase in my last year [1964]," Williams chuckled. "So I knew what most of the guys could do.

"And I knew I could count on Yaz for leadership on the field. I was aware that he never really wanted to be captain. But even *I* didn't expect the kind of year he had in 1967. He had as good a year as any ballplayer I have ever seen," Williams insisted.

Carl Yastrzemski could prepare for the 1967 season without worrying about the ambiguous duties of a team captain. More importantly, Yaz reported to camp in the best shape of his professional baseball career. During his first six seasons in the big leagues he had won an American League batting title and he had achieved All-Star status three times. Now, at age 27, he appeared ready to take his place as one of the elite players in the game.

"One of the big differences in 1967," Yaz told me 45 years later, "is that I was able to work out the preceding winter. In earlier years, I was finishing up my college work in the off-season. But I had completed my degree at Merrimack College so I had time to focus on my conditioning. I reported to spring training in the best shape I had ever been in."

The previous winter Yaz had traveled regularly from his home in Lynnfield to the Colonial Resort in Wakefield, Massachusetts, working out under the direction of physical therapist Gene Berde. "Gene worked with me all winter. He let me know that he didn't think I was in great shape when we first started," Yaz recalled. "He really worked me hard and it paid off."

The intensive regimen improved his stamina and made Yaz stronger at the plate. "I had good spring training. I noticed right away that I had more power. The ball was going another thirty or forty feet. That's when I decided to become a pull hitter," he said. "I felt I could help the ball club more by being a power hitter, so I made the transition in hitting style," Yaz remembered.

Dick Williams knew that Yaz would be his every-day left fielder, and he felt the same way about twenty-two-year-old right fielder Tony Conigliaro. When Williams was introduced to the media the previous October he was asked to identify his regular players. The first name he mentioned was Yaz, and the second was Tony C. "I knew what Tony could do," Williams acknowledges, "And I wanted his bat in the lineup every day. There was never any question of who my right fielder would be."

Local boy Conigliaro was beginning his fourth season with the Boston Red Sox. His right-handed swing was seemingly tailor-made for Fenway Park, and he had topped the American League with 32 home runs in 1965. Tony got off to a great start in March 1967, homering in the Grapefruit League season opener in Sarasota, Florida, against the Chicago White Sox. Then four days later, when the White Sox came to Winter Haven, he greeted them with a home run and two doubles.

But the Red Sox and Tony got a scare on March 18 when teammate John Wyatt drilled him in the left shoulder with a batting practice fastball. He was flown back to Boston where x-rays showed a slight crack of the shoulder. It was the fifth time in four years with the Red Sox that Tony had a bone broken by a pitched ball. Fortunately, the injury was not serious. Conigliaro returned to Florida and resumed his slugging ways.

Dick Williams didn't want a team captain, but he did want someone to take charge of the infield. And he recognized that Rico Petrocelli, who was beginning his third season as the regular shortstop, had the potential to fill that role. Williams told the writers, "This I believe would be a perfect job for Rico. He's an intelligent ballplayer and I want him to have some authority out there. So I told him that I want him to take over in tight spots."

Williams was a tough disciplinarian but he also was an astute judge of talent. And he understood that some players needed special handling. He and coach Eddie Popowski went out of their way in spring training to make sure that Rico was comfortable.

Looking back, Rico remembered how much being selected as "captain of the infield" meant to him. "Dick showed a lot of confidence in me, and gave me a lot of responsibility. It really meant a lot to me. For the first time," Rico said, "I felt like a big leaguer, like I really belonged out there."

Another infielder that Williams singled out as a likely regular was third baseman Joe Foy. Foy had been a key player for Williams in Toronto in 1965, when Joe was named the Most Valuable Player of the International League. After a slow start as a rookie with the Red Sox in 1966, he came on strong in the second half and led the team in runs scored.

Dick Williams was watching Foy's weight almost as carefully as he was watching George Scott on the scales. Foy had reported at 211 pounds and the manager wanted him to drop at least 6 pounds. Williams told reporters, "We want to avoid another slow start for Foy, and the best way to do that is to make sure he is in playing shape."

Tony Horton continued to get playing time at first base throughout the spring. Both Williams and Bobby Doerr liked his swing and the Red Sox were showcasing Horton for a possible trade. George Scott swapped off with Horton at first, spent some time at third base where he had played five games in 1966, and he made several appearances in the outfield.

Scott's outfield adventures came to an end on March 23 when the slugger knocked himself unconscious running into the right-field wall in Winter Haven. "He was out cold for one minute," trainer—and future Red Sox part-owner—Buddy LeRoux told reporters. "He moved the wall from 330 feet to 332," second baseman Mike Andrews offered.

Scott was kept overnight at Winter Haven Memorial Hospital as a precaution, but his only injury was a bruised wrist. On March 28 Dick Williams announced, "As soon as Scott is ready to play, he will go immediately to first base."

In addition to Russ Gibson and Joe Foy, there were several other candidates for spots with the 1967 Red Sox that had played for Dick Williams in Toronto. Mike Andrews was likely to take over as the regular second baseman and Reggie Smith was positioned to become the starting center fielder. Both players had excelled in Toronto, but both knew that Williams wouldn't show them any favoritism.

Mike Andrews remembered that the success in Toronto carried over to training camp in 1967. "Reggie Smith, Russ Gibson and I were all rookies in 1967, and we had won the International League championship the year before in Toronto, so we didn't think about losing. And we knew

Dick Williams hated losing. I don't think any of us thought about the second-division that spring."

Reggie Smith was twenty-one years old when he reported to training camp at the end of February. When Dick Williams looked back on 1967 he talked about Reggie Smith's athleticism. "Reggie was probably the best athlete on our team," Williams believed. "He really could do it all.

"I know when he was taking some headfirst slides in spring training games that he opened some eyes. When Mike Andrews came down with a bad back I put Reggie at second base. He was such a good athlete that I knew he could handle it."

Dalton Jones, who had spent the three previous seasons with the Red Sox, was the obvious choice as the team's backup infielder. The versatile George Thomas was slotted as a spare outfielder and to play in the infield if needed. In fact, when the writers were pressing Williams to name his regular lineup, Williams, answered "possibly George Thomas" for all nine positions.

Haverhill, Massachusetts, native Mike Ryan had caught 116 games for the Red Sox in 1966 and he was highly-regarded for his defense. It seemed clear that Ryan and Gibson would share the catching duties, leaving veteran receiver Bob Tillman for spot-duty behind the plate.

When spring training camp opened, Dick Williams' number one concern was his pitching staff. "I knew we would score runs, that we had a strong lineup. And I thought we could improve our defense. But I wasn't sure about our pitching." Echoing a time-honored refrain, he added, "You can never have enough pitching."

One pitcher that Williams was counting on was right-hander Jim Lonborg, who had shown lots of promise during his first two seasons with the club. "Lonborg was one player who I had never seen. I didn't play with him and I didn't manage him. But when I got a look at him that spring I knew he would help us. He had good stuff and he was a hard worker," Williams observed.

Lonborg was determined to have a good year in 1967. He had pitched winter ball in Venezuela and he reported to camp in great shape. He remembers how organized the camp was that spring. "Dick [Williams] was very purposeful. If we weren't throwing or running wind sprints, he had us playing volleyball. He kept us focused all season long."

Lonborg won his third game in three decisions on March 20, and he was emerging as the ace of the staff. He told reporters, "I want to be the Opening Day pitcher. It would be quite an honor and it would mean the manager thinks I'm the best on the club." He added, "I'd like to pitch between 260 and 270 innings this season."

Williams made it clear to his players and the media that he had no patience with sore-armed pitchers. In mid-March he told writers that he intended to carry "three catchers, six outfielders, seven infielders, and only healthy pitchers." At that time he listed Lonborg, Santiago, Darrell Brandon, Lee Stange, and Hank Fisher as his likely starters.

One unheralded rookie pitcher who was making an impression was skinny, 21-year-old Billy Rohr. The lefthander made several strong appearances in exhibition games and appeared likely to pitch his way onto the roster. Veteran pitchers Dan Osinski and Don McMahon, along with young lefthander Bill Landis, were the leading candidates for middle relief.

John Wyatt was a lock to close games for the Red Sox if he could ever find his way out of Dick Williams' rather large doghouse. Hitting Tony Conigliaro in batting practice had brought down his manager's wrath, and he was still working his way back into Dick Williams' good graces.

The Boston Red Sox finished their spring exhibition games with a record of fourteen wins and thirteen losses. And while they had tried their manger's patience at times with fundamental missteps, in general Williams was pleased with his team. "I liked the way we had come together as a unit. As the spring went on I saw players pulling together more and more. That had been missing from other Red Sox teams," he emphasized.

Veteran *Boston Globe* columnist Harold Kaese penned an upbeat assessment of Williams and his ball club in late March. "Williams is away to a good, though somewhat controversial start," Kaese told readers. "The Red Sox are probably playing more inside baseball now than they have for any manager since Bill Carrigan [Red Sox manager from 1913-

Rico Petrocelli squeezes the last out of the 1967 season.

1916 and 1927-29]. Williams has his players doing more than swinging bats. He has them running, bunting and thinking."

As spring training came to an end, the Boston writers pressured Dick Williams for his prediction on the upcoming season. Williams finally offered one of his most-remembered quotes: "We will win more than we lose." For a club that had lost ninety games the year before that seemed like a very optimistic forecast.

The 1967 Boston Red Sox did indeed win more games than they lost. But they did so much more than that. They captured the hearts and minds of New England fans and they restored a regional pride in the Boston Red Sox. *And they built the foundation that Red Sox Nation rests upon today!*

Chapter 2

Russ Gibson Catches the Season's First Magic

Boston Red Sox vs. New York Yankees, Friday, April 14, 1967

Russ Gibson, one of the most heralded schoolboy stars in the history of sports-crazed Fall River, Massachusetts, played his first major league game when the Red Sox met the Yankees in New York. It was the third game of the season for the Red Sox but the home opener for the Yankees, who sent their ace pitcher, Whitey Ford, to the mound to ensure an initial victory before the home crowd of some 14,375. Gibson, who had labored in the Red Sox minor league system for a decade as a catcher, was teamed with Billy Rohr, a 21-year-old rookie lefty, who was also appearing in his first major league game. To Gibson, then age 27, the years of striving were about to pay off by placing him within one out of catching a no-hitter in his major league debut.

Friday, April 14, 1967, dawned sharp and clear in New York City. The sun's ray fought with the lingering cold of winter to produce a typical spring baseball day in the Northeast.

The weather may have been typical but the events of the day would be anything but. For rookie catcher Russ Gibson and rookie pitcher Billy Rohr just waking up in the Biltmore Hotel in Manhattan was an adventure. The fact that they would both be making their major league debut at Yankee Stadium that afternoon seemed quite implausible.

Gibson had learned late Thursday that he was going to catch for Rohr against the Yankees shortly after manager Dick Williams finished castigating the team in the clubhouse for its 8-5 loss to Chicago. Williams was particularly upset because his players had committed five errors and given up five unearned runs in the top of the ninth. Third baseman Joe Foy caught a lot of the steam for his two errors. The loss put the Red Sox at 1-1 for the early season.

"Dick came over to me after the meeting and told me that I was going to catch the next day. This was after Mike Ryan had caught for the team in the first two games against Chicago. The next day meant the Yankees in New York. I could only say, 'Great!' The fact was that I couldn't wait to get into the lineup and see major league action."

Actually Gibson was glad that Williams hadn't started him in Boston because the few days off helped to settle him down and shake off any nervousness about playing in the majors.

"Dick was smart that way, the way he handled his players. He had a lot of confidence in me. Knew how I played and I had all that experience from the minors, but still he let me unwind by sitting out our first two games. To tell you the truth, I was glad that I didn't catch the opener at Fenway. With all the hometown crowd, the family and friends who'd be up from Fall River; I'd probably have been very nervous. Yeh, I really was glad."

For Russ Gibson, who was born in Fall River, MA, on May 26, 1939, and grew up in that old New England blue collar city, it was a dream that seemed impossible just two short years earlier. Not that he lacked the tools to do the job behind the plate at the major league level. That was never in doubt. Sure you would like to see a little quicker bat and a bit more power. But Russ Gibson could call a game with any of them and he could handle pitchers. That was a given.

Two years earlier in 1965, Gibson had been a victim of the Red Sox depth chart at catcher. He was invited to spring training with the major league club coming off an outstanding year at the Red Sox Triple-A club in Seattle. He had batted a solid .276 with 17 home runs and anchored a young pitching staff for 130 games behind the plate. After eight years of riding buses in the bushes, Gibson was more than ready for "the show."

The newly-married Gibson put on a show of his own in Scottsdale, AZ. Still a few months shy of his 26th birthday, he was in his prime and he showed it with his defensive ability and with his bat. Surely the top brass on Jersey Street (now Yawkey Way) couldn't ignore his performance.

But ignore it they did. Six-foot-four Bob Tillman had batted .278 in 131 games for the Red Sox the year before and he was penciled in at number one before spring training even started. Mike Ryan, another local boy, from Haverhill, Massachusetts, was two years younger than Gibson, a little bigger than he, and the brass wanted to see what he could do in the big leagues. Besides, the new manager in Toronto, Dick Williams, was only 35-years-old and he could benefit from the presence of a seasoned veteran. And if Russ Gibson was anything, he was an organization man to the core. Ryan would go north to Boston and Gibson would go farther north to Toronto.

It's a long ride from Scottsdale, AZ, to Toronto, Ontario. And it's even longer when you've just sent your new bride home alone. Home as in Fall River, Massachusetts, just an hour drive from Fenway Park, home of the Boston Red Sox. Your home team.

To get to Toronto from Scottsdale, you have to go through North Carolina, and if you're Russ Gibson you think about 1959-61 in Raleigh and Winston-Salem. As you head further north into Pennsylvania and New York you think about Corning, New York, in 1957 and York, Pennsylvania, in 1962. Certainly Toronto is a lot closer to Fenway than Seattle was in 1963 and 1964. But in April of 1965 the locals would be much more interested in hockey star Frank Mahavolich of the Toronto Maple Leafs than the arrival of journeyman catcher, Russ Gibson.

A five-day car ride gives a man a lot of time to think. Especially if you've already logged as many miles on the highway over eight years in the minors as your average Greyhound bus driver. In a very short time Gibson had gone from the dead of winter in Fall River to the false spring of Scottsdale, AZ. As the seasons reversed themselves again and he headed back to the lingering winter in Toronto, Gibson had come to a difficult conclusion.

Two years later, Gibson was standing in the lobby of the Biltmore thinking about the game with the Yankees that afternoon. He could look around and see veterans like Carl Yastrzemski, Rico Petrocelli, and Tony Conigliaro who thrived on the limelight of New York. He could look over and see fellow rookies, Mike Andrews and Reggie Smith, who had been teammates on last year's championship Toronto club. And he could see rookie manager, Dick Williams, who had been his manager and mentor in Toronto for the past two years. In some ways, Williams was the man who was most instrumental in Gibson's starting assignment that day.

When Gibson arrived in Toronto in April of 1965, he reported directly to manager Williams' office. Almost the first words out of his mouth were, "If I can't make it to the majors after eight years in the system and the spring I had, I think it's time to hang them up." Williams responded with, "Look, I'm new at this job and I need some help. I want you to stay here as a player-coach. I expect that my time will come in Boston soon and I'll do everything I can to take you with me. Take a few days off to play golf and then come back and let's get to work."

Gibson played a little golf—you can get some good drives off when the ground is still frozen—and thought it over. He came back and helped Williams and Toronto to two consecutive championships. Now he was getting ready for Opening Day in Yankee Stadium and he knew he had made the right decision.

Gibson never talked about his first game in the majors without recalling a humorous anecdote. "All those years in the minors, Corning, Lafayette, Waterloo . . . Raleigh and Winston-Salem, York and then on to Seattle and Toronto . . . no matter where we went to play, it was almost always by way of bus. Every type of bus you can imagine. Now, finally,

I'm in the big leagues, the majors, and I'm thinking that wherever the team goes, it'll be first class and by air. So what happens? When I'm told that I'm to catch the next day in New York against the Yankees, the Red Sox take a chartered bus at night to go down to the big town. Boy, what a letdown. It's 1967 and we're going to New York for their season opener and there I am back in the bus, for Pete's sake!"

When the Red Sox went out to Yankee Stadium Friday, Gibson, a husky six-footer with hands like bear paws, felt calm and confident, ready to do the job. It was his first major league start, but the Red Sox were away from home and as always puffed up to do battle with their traditional foes, the pinstriped Yankees.

"It didn't bother me that I was going to catch because we were in New York and I'd be more relaxed, at least that's what I thought until I walked into Yankee Stadium. As soon as I came out of the dugout and could see the size of the field, all I could think was, 'God, this is unbelievable!' They had all the plaques of the great Yankees . . . Ruth, Gehrig, DiMaggio, all those guys: and the size of it. And all the fans who were out for the opener. It was beautiful! Fantastic! But it's like everything else, believe me. I'm a pro and as soon as the National Anthem was over, I knew I had a job to do and looked forward to it."

Gibson knew his pitcher, Billy Rohr, would be subject to the jitters. Like Gibson, it was his first major league start. Russ, though, had ten years playing time in the minors against many top caliber players who had gone up to major league teams, so he wasn't so overawed by big leaguers and the crowd.

Rookie southpaw Billy Rohr's route to the majors was much less bumpy and had almost no U-turns. Rohr had been a high school phenomenon at Bellflower High School in Garden Grove, California. His portfolio in his senior year included three no-hit games. The Pittsburgh Pirates signed the 17-year-old Rohr for $40,000 immediately after graduation. Serious money in those days.

Rohr and Gibson took very different paths through the minors. Gibson reported directly from graduation to Corning, New York, in the New York/Pennsylvania league. He got four hits in his first two games and was told to report to Lafayette in the Midwest League. Corning wanted

Russ Gibson at 1967 Spring Training.

to use someone else as their catcher. Rohr reported to Kingsport, Tennessee, in the Appalachian League and was told that he was too valuable to pitch in games. His routine was to pitch batting practice and then watch from the stands. The Pirates were trying to hide him. The Red Sox weren't fooled. When the Pirates failed to protect him by putting him on their expanded major league roster, the Red Sox snapped him up for

$8,000. It would appear that Pittsburgh paid $32,000 to provide King-sport with a batting practice pitcher!

While Gibson had to work his way up the minor league rungs over ten years, Rohr was assigned immediately by the Red Sox to their Tri-ple-A farm club in Toronto. Once again, the system's depth chart had come into play. The pitching-thin Red Sox were ready to throw any strong, young left-handed arm into the breach. Rohr showed a great deal of promise in Toronto but he was a long-shot to stick when he arrived in Winter Haven in the spring of 1967. A strong showing in Florida and Dick Williams' belief in his potential had earned him the starting nod for Opening Day in Yankee Stadium.

"I could tell from his initial practice throws that he was nervous and it was up to me to settle him down. Hey, he was just this tall, skinny kid . . . part Indian, Cherokee, if I remember . . . and it was just a matter of talking to him. Billy had shown a lot of good stuff in spring training and he and I had talked about the batters we'd be facing and how he should pitch to each one. I went out to talk to him. 'Just put 'em between the lines, Billy, and we'll take each out as it comes along.'"

Gibson reminded Rohr, whose best pitches were a fast sinking ball and sharp curve, that Yankee Stadium was a great park for him to pitch in, particularly where it was his first major league start. Even 400-foot fly balls could be caught for easy outs in the old Yankee Stadium.

Gibson recalled, "Billy's ball moved a lot. He had a sharp curve that came in on right-handed hitters and a fastball away. In fact, the ball moved so much that it looked like it was right over the plate. But by the time you took a cut at it, swung away that is, it was down and away. Billy, that day, once he got his rhythm, had them hitting a lot of ground balls, ones our guys could easily scoop up."

Gibson had one edge over the typical rookie debuting in New York. As a teenager, he had been a three-sport start at Durfee High in Fall River, Massachusetts. Sports consumed this old New England town—they still do—and Russ was the super star of his era. He quarterbacked the foot-ball team, turning down several football scholarships to join the Red Sox immediately after graduation. Gibson was a sparkplug on the Durfee High basketball team leading them to the New England schoolboy championship in his junior year. But his first love was baseball and his natural position was behind the plate.

In 1946 through 1965, the Hearst Corporation sponsored an all-star series throughout the United States starting at the local level. This culminated in a national all-star game bringing the 50 best high school ball players in the U.S. together. Gibson excelled at all regional levels and three hits at Fenway Park earned him a trip to the Nationals. The game was played at the old Polo Grounds in New York and Gibson was on the receiving end of three innings of shutout baseball thrown by Mike McCormick, who went on to a distinguished career with the San Francisco Giants.

If Gibson was a little nervous, Rohr was nearly a basket case. Rohr had sought to prepare for his moment of glory by switching roommates from catcher Bob Tillman to the ace of the pitching staff Jim Lonborg. Lonborg took him out for dinner to go over the Yankee hitters. According to Lonborg, "We were there for two hours, and for an hour and three quarters, he didn't say a word. I talked and he just listened."

Rohr took a sleeping pill but he was up and about at 7:00 a.m. the next morning. "We talked about their hitters some more, had breakfast, then went to the park. I knew he was nervous," said Lonborg.

The opening day crowd was small by New York standards: only a shade over 14,000 fans. But there was an ample mix of celebrities. Jacqueline Kennedy was there with her six-year-old son, John Jr. Quincy-born movie star, Lee Remick, was there. Tony Conigliaro sent her a note before the game suggesting that if she wanted to date a real star she should meet him after the game.

The 1967 Yankee team will not go down in the annals with the 1927 Yankees, or the 1936 team or even the 1961 Yankees. There were no Ruth's, no DiMaggio's, not even a Phil Rizzuto. But there were some decent bats in the lineup. Tom Tresh and Joe Pepitone could still swing a bat. Ellie Howard was nearing the end of an outstanding career, but as he would later dramatically prove, he could still get around, and the sight of No. 7, Mickey Mantle, pinch hitting in the eighth inning would strike fear in the heart of Russ Gibson.

"Alright, Billy-baby, settle down. Easy out there. Just keep it between the lines," Gibson yelled through his mask to his battery mate atop the mound. Despite his nerves, Rohr got the Yankees one, two, three in the first inning and began to relax because by then the Red Sox had a 1-0 edge from Reggie Smith's lead-off homer.

Once the game began, the only real sign of nervousness from Rohr was the rapidity with which he pitched. Gibson remembers "every pitch was right at my target . . . I didn't even have to move. His control was unbelievable and his fastball was really sinking. They couldn't do anything with him."

Gibson could sense his pitcher settling down as he retired the first ten Yankees in the giant stadium before walking a man. "Yeh, he was still a little nervous, but you could almost see the wave of confidence taking over him," Gibson recalled. "He was remembering what Jim Lonborg had told him about the hitters and the stuff about them that we'd discussed before the game and between each inning as we went along. 'Course because you got 'em out with one type of pitch one time, didn't mean that you'd call for the same pitch against him every time. You sort of have to pitch them a little different every time. If you get a hitter out on fastballs, you can't throw him ten of them in a row. He gets the big picture and soon will hammer one away. No, you have to mix it up."

Gibson had some success at the plate as well. Facing the wily veteran, Whitey Ford, Gibson was prepared for anything in his first at bat. Gibson remembers that "Whitey's ball moved a lot. I got one that I could handle and lined it right up the middle." Not a bad start for a guy who was ready to give up the game two years earlier.

Gibson was too concerned about keeping his pitcher under control to think about his own situation. "Fact was I really wasn't nervous, especially after a couple of innings of play. Sure it was the Yankees and we were on their home turf, but it was easy for me by then. I began to think of it as any other ballgame where I always wanted to win. When we got the lead on Reggie's homer, and I got a hit my first time at bat it helped a lot. Meanwhile, Billy was just pitching a hell of a ballgame."

Rohr had the ability to throw the ball where he wanted it to go. "It was unbelievable," Gibson recalled, "I couldn't believe it for a kid like that in his situation. He had such good control. The only pitch that got away that I can remember is the one in the ninth."

After five innings, both teams and the fans became aware of what was transpiring. With each succeeding inning, the tension built in the stands. As is baseball tradition, no one on the Red Sox bench mentioned even the words "no-hitter."

"All the players stayed away from him in the dugout," Gibson remembered. "Billy was a little confused by that but I told him they didn't want to jinx him. But we talked about the fact he was pitching a no-hitter. We were playing our first big league game in Yankee Stadium. Of course we talked about it!" Russ chuckled.

Gibson concentrated on going over the hitters between innings. It was a tight game and there was no time to focus on individual glory, just the task of winning the game.

Rohr entered the sixth inning without anything against him even resembling a base hit. And he was nursing a slim 1-0 lead. To pitch a no-hitter you need outstanding "stuff" and a great deal of luck. There is more than one pitcher in the Hall of Fame who never put that combination together. But Rohr was working so quickly that it appeared the game would soon be over. And he was about to catch a bit of luck.

The first ball hit hard off of Rohr was a line drive from the bat of Horace Clarke. It was a solid smash, but it went on a line to Carl Yastrzemski. A portend of more good fortune to come later.

There was even greater drama in the sixth inning. Bill Robinson was pretty much a journeyman ballplayer, but he could hit his pitch. And hit one he did in the sixth. Hit one right at Rohr. Hit one right off Rohr. Baseball is the game that has benefited the most from the instant replay. Plays of multiple dimensions happen in a flash and given the game's elegant pauses, there is time to freeze-frame the action and figure out what really happened.

Picture Rohr's ninety-mile-an-hour fastball reaching Robinson in less than one-half second. Imagine Robinson's bat responding in milliseconds. His line drive goes directly back at Rohr faster than the speed of the pitched ball. It careens directly off Rohr's shin and in less than one second it has been redirected to Joe Foy at third base. Foy grabs it and fires it to George Scott at first base and Robinson is out by an eyelash. Perhaps five seconds have elapsed from the time the ball has left Rohr's hand. Miraculously, it seems Rohr's flirtation with immortality has been preserved. Such is the perfection of baseball's dimensions and the combinations that are played out.

Gibson was already headed for Billy who was dancing around the mound in pain. Right behind him came Williams and trainer Buddy LeRoux. Elsewhere in the stadium, the crowd roared its appreciation for the great out.

Williams recalled later that he "asked the kid to roll down his stocking. He was on television. He has the skinniest legs you ever saw. I knew he was hurt. I was thinking of taking him out but I left him in."

"I had mixed feelings on my way to the mound," Gibson said. "I was happy for Foy's great play but also very concerned for Billy. That ball had ricocheted like a cannonball off his leg. But he sort of waved us off. Kept saying he was okay. Williams was not completely convinced. He thought maybe Billy should come out because he might hurt his arm by favoring his leg. Billy said it wouldn't be a problem. He wanted to stay in. Dick cautioned me to let him know immediately if Billy began to favor his leg and he'd have to pull him."

After taking a few pitches, Billy signaled that he was okay to pitch. The crowd gave him a big hand while Gibson scrutinized his pitching performance.

"He looked good to me. Far as I was concerned he was tossing better pitches than before that grounder hit him. I told Dick that when we came off the field and he left him in."

From Rohr's perspective, it was the ultimate "bang-bang" play. He told Cliff Keane of the *Boston Globe* after the game, "I never saw the ball come back at me. It hit my leg and it hurt. I looked and saw Joe Foy take the ball by third base with his bare hand and he threw out the runner."

When a pitcher goes five innings without a hit, everyone gets interested. You're past the half-way point. When a pitcher reaches six innings without a hit, everyone gets serious. Only nine more outs to go: a very manageable number. Two-thirds of the way there.

Gibson said that he first became a believer in a Rohr no-hitter after that sixth inning. "I think everybody by then was having thoughts about such a possibility. You just had to know it was possible, but no one said a word about it. We just kept going along through the seventh and eighth innings and Billy just kept setting them down."

There was a certain amount of tension on the Red Sox bench but after all these were all professional athletes not schoolboys. Their pri-

The young lefty, Bill Rohr.

mary focus was on squeezing out a victory. Gibson recalls being very aware of the no-hitter in progress, but he was more concerned about being on the right side of a tight 1-0 lead. He continued to go over the hitters with Rohr and to urge him to bear down. The ultimate pros find a no-hitter in progress to be a distraction. Their only interest is in putting a "W" on the board.

When the Red Sox failed to score in the top of the seventh, the New York crowd rose for the traditional home seventh inning stretch. While they were Yankee fans, their sentiments were clearly with Rohr as he marched to the mound and towards history. Rohr faced the meat of the Yankee order and he dispatched them just as quickly as if he were still pitching for Bellflower High School against a local nine. Three up, three down and only six to go.

This was getting very serious. Gibson had to shift his attention from the eighth inning Yankee lineup to his turn at bat. He would leave young Mr. Rohr in the capable hands of pitching coach, Sal Maglie.

Catchers will tell you that they don't hit for higher averages because they have to concentrate so much on the defensive part of the game. Yankee pitcher Whitey Ford had Gibson's full attention on this at-bat, however. Gibson knew that Whitey remembered he had thrown him his best pitch on his first at bat and had been burned with a hit. He figured Ford would try something else so he went up "thinking curve." Curve him Whitey did and Gibson touched him for his second hit.

Perched on first base, Gibson had to be glowing. He had toiled ten years in the minors to get to this place. Now two hours into his first game he's hitting .500 — off of Whitey Ford, no less — and catching a no-hitter. Which direction is Cooperstown anyway?

Reggie Smith failed to advance Gibson who represented a cushion for their 1-0 lead. Young third baseman, Joe Foy, a native of the Bronx, stood in against Ford. No respecter of future Hall-of-Famers, Foy sent a Ford delivery smartly into the left-field bleachers. The Red Sox bench, sensing victory, jubilantly welcomed local-boy-made-good Foy. With a three-run margin, the tension was eased a little.

Rohr appeared to be ideally positioned as he took the mound in the bottom of the eighth inning. With a three-run lead, he could go for the perfect pitch. If he cut it too fine, a bases empty home run would still leave him with a two-run lead. Not only that, but he was working to the eighth and ninth batters before rolling over to Horace Clarke at the top of the Yankees' batting order.

With shortstop John Kennedy due up to the plate, catcher Gibson was startled by the loudest roar from a crowd that he had ever heard. He looked beside him to see a large number seven and the most imposing looking hitter he had ever seen. The legendary Mickey Mantle had been announced as a pinch hitter. Mantle wasn't huge—only about 5'11"—by any standard, but he looked as if he had been carved from clay and fitted with Yankee pinstripes. If anyone could put an end to Rohr's epic effort, Mantle could.

But 21-year-old native Californians are not awestruck by New York legends—at least not young Mr. Rohr. Mantle, whose days of terrorizing American League pitching were several years behind him, flied out routinely to Tony Conigliaro in right field. Another major threat had passed and Gibson breathed a sigh of relief.

As Rohr walked off the mound after retiring Clarke to the end of the eighth inning, reality began to set in everywhere in Yankee Stadium. The reality to the fans that he was only three outs away from immortality. The reality among his teammates that the kid might just do it. Nowhere was reality more in evidence than in the Press Box. Reporters were flipping through record books to see if any rookie had ever pitched a no-hitter in his first game. Phone calls were made back to the sports desks in New York and Boston. Someone said, "How about Bobo Holloman?" That turned out to be wrong. Holloman had pitched a no-hitter for the St. Louis Browns as a rookie in 1953, but he had made four previous, brief relief appearances. No one had a nominee, not even the most senior reporter, but no one had a definitive answer either.

Dick Williams was interested in Rohr's no-hitter but he was much more concerned about getting an insurance run or two. After all this was his New York debut as a manager and he had promised that his 1-1 team would win more than they would lose. This wasn't the Yankees-Red Sox of *The Summer of '49*—these teams had finished one-half game apart in tenth and ninth places respectively in 1967—but this was an important game to his young team.

"Then there we were at the top of the ninth," Gibson recalled, "and all our guys went down in rapid fire order. But it was okay because we led 3-0. And Billy and I looked at each other and without a word we walked up from the dugout. Boy, for a kid, he sure had a serious expression on his face. It was strange; everyone was standing to watch Billy go to the mound but no one was cheering. It was like no one wanted to do anything that might snap the no-hitter, even the Yankee fans."

Gibson reviewed the three Yankee hitters due up in the top of the ninth. The three best Yankee hitters. Tom Tresh, batting in the third spot, was only about a .250 hitter but he had power. He had hit 27 home runs in 1966 and he was good in the clutch. Tresh could be the one to stop it. Joe Pepitone was worrisome. He was another .250 hitter with power and he was unpredictable. He might strike out or he might hit one into the right field bleachers. Joe was a problem. Elston Howard was a cause for concern as well. Although Howard was then 38-years-old, he had been a tough out for 13 years in the big leagues. He had hit .313 as recently as 1964 and he had the experience of playing under pressure in 47 World Series games. Ellie was a real threat. Three tough outs: all pitchable but not one sure thing in the bunch.

Standing tall and thin atop the mound, the young Boston lefty looked about like some imperial potentate on his lowly subjects, checking to be sure all eight were positioned to his taste. Each in turn gazed back at him as though he was some demi-god who was about to perform a magical feat that would bring them all lasting fame.

Forty-five years later I asked Billy Rohr if he was checking the positioning of his fielders. "That wasn't it at all," he told me. "I just realized that there would be a day, maybe when I was a 65 year old, when I would want to remember it clearly." He added, "I'm glad I had the foresight to do that. It's a special memory."

"Their left fielder, Tom Tresh, was first up for New York," Gibson said. "I give Bill the signal for his fast sinking ball and he lets it go and Tresh catches it clean and hard on his bat and it takes off like a rocket to left over the heads of the infielders. I cursed. There was no way that ball was going to be caught. It was a white blur on a course to rip right over Yastrzemski's head. There goes the no-hitter!"

Yaz, however, wasn't buying it. While the crowd groaned, he took off like a shot towards the fence on a line with the white blur that was headed right for the space far above him. He was running all out when he leaped like a yearling deer into the air to spear Tresh's ball with his splayed glove.

Yaz came to earth with a thump and absorbed the impact by going into a full somersault. The crowd held its breath! Did he have the ball? He rose triumphantly to hold the ball safely in his glove for all to see. It was a catch for the all-time archives and all the more so in such a game. The cheers from the crowd seemed to swell their numbers.

Three to nothing, Boston. Last of the ninth. One out. Now only two outs away from an historic no-hitter. The thunderous roars and applause was not only for Yaz but mostly for Rohr's working no-hitter which he had saved. The genie was out of the bottle. The forbidden word was being spoken: NO-HITTER! All hoped that they'd see history happen right before them that day.

"Billy was more relaxed, looking good," Gibson said. "The grim look had faded with Yaz's spectacular catch. He was beginning to believe that he might just pull off the unthinkable—a no-hitter in his first major league game. We were working very good, getting the pitches right to the target."

The next batter up for the Yankees was right fielder Joe Pepitone, who hit a fastball in the air to right field. Tony C. hardly had to extend himself to make the catch. The crowd again sundered the air with their whoops of delight. A historic moment lay ahead and they would be part of it for the ages.

With two outs in the bottom of the ninth and losing 3-0, catcher Elston Howard, a solid, muscular slugger who had gone zero-for-three-at-bats, prepared to face young Billy Rohr. Before he got to the plate, Williams hurried to the mound to caution Rohr to watch his first pitch, "Howard's a dangerous batter on the first pitch."

Years later Williams said, "I wish I had stayed in the dugout. The kid had a good rhythm going. He had retired the first two batters and I went running out to put my two cents in." He told me with all sincerity, "I don't know how many times over the years I've kicked myself for doing that. I worry that I cost the kid his no-hitter."

Now there wasn't a sound to be heard but the encouraging chatter of the Red Sox players as they hovered expectantly about their positions in anticipation of Rohr's initial pitch. The count went to two and two on fastballs and the stadium was set to explode. The unthinkable was going to become reality. Get ready for it!

Rohr wound up, all arms and legs whirling about, and threw his next pitch. "It was a strike! Right on!" Gibson said. "It was the final out of the game. Then, I couldn't believe it."

But believe it he had to. The umpire, Cal Drummond, called Billy's toss a ball to bring the count to three and two. For the next 40 years Gibson insisted that the umpire blew the call. "It was that close between our rookie battery and the veteran batsman. He obviously felt that he had to give it to Howard."

Gibson only mildly contested the call. "I knew Billy was thinking three and two and that he really wanted to get on top of the curve ball and get it over good to put Howard away. Up to the ninth we hadn't thrown a curve at him. Billy and I figured it was time to toss one up on his first pitch. It fooled Howard, making him swing in the dirt for it. Now with the three and two count we figured it was time to throw him another one."

Rohr appeared so confident on the mound that Gibson never went out to speak to him at any time during the ninth. "His control was just that good. We had Howard to three and two and agreed on the second curve. Billy wound up and threw the ball but I knew immediately that he held it too tight and it sort of squirted out on him. What the hell! One pitch that hung a fraction too long!"

When Howard hit the ball to right field toward Tony C., Gibson knew it was in there, a clean base hit. The good thing was that there was no doubt about it. It was a solid, well-stroked hit, leaving Tony without any chance of making a play.

"It was sort of a letdown," Gibson said, "but what the hell, we're still in a 3-0 game and you can't let down too much because I've seen games turn around pretty damn fast. Once the no-hitter was gone, the idea was let's win the game and get out of here."

As for the young lefty for Boston, he hardly changed expressions as he watched Howard's single bounce into right field. If he was disappointed, he didn't show it. His attitude like Gibson's was matter-of-fact like, "Hey, that's baseball. Next batter."

While Gibson and Rohr stood silently with nonplussed expressions, the throng in Yankee Stadium howled in dismay at the loss of "their no-hitter." Hometown hero, Elston Howard, was the villain although he was only doing what he was paid to do—hit the ball. The boos filled the huge expanse of the stadium. Later Howard would recall that "my job is to hit the ball and I've got three kids to feed and that's what I do. I looked over at Rohr when I got to first base and I could see that he was hurting, but I wasn't sorry a bit." After reflecting for a moment he said, "That's the only time I was ever been booed in Yankee Stadium for getting a base hit."

With Howard at first base, Charley Smith, New York's third baseman came up to the plate. The fans' boos continued to wrack the air. Smith took his cuts and soon was retired for the final out. Rohr had a one-hitter.

Almost instantly, the roars of disapproval directed at Howard for getting a hit before his hometown crowd turned to cries of congratulations for Billy Rohr. The fans were baseball lovers first before partisan diehards and showed their appreciation for his great pitching effort with their sustained applause.

Rohr and his fellow players dashed toward their dugout only to run into their own teammates who rushed out to congratulate their pitcher. All were soon swept away into the dugout and the clubhouse by hordes of policemen, the media and fans that had broken through police lines.

In the midst of all the excitement and whooping, Jackie Kennedy and her son, John Jr., came by to congratulate Rohr.

When things began to calm down Rohr told the press he first "thought about a no-hitter about the fifth or sixth inning. Nobody on the bench talked about it and neither did any of the Yankees." In ironic acknowledgement of Howard's lone hit, he added, "Sure I'm a little disappointed that Howard got the hit. But he gets paid more to hit than I do to pitch, so how can you begrudge him one. When he was on first I looked over at him. Yeh, I was disappointed but I wasn't mad at all."

According to Gibson, Red Sox manager Williams was "happy about the win. He congratulated us on a good game. His attitude was to win a game any way you can. No-hitter or one-hitter, it still went into the books as a win. And Dick was determined the team was going to win more than it lost in 1967."

Rohr, of course, was "on top of the world," according to Gibson. "It was a great thrill for him. I'm sure he definitely wanted the no-hitter, but as a professional you do the best you can. And Bill certainly was on that day."

When Gibson was informed by Williams that he wouldn't be catching again until Sunday, he joined Yaz, Mike Andrews and the pumped up Billy Rohr on a trip downtown to a Wall Street pub.

"We were all on a high, coming off such a spectacular win over the Yankees in New York. We felt like we owned the town. A radio broadcast truck came by and we flagged it down."

They told the driver that they wanted a lift downtown to a Wall Street restaurant. When he demurred, Gibson said to the driver while pointing at Billy, "You know who you got here? Billy Rohr, the Red Sox pitcher who threw the one-hitter today at Yankee Stadium. Only tossed 122 pitches against your big guy, Whitey Ford. Billy here, it was his first major league outing. Your guy, Ford, was making his four hundred and thirty-second."

Once the truck crew realized the quality of their catch they insisted on taking the Red Sox players to their radio station for a live interview. Only then did they transport the Boston quartet to their eatery on Wall Street.

High on the list of congratulatory messages Rohr received was a telegram from Boston Mayor John Collins: "You gave Boston an unforgettable day. Red Sox fans everywhere salute you and congratulate you on a fine pitching performance. May today's victory be the first of hundreds in your major league career."

Sadly, it was not to be so for the lanky lefthander. For though Billy Rohr was swept victorious off the mound with his one-hitter that day in Yankee Stadium, he was to win only one other game in 1967, ironically against the Yankees again in Boston, and an additional game in 1968, pitching for the Cleveland Indians. Incredibly, Rohr's career began and peaked on that cold April day.

In another ironic twist, Yankee catcher, Elston Howard, who got the lone hit off Rohr in the 3-0 Boston victory, was traded late in the season to Boston and made a significant contribution to their miracle finish. By the time he joined his Boston teammates in August, young Billy Rohr had been exiled to the minors.

This most improbable of starts on opening day in Yankee Stadium was the first clue that this was perhaps a team of destiny. Time and time again they would be counted out only to rise again from the canvas. It would take another 159 games, however, to determine how the drama would be played out.

"It's still incredible," Gibson said, "when I think of the game that Billy pitched. To pitch a one-hitter and then win your second game again against the Yankees. And then not to win another game until 1968 and only one and then he disappears. He was traded to Cleveland the next year and couldn't perform on the mound."

Gibson surmises that "when you're a sinker ball pitcher like Billy, you lose your sinker ball if you don't throw hard. Billy didn't really throw that hard. He threw fairly hard, but he lost his sinker. When he lost that his ball stayed flat. They killed him because with his best pitch, the ball moved. When he stayed on top, the ball sank. Once he lost whatever he lost, the sinker went in straight. The same thing happens to a lot of pitchers in the majors. With Billy, bingo, he's gone! He's out of baseball two years later. How do you figure it?"

Gibby and Billy Rohr always stayed in touch. "Billy was a great kid," Gibson said in our 2007 interview. "After he left baseball he put himself through college and law school. He's a very successful attorney in southern California now."

Every year until Gibson's death in 2008, Billy would call Gibby on the anniversary of his near no-hitter. "He called every year and he always said the same thing: 'That sure was a lousy pitch you called for Elston Howard!'" Now Billy Rohr calls Russ' sons Greg and Chris every year on April 14.

Russ Gibson had a number of thrills ahead during the 1967 season. In July, the good people of Fall River organized "Russ Gibson Day" at Fenway Park. An estimated 6,000 residents of Greater Fall River made the trek to Fenway Park to honor their local hero and they presented Russ with a new car.

"I got a lot of grief from my teammates about that day," Gibson recalled. "Yaz said, 'I've been here seven years and I've never had a day in my honor. Why are they doing this for a .220 hitter?'"

Gibson's biggest worry was that Dick Williams would leave him on the bench on his big day. "I was in Dick's doghouse for some reason and at one point he said, 'I don't even know if I'm going to play you that day.' I said 'Dick I have to tell you, there will be some pretty tough guys on those buses and they won't be pleased with you if I don't play.' I don't know if he realized how serious I was, but he [Williams] did start me."

His other great thrill was being named as the starting catcher in Game One of the 1967 World Series. "I had been a Red Sox fan all my life. And there I was, a regular guy from Fall River playing in the opening game of the World Series. What a thrill that was," he marveled.

Gibson remained with the Red Sox through the "Impossible Dream" year and all of 1968 and 1969. "I was probably as close as anyone to being a regular catcher, playing in eighty to ninety games each of the last two years. My hitting was improving, .225 in 1968 and .251 in 1969."

Unfortunately for Russ, when Dick Williams was unceremoniously fired in late 1969, Gibson's days with the Red Sox were numbered. "When I heard that Dick got fired I knew I was gone. He, in effect, had been my mentor going back to Toronto, and it was just a matter of time."

Gibson's time came at the end of spring training in 1970 when he was "leading the team in hitting in the Grapefruit League. I was the top catcher, headed for my best season ever. I remember that I was hitting something like over .400."

Despite his great spring, the Red Sox traded Gibson to the San Francisco Giants. To add insult to injury, he was traded for a player to be named later and that old Red Sox nemesis—cash. "Hell, they didn't even trade me for anybody. What a comedown."

Russ played with the Giants for three seasons as a backup catcher. He missed being in Boston with the Red Sox but he enjoyed his time in San Francisco. "The Giants owner, Horace Stoneham, was a very classy guy. Everything was done right. I was lucky playing for Tom Yawkey in Boston and Stoneham in San Francisco."

His playing time was limited with the Giants, but Russ was philosophical about that. "If it was raining I got to play. They didn't want to take a chance that the regular catcher would get hurt!"

Russ had one ironic experience while pitching for the Giants. "I caught Mike McCormick in the Hearst All Star game in 1956, when we were both 17 years old. And Mike McCormick was the last San Francisco Giant pitcher [1972] I caught in the major leagues. I guess what goes around really does come around," he laughed.

When his playing days were over Russ and his family stayed on the west coast for about ten years before returning to southeastern Massachusetts. Russ worked as a sales representative with the Massachusetts Lottery, retiring after 20 years in that position.

What did it mean to Russ Gibson all the years since he was a member of that wonderful winning team of 1967? "I can only tell you that something like that changes your life as far as the way you live. Everybody knows you no matter where you go. People are always sending you cards, letters, whatever, asking for autographs. They want you to speak at banquets. People act like the 1967 season was just yesterday.

"It's funny though," he reflects. "Almost everybody says, 'I was a little kid in 1967 when you played.' I keep wondering where all the older people are. I know they're out there. There were 30,000 of them in the stands at Fenway Park almost every night!"

Ultimately, Gibson said, "It's like a love affair because we shared so much together that season . . . a love affair not only with the fans but with the players who shared so many ups and downs with you and who became a close bunch of guys."

John Russell "Russ" Gibson died on July 27, 2008, at age 69, after a long illness. He was survived by his sons, Greg and Chris, and four grandchildren.

A final reflection about my pal Russ Gibson: old-time baseball manager Leo Durocher wrote a bestseller many years ago entitled, "Nice Guys Finish Last." Russ Gibson was proof that nice guys can, in fact, finish first.

Chapter 3

George Scott: Lowering the Boom with a Bat and a Mitt

Boston Red Sox vs. Detroit Tigers, Doubleheader, Sunday, May 14, 1967

George Scott, the Red Sox twenty-three-year-old first baseman, was born and raised in Greenville, Mississippi. On this Sunday in Boston, he was a long way from home in more ways than one. The one thing Boston and Greenville had in common was a love for baseball and for George Scott. Scott was beginning his second year with the Red Sox and the fans loved his enthusiasm for the game and his colorful quotes. George had hit 27 home runs as a rookie in 1966, but he also led the league in strikeouts with 152. So far in 1967, he had shown signs of becoming a more disciplined hitter and he was playing like a potential golden glover as the everyday first baseman. There was every reason to believe that George had a very bright future ahead of him.

The Red Sox began Mother's Day 1967 in eighth place with a record of eleven wins and fourteen losses. Dick Williams' spring training prediction that the Red Sox would win more than they would lose was beginning to look like a dubious proposition.

The Red Sox had followed Billy Rohr's near no-hitter in New York with a tough 1-0 loss and then a heart-breaking 3-2 defeat in eighteen innings to the Yankees. But they had shown some good pitching and they had demonstrated more determination than any Boston team in years.

Williams took out most of his frustration over the two losses to the Yankees on George Scott. George had gone one for eight in the third game of the series and left seven runners in scoring position. At that point in the season, he was hitting .185 and had produced no extra base hits and no RBI.

Williams decided that Scott should sit down in favor of Tony Horton for their unusual one game trip to Chicago's Comiskey Park. Williams fumed "the last three times up, he struck out with men on base." Then he uttered a quote that haunted both men for nearly fifty years, **"Trying to talk to him is like talking to cement."**

Dick Williams told me in a 2006 interview, "I wish I had never said that. I was trying to get George to focus and become a better ballplayer. But that was too harsh. I was frustrated because I knew how talented he was and how good he could be. We really wanted George to be more selective about what he was swinging at. Dick O'Connell [Red Sox GM] went to one of the Boston TV stations and got them to loan us their video equipment. We taped George in a couple of games and sat with him to show that he was swinging at bad pitches," Williams remembered. "When the tape was over, George said, 'That's not me.'"

Tony Horton was not the answer to the Red Sox' early season woes as they fell to Eddie Stanky's White Sox on April 18, by a score of 5-2. Darrell Brandon took the loss for the Red Sox.

The Red Sox came home to play their annual Patriots Day doubleheader on April 19. The Red Sox were scheduled to play a doubleheader with the Washington Senators including the only morning game scheduled in the major leagues followed by a separate admission afternoon game. But playing baseball in Boston in April is a dicey affair and the games were cancelled due to snow.

Williams's temperament was as foul as the holiday weather. He took the occasion to lambaste Scott and third baseman, Joe Foy, for being overweight. Scott, a large man with an enormous frame, weighed in at 221 pounds. At 6' 2" this was probably fifteen pounds more than ideal for him. This theme of Williams' harping on Scott's weight would prevail all season long.

The next Red Sox game was scheduled for Friday night, April 21. Billy Rohr was the announced starter and 25,603 fans showed up to see if he could repeat his magic of a week earlier.

Rohr didn't have another miracle up his sleeve but he evoked memories of the Red Sox left-handed star of the '40s and '50s: Mel Parnell. Rohr pitched a complete game and shut down the Yankees for the second time in eight days with a 6-1 win. At that point, Rohr's lifetime stats read: two wins and no losses; nine hits in two games; ERA 0.50. Not a bad start.

The Red Sox split the next two games with the Yankees taking the series two-games-to-one. Ten days into the season the Red Sox were 4-5, tied for seventh place but only a game and one-half out of first place.

The Red Sox then journeyed to Washington where they won both games behind the relief pitching of John Wyatt and a complete game by Hank Fischer. From there they returned to Fenway Park where they took two-out-of-three from the Kansas City A's including a fifteen-inning, 11-10 slugging contest.

As April came to a close, the Red Sox had edged up to third place, trailing the league-leading Detroit Tigers by one game. Both Carl Yastrzemski and Rico Petrocelli were hitting .330 and Lonborg, Rohr, and Wyatt were all 2-0. It appeared that a lot of the pieces were fitting together.

The Red Sox began May with their first western road trip: always a test for a Boston team. Lefthander Dennis Bennett got things off on the right foot against the California Angels with a 4-0 win in which he also contributed a three-run homer. That high note was more than offset by two tough one run losses to the Angels.

Shortstop Rico Petrocelli still remembers their 2-1 loss in the last game of the Angels series. "Lonborg had pitched really well, and as we were walking off the field I said, 'Nice game Lonnie. Tough luck!' Dick Williams overheard our exchange and snapped, 'Don't you be congratulating anyone, we lost.' Right then and there I knew it would be a different kind of year."

The Midwest proved no more hospitable to the Red Sox. Jim "Mudcat" Grant picked up his first win of the season in the series opener and Dean Chance five-hit them in Saturday's 4-2 Twins'victory. At this point the Red Sox had lost four in a row and five of their last six.

The Red Sox salvaged one game from the Twins as their bats came alive the following day in a 9-6 win. Williams raised a few eyebrows by not starting Yaz and then using him as a defensive replacement in the ninth. As the Red Sox boarded their plane to fly to Kansas City, they were 10-10 and three games off the pace.

The Red Sox split the doubleheader opener of the series to maintain their .500 record. They were actually in danger of being swept, trailing 2-0 going into the ninth inning of the night cap, but rallied for five runs as John Wyatt picked up another "W." These last inning heroics were quickly forgotten as the A's won the third game of the series, 7-4. The Red Sox staggered home on May 10, with a 3-6 record for their trip and more than a few pieces to the puzzle still missing.

The Detroit Tigers came to town as clearly one of the American League's bona fide contenders. The Tigers were led by future Hall-of-Famer, Al Kaline, who was recognized as the premier right fielder in the league. Dick McAuliffe anchored a steady infield from his second base position and Bill Freehan gave the Tigers an All-Star behind the plate. The pitching staff featured former Red Sox right-hander Earl Wilson, who had won 13 games in 1966, Mickey Lolich and Denny McLain.,

The Tigers had won 88 ball games in 1966 even though they endured 3 different managers. Given the stability of veteran manager Mayo Smith, they were well-positioned to make a run for it in 1967. They were off to a great start and brought a 15-7 record into Fenway Park.

Detroit was soon to make it 16 wins as the Red Sox fell by a score of 5-4 on Friday night. The low point of the evening occurred when Red Sox catcher, Bob Tillman, attempted to catch Kaline stealing in the eighth inning. Tillman was so intent that he managed to drill relief pitcher John Wyatt flush in the forehead. Wyatt was down for the count, and Kaline made it to third from where he eventually scored the game winner on a sacrifice fly. Tillman was buried so deeply in Dick Williams' doghouse that he never really escaped until he was sold to the Yankees in August.

Saturday afternoon was no better for the Red Sox or for John Wyatt. He pitched well in the seventh inning, coming in for relief and held the fort in the eighth. Wyatt ran out of gas in the ninth, but Williams left him in to endure a six-run drubbing. The Red Sox lost again, 10-8, and Wyatt must have wondered what was going to happen to him next.

There was an undertone of chirping in the clubhouse over Williams' treatment of Wyatt. Wyatt shrugged it off saying, "I'm a pro and I've got to eat. I don't say nothing man."

As George Scott got ready for the Sunday afternoon doubleheader, he knew he would be facing a right-hander, McLain, in game one. He hoped he would play the second game. Williams had been penciling him in for every game for a while, so he could face the left-handed Mickey Lolich. George loved to hit against left-handed pitchers.

While Scott had a serious communications problem with manager Williams, he had a wonderful relationship with third-base coach, Eddie "Pop" Popowski. Popowski had been in the Red Sox organization since the 1930s and he was universally beloved for his low key style and good nature. He and manager Williams played "good cop/bad cop" more than once in 1967.

Pop had been George's manager in 1965 when Scott played for the Double-A Pittsfield Red Sox in the Eastern League. That was the season when George put it all together, batting .319, and winning the Triple Crown. George said, "I really learned how to play baseball the year I played for Pop."

Pop would talk to George before the games and counsel him on what to look for. He would tell him that Williams just wanted to see him reach his potential and not to take it personally. Pop was on him constantly to stay alert.

The Red Sox starter in game one was their ace, Jim Lonborg; Jose Santiago would start game two. Given the pitching selections and the early season weather it looked like a long afternoon of defense with modest offense. What transpired was quite the opposite.

George Scott shows his home run swing.

Both Lonborg and McLain were touched for a run in the first but this is fairly common. Power pitchers often need an inning to settle down and find their rhythm.

There were indications in the last of the second that McLain might not settle down and just might not have it this day. Rico Petrocelli took him into the left field net and the Red Sox were out to an early 3-1 lead.

McLain finally found his groove and shut the Red Sox down in innings three and four. Meanwhile, Lonborg had simply put it on cruise control and held the Bengals at bay during innings two, three and four. He came a little unglued in the fifth as the Tigers touched him for two more runs. As the game reached the halfway point, the score was knotted at three. Visions of a "pitchers day" were starting to become blurred.

When George Scott came to bat in the fifth, the score was still 3-1 but the bases were filled with Red Sox teammates. Two were gone but "Scotty" relished pressure situations. Recognition was important to him and he was delighted that he was batting clean-up in the opener.

McLain had been wild throughout the game and George disciplined himself to wait for a pitch he could drive. Pop had preached to him over and over that he could raise his average 50 points if he could learn to be patient.

Scott worked the count to 3-2 and he dug in knowing that McLain would have to come across the plate. The most exciting recurring moment in baseball may be the 3-2 pitch when the bases are loaded with two men out. Baseball is a game of waiting for action but at this point, everyone in the ballpark knows something must happen. With the windup of pitcher, Denny McLain, all three runners were off knowing there was no reason to hold their base.

Scotty launched a tremendous blast in the direction of Kaline in right field. Kaline was one of the better right fielders in the game, but Scott's drive was a rocket and Kaline simply couldn't run it down. The three base runners were heading for home as the ball was retrieved and Scott was barreling for third. He moved well for a big man and when the dust cleared, he was safe with a rare Fenway triple. The beleaguered McLain gave way to relief and the Tigers got out of the inning without further damage. But the horse was already out of the barn and Lonborg took the mound with a 6-3 lead.

This would not be Lonborg's finest day. He staggered through the sixth allowing the Tigers another run. Williams had reliever Hank Fischer, who the Red Sox had picked up at the end of the 1966 season, warming up during the inning. When Williams sent Dalton Jones up to pinch hit for him, Lonborg left the game having given up nine hits and four runs, all of them earned. Not a bad day's work for most pitchers, but well below the standard that he would set in 1967.

The Red Sox had scratched out another run in their half of the sixth and the right-handed Fischer was brought in with a 7-4 lead. Fischer was a 27-year-old-native of Yonkers, New York, who was in his sixth major league season. He had pitched four plus years for the Braves and a part of the 1966 season for the Cincinnati Reds who dealt him to the Red Sox at mid-season.

Fischer shut down the Tigers in both the seventh and eighth innings and the Red Sox added an insurance run in the bottom of the eighth. He weakened in the ninth, giving up a homer to third baseman, Don Wert, but proved equal to his nickname of "Bulldog" to preserve the win.

Lonborg got credit for the win and Hank Fischer earned himself a save. Hank Fischer appeared in a total of nine games in 1967 and picked up a win to go with his save. The Red Sox gave him his outright release in mid-season and he never pitched in the big leagues again.

Scott was pleased with his performance in game one. His triple had proven to be the winning hit. He had also added a single, which was more evidence that he was getting over his tendency to try to hit every pitch out of the ballpark.

George Scott was born in Greenville, Mississippi, in the heart of the Mississippi Delta on March 23, 1944. The youngest of three children, his father died when George was two years old. He grew up on a small farm and he was raised by his mother Magnolia.

"When you grow up on a farm you learn to work hard when you are young. My mother worked three jobs to keep us together. She was the greatest influence in my life," he said emphatically. Magnolia Scott was so busy working to provide for her family that she never got to see George play baseball until he played for the Boston Red Sox.

Young George Scott played Little League baseball but he was so big and so much better than the others that he was actually suspended for a time while officials checked his age. He was the quarterback on his football team and he led Coleman High School to the state title in football and basketball. "Basketball was actually my first love," George told me. "I was told that Coach [John] Wooden was interested in having me play for UCLA when I was a senior."

Scott was well-known as a three-sport star at Coleman High School in Greenville and he was identified as a prospect for the Red Sox by scout Ed Scott—no relation to George. Ed Scott had been hired by the Red Sox with the specific mandate to identify African-American prospects. When it was time to sign George to a Red Sox minor league contract, Ed Scott brought in fellow Red Sox scout Milt Bolling. Bolling, a former Red Sox infielder, accompanied George's mother to the Greenville High School graduation. Bolling told me, "I felt badly that I was brought in to finish the deal. Ed Scott had done all the work and he earned the signing. But the front office [Red Sox] wanted me to handle it."

While Bolling and Scott's mother were walking home, Bolling, knowing that he was about to offer a sizable bonus, asked George if there was anything he wanted; he was thinking George might ask for a car. When Scott replied: "Yes, a basketball," Bolling stopped at the local sporting goods store and bought him one. George spent the rest of the walk home palming the ball with either hand.

George told me many years later, "I picked baseball and signed with the Red Sox for the money. It just didn't seem right to go to college all the time watching my mother continuing to struggle. I wanted to make money and help her out."

George Scott's journey to Boston began at the Red Sox minor league club in Olean, New York in 1962. The following year he graduated to Wellsville, where he played with Red Sox prospect Tony Conigliaro, and hit 15 home runs in only 106 games. "I was very confident coming up through the minors but Tony was the most confident ballplayer I ever knew. Tony was my friend. I miss him very much," Scott said.

His next stop was Winston-Salem, North Carolina, in 1964. To this point, he had played second base, shortstop and third, but he hadn't spent any time at his ultimate position, first base. His Triple Crown season with Pittsfield under Pop Popowski in 1965 made him a long-shot to stick with the big club in 1966.

George Scott impressed everyone with a spectacular spring training performance at Winter Haven, FL, in 1966. Scott had been the MVP of Double-A in 1965, but Joe Foy, who had been the Triple-A MVP while playing for Dick Williams in Toronto, was ahead of him on the Red Sox depth chart. But Scott played so well in the spring training games that he was the starting third baseman for the Red Sox in 1966. About one week into the season Scott moved across the diamond to become the regular first baseman and Joe Foy took over at third base.

He had started his rookie year in 1966 on a home run tear that drew favorable comparison with old Double X: Jimmy Foxx. Scott played so well in early-going that he was named to the American League All-Star team and he played in the game in St. Louis. Looking back on his participation in the 1966 All-Star George told me, "My legs were like spaghetti, I was shaking so much. I'm sitting in the dugout, everybody else is running around having fun, but I can't take my eyes off the field. I'm watching Willie Mays, Clemente, Stargell, Koufax, and I'm saying to myself, 'Are you in the right place?'"

In the second half of the 1966 season word went 'round the league: don't give this kid a fastball that he can hit; he'll kill you! Give him slow breaking stuff until his tongue is hanging out. Then give him a fastball way outside and he'll chase it. The "book" on Scott had been perfect. He continued to chase pitches outside the strike zone and his home run

George Scott hit .303 in 1967, good for fourth in the league.

output diminished along with his batting average. He finished the year with twenty-seven home runs and a .246 batting average. Respectable numbers for a rookie, but a far cry from his torrid start.

Pop took him under his wing in spring training in 1967 and urged him to become a smarter hitter. "Wait for your pitch. Don't swing at their pitch. Go where the ball is pitched. If it's outside, take it to right field. With your strength you can hit it out to the opposite field or drive it into the gap in right center. Don't try to pull every pitch."

All of Pop's advice on hitting was good advice. Scotty was starting to hear it and apply it. And the results showed as his average began to climb towards .300 from its low of .185 on April 17.

And where did George come up with "Taters" for his long home runs? "You have to remember that I played against guys like Reggie Jackson, so I needed something," George told me. "Growing up on a farm where I loved sweet potatoes, Taters seemed like a natural."

Scotty was delighted when he saw his name on the lineup card at first base against Lolich. He had been dropped to the fifth position in the batting order, but he told himself he was still in the heart of the order. A seemingly simple man, he was actually quite complex and sensitive. He took tremendous pride in his baseball skills and his ego was easily wounded by a Dick Williams' barb.

Scotty relished the thought of facing the left-handed Lolich. George was a pure fastball hitter who had trouble with breaking pitches. Naturally, he was fed a steady diet of curves, slurves and sliders, almost all of them off-speed deliveries. Although the breaking ball bothered him, thrown by a lefthander the pitch broke in towards him and he found it easier to time his swing. George relished the thought of going up against a southpaw, particularly in Fenway Park with its attractive power alleys.

The big guy was known for his hitting and power. To the fans he was "Boomer," a nickname inspired by his prodigious home runs. But George was a complete athlete and an outstanding fielder. For a big man, he moved with catlike grace.

George was a natural first baseman, as good a glove man as has ever been seen at that position for the Red Sox. But his athletic skills were such that he performed credibly at third base when the Red Sox had asked him to fill in there. Scotty kept his fielder's glove, but his first love was his dependable first base mitt.

The Red Sox basically went with the same lineup in game two as they had in the opener. The big surprise was catcher Mike Ryan getting the call in both ends of the twin-bill. Manager Williams had been juggling

Russ Gibson, Bob Tillman and Ryan at the position. Mike's three hits in game one caused "Riverboat" Williams to see if Ryan had been dealt the hot hand. The Red Sox lineup was packed with eight right-handed hitters to face southpaw Lolich.

After starter Jose Santiago disposed of the Tigers without incident in the top of the first, Red Sox hitters took dead aim on the portly Lolich. Joe Foy got things rolling with a double. Yaz moved Foy over to third with a single. George Scott came to the plate thinking, "Hit the ball where it is pitched. You can hit this guy if you wait for your pitch." And that is exactly what he did. Scott lined sharply into center and Foy was home for the first run. Rico Petrocelli added a double off the wall and the Red Sox had jumped ahead 3-0. The fans had just begun to enjoy this cushion when Santiago found himself in hot water. Norm Cash had touched Jose for a solo homer, and before anyone realized what was happening, the Tigers loaded the bases with one out. The dangerous Don Wert was at the plate and the key play of the game was about to occur.

George Scott prided himself on his fielding instincts but the upcoming play was a unicorn for him. Wert hit a bouncing ball to Scott and you could almost see him start to turn towards instant to go for the standard first-to-second-to-first double play. At the very last instant, the ball took a weird hop, handcuffing him. Scotty immediately reacted and pegged a strong overhand throw to catcher Ryan for the force at the plate. Ryan's rifle return to George at first doubled up Wert. The Red Sox were out of the inning and a Tiger outburst had been squelched.

The first-to-home-to-first double play is not unheard of, but few first basemen in the game could have converted the double play on Wert's ball. Scott told Cliff Keane of the *Boston Globe*, "I never made that play before in my life."

Scott's defensive gem seemed to energize the Red Sox bats. They drove Mickey Lolich to an early shower in the second with two more runs. Detroit manager, Mayo Smith, said after the game, "I will never start another lefty in Fenway Park. The last guy to win here was Mel Parnell."

Meanwhile, Santiago was pitching just well enough to keep the Red Sox safely ahead. His effort was a mirror image of Lonborg's outing in game one. The day had truly turned into a hitter's paradise. The Red Sox came to bat in the last of the fifth with a 6-3 lead. Few present felt it was

Scotty slides towards Angels' second baseman Jerry Remy in 1977.

enough. Happily for Red Sox partisans, Detroit reliever, George Korince was about to unravel. George would only make nine appearances for the Tigers in 1967 but two of them would be on May 14, 1967, relieving both McLain and Lolich.

"Moose" Korince was no mystery to Red Sox hitters and they tallied five runs in the fifth. Joe Foy sparked the uprising with a two-run homer. George Scott contributed another key single as the Red Sox made the most of Korince's wildness and five base hits.

Jose Santiago staggered into the eighth inning with a seemingly safe 12-4 lead. But perhaps Jose was worn out from watching all the balls fly around Fenway. He had given up homers to Cash, Willie Horton and Bill Freehan. He had gotten into the spirit of the day with one of his own in the second, the only home run he hit during the regular season in his eight year major league career. Jose gave way to veteran Don McMahon in the eighth with two men on.

McMahon was a 37-year-oldster who was in his 11th big league season. At this point, he had made over 600 appearances in the major leagues—all but two of them in relief. While he would end a distinguished career in 1974 with 153 saves, this was just no day for pitchers.

McMahon barely made it through the inning as the Tigers tallied five runs to move within striking distance.

The Red Sox added a final insurance run in the eighth. Only in Fenway could the thirteenth run of the game be an insurance run. Dick Williams took mercy on McMahon and brought in the fresh arm of Galen Cisco for the ninth. Cisco had started his career with the Red Sox in 1961, had been sentenced to four years with some truly dreadful New York Mets teams and had returned from exile in 1967. Maybe the Tiger hitters were simply exhausted, but Cisco set them down in order to preserve the Red Sox 13-9 win.

The official scorer needed a calculator to tally the offensive carnage for the day. Thirty-five runs had been scored, twelve home runs had been hit (six for each team), and fifty hits had been registered. Most significant of all, 28 extra base hits had been struck. The 16,436 fans on hand witnessed American League history in the making. The 28 extra base hits was a new record for one day, eclipsing the mark of 27 set by the Red Sox-A's 62 years earlier in 1905. A pitcher's day indeed!

The day was a memorable one for the emerging Red Sox team as well. The doubleheader sweep of a strong Tigers team was important. It established the young Red Sox as a team to contend with. Not necessarily a contender, but one that would be heard from. The sweep also propelled them from eighth place to a tie for third place. While they were still six games out of first place, they would never fall more than seven games off the pace for the rest of the season.

The game was an important one to George Scott as well. He had performed well at the plate. His stats showed four hits and five key RBI. More significantly, the doubleheader had showcased his newly discovered versatility. On this day of extra base hits, three of his hits were well-placed singles. He had run the bases well and he had executed the fielding play of the day.

Veteran sports reporter Cliff Keane of *The Boston Globe* did his best to summarize the day's highlights. "Who was the big guy to single out in the doubleheader?" Keane wrote. "There were enough to fill two columns of type." Keane then went on to identify Scott as the number one star of the day, and spent three paragraphs describing George's eye-popping double play in game two.

Dick Williams didn't have anything to say to the media about George Scott's outstanding play in the doubleheader. In fact, Williams didn't have anything to say to the media at all. The Boston press, which had been generally favorable to Williams until then, had really roasted Williams for letting Wyatt absorb a beating in the ninth inning of the previous game. Williams responded with the silent treatment on Sunday.

Scott's 14-year major league career would prove to be distinguished, but it would be filled with ups and downs as well. In many ways, 1967, his second year, would be one of his more memorable years. He continued to field flawlessly, he raised his average by 58 points to finish at .303 and he still managed to hit 19 homers and drive in 82 runs. His .303 batting average ranked 4th in the American League and his 82 RBI were good enough for 6th in the league. George Scott truly did it all in 1967.

And Red Sox fans loved George's enthusiasm, his slick fielding and his colorful quotes. He makes the top-ten favorite list of many long-time Red Sox fans.

But the following year, George's average plummeted an astounding 132 points to a dismal .171. This was no injury-riddled, shortened season. George came to bat 350 times and managed only 60 hits, 3 home runs and a paltry 25 RBI. Keep in mind that George finished his career with a lifetime batting average of nearly .270, 271 home runs and over 1,000 RBI. With these figures in mind, his 1968 offensive output may represent one of the weaker single-year performances by any bona fide major league slugger.

George's incredible descent puzzled everyone and yet everyone had a suggestion. There probably were too many suggestions. Some felt that his futility stemmed from personal confusion off the field. Others felt he was getting bad off-the-field advice to swing for the fences on every pitch. Whatever the cause, George was simply hopeless at the plate. Dick Williams was quickly running out of patience. The former Boomer spent most of the last two months of the season on the bench.

Scotty rebounded to .253 and 16 home runs for the Red Sox in '69. It was no repeat of '67, but it was a big improvement over 1968. George continued at a steady clip for the Red Sox in '70 and '71. In 1970 he batted a commendable .296 and the following year he socked 24 home runs.

On October 11, 1971, almost exactly four years after the final game of the 1967 World Series, George learned that he had been traded to the Milwaukee Brewers in a massive trade. He, Jim Lonborg and four other players, including Tony Conigliaro's brother, Billy, and George Brett's brother, Ken Brett, had been traded for four Brewers.

Scott was devastated by the trade. The Boston fans had always treated him well, even in the dark days of 1968. The Red Sox had been his only team and he had made a lot of friends in the city.

"I hated to leave Boston. But Milwaukee turned out to be good for me. It's a good baseball town with good people."

Scott did finally accept that a change of scene might be good for him. The Brewers' fans recognized his boyish enthusiasm (even at age 28) and took him to their hearts.

George flourished in Milwaukee. There was less media coverage and fewer opportunities for misinterpreted "Scottisms." Milwaukee is a blue-collar city and George Scott was a regular guy. His defensive prowess also began to achieve recognition around the league.

Scott had five good years with the Brewers. In 1973, he achieved his high water mark of a .306 batting average and in 1975 he led the league with 36 home runs and 109 RBI. He played in more than 150 games each year that he was there.

But George was thrilled when he was traded back to the Red Sox after the 1976 season. Ironically, he was traded by the Brewers along with Bernie Carbo. Never before have any two players been happier to be traded to the Red Sox. This trade marked the return of the prodigal sons to Boston.

Scott played extremely well for Boston in 1977. It was as if he was reborn. He bashed out 33 "taters" and scored 103 runs. But, in 1978, that heart-breaking of years, George's skills showed signs of erosion. He had lost a step in the field, his average fell to .233 and his home run output fell to 12.

Scott started his last year in 1979 with the Red Sox but was traded to Kansas City and finished up with the hated Yankees. When the year came to an end, George Scott's MLB career was over at age 35.

Unable to land a position with a major league team George gravitated to the Mexican League, playing for Yucatan in 1980 and Mexico City in 1981. Eventually he earned a job as player-manager and he continued in that role through 1984.

George returned to the United States and managed a number of teams in the Independent Leagues from the mid-1980s through 2002. When I interviewed George as the manager of the Massachusetts Mad Dogs in 1999, he seemed like a man who had found a home. As we sat together in the manager's office George fielded calls from players looking for a job and then prepared the barbeque concession at Lynn's Fraser Field as well.

"As a manager I borrow a lot of what I learned from Dick Williams," Boomer chuckled. And where did the nickname "Boomer" come from? "Joe Foy [Red Sox third baseman 1966-1968] put that on me when we were both rookies in 1966. I hit a long home run and after the game Joe said, 'You really put a boom on that one.' It stuck and eventually I became The Boomer."

The Massachusetts Mad Dogs went out of business at the end of the 1999 season and George Scott ended up managing in the Texas-Louisiana League. After managing the Berkshire Black Bears of Pittsfield, MA, in the Northern League in 2002, George retired from organized baseball almost exactly 40 years from the date his baseball career began in Olean, NY.

George Scott was inducted into the Red Sox Hall of Fame in 2006. Ironically, his entry coincided with the induction of his former nemesis and manager Dick Williams. The pair greeted one another like long-lost friends, having resolved their differences at Old-Timers games over the years.

Before the ceremony in 2006, George told me, "I didn't realize in 1967 that Dick [Williams] was just trying to make me a better player. I was young and I think that's why I took it to heart."

Dick Williams added, "George and I are fine. He knows that everything I said was intended to help make him a star. I knew what he could do if he took some instruction."

In 2012, the Boston Red Sox announced their All-Fenway Team as part of the celebration of Fenway Park's 100th year. George Scott was named as the second reserve first baseman behind Hall-of-Famer Jimmy Foxx and Mo Vaughn. He played his last game for the Red Sox in 1979, but in 2016 he still ranked in the top 20 for Red Sox career leaders in games played, at-bats, and home runs.

When Red Sox fans that experienced the 1967 season look back on the Impossible Dream team the first player they think of is Carl Yastrzemski. From his great tumbling catch at Yankee Stadium in April to keep Billy Rohr's no-hitter alive through his four hits in the final game of the regular season, Yaz set the tone and kept hope alive.

The second player from the 1967 season that Red Sox fans think about is "Gentleman Jim" Lonborg. Time and time again Jim stopped a losing streak or pitched an outstanding game when the team had to have a win. And their lasting memory of that glorious season is Lonborg being carried on the crowds' shoulders after the win against the Twins in the final game of the regular season.

And the third player from the 1967 season that Red Sox fans think about is George "Boomer" Scott. From the beginning of his career in Boston in 1966, Red Sox fans were captivated by his legendary "Taters," his stellar play at first base and his colorful quotes. Fans followed Scott's weight battles with Dick Williams as closely as they followed the AL standings. With George in 1967, there was always a sense that he would surprise us somehow with a home run, a spectacular play at first base, or with a malapropism that we all knew what he meant.

When you look at George's offensive statistics from 1967, you realize that Scott was loveable **and** he produced. Scott led all AL first basemen in putouts, double plays started, and he received the AL Gold Glove for first basemen in recognition of his defensive prowess. By any measure George Scott had a season for the ages in 1967.

George retired to his native Greenville, Mississippi, when his baseball career ended in 2002. He was in failing health for a number of years having been diagnosed with diabetes and a number of other ailments. George Scott passed away in Greenville on July 28, 2013, at the age of 69.

Nobody ever loved baseball more than George Scott.

Chapter 4

Joe Foy's Fast Start and Sad Finish

Boston Red Sox vs. New York Yankees, Wednesday, June 21, 1967

For *Joe Foy*, 1967 was a season of ironies. Foy had been the regular third baseman in 1966, his rookie year with the Red Sox. He had appeared in 151 games as a rookie and batted a solid .262 with 15 home runs. He had come to the Red Sox after being named MVP of the International League for Toronto in 1965. At age 24 he was clearly the Red Sox third baseman of the future, but before 1967 came to a close, Foy would find himself sharing third base with both Dalton Jones and Jerry Adair. It was a further irony that Foy was originally signed by and played in the minors for the Minnesota Twins. As the season came down to the wire, the Red Sox and Twins would emerge as the prime pennant contenders. And what was the Twins' biggest weakness? A lack of a regular third baseman! In the greatest irony of all, as the Red Sox arrived in New York for their series with the Yankees on June 19, Foy discovered his parents surrounded by flames in their Bronx home seven blocks from Yankee Stadium. Their home was a total loss and Foy lost all of his trophies and memorabilia. But for Foy's quick actions, his parents might have lost their lives as well.

As the Tigers left town on May 14, with their tails between their legs following their doubleheader loss at Fenway Park, the Red Sox prepared to establish their legitimacy. With better than a month of the season gone, they had gotten a chance to get used to their new skipper, Dick Williams, and to one another. On more than one occasion, their starting line-up had included four rookies.

The struggling Baltimore Orioles followed the Tigers into Fenway for a two-game series. The reigning World Champions were off to a terrible start and the Red Sox hoped to take advantage of the faltering Birds.

When the last Baltimore runner had touched home on May 17, it turned out that the Red Sox pitching staff was the one that took the pounding. The Orioles racked Red Sox pitching for 20-runs as they swept a pair. Reliever John Wyatt, who had been unhittable during the first month of the season, was hammered in game one's 8-5 loss. A variety of Red Sox pitchers, principally Galen Cisco and Bill Landis, were handled easily by the O's in a 12-8 loss in the second game.

Twenty-nine games into the season, one had to wonder about the Red Sox pitching. Any team that gives up 56 runs in 6 games against the Tigers and Orioles has a suspect staff. The Red Sox hitters looked sharp but no amount of slugging could overcome that defect on a consistent basis.

Red Sox hopes were boosted when the home team took three games out of four from the visiting Cleveland Indians. Jim Lonborg gave the Red Sox bullpen a much needed rest in the series opener with a four-hit, 3-2 victory. The Red Sox rebounded from a disheartening 4-3 loss on Saturday with a doubleheader sweep the following day. George Scott's two-run homer was the key hit in the 4-3 opening game win and Bucky Brandon pitched a complete game in the 6-2 nightcap win. At 16-17, the Red Sox were close to Dick Williams' spring training prediction.

The Red Sox moved one step closer to Williams' pledge by opening a three-game series in Tiger Stadium with a 5-2 win. Free-spirit Dennis Bennett pitched well enough to win and to avoid permanent banishment to Dick Williams' doghouse.

Lonborg carried the day in the second game of the series. All he did was go the distance, strike out eleven Tigers, and earn his fifth win with a 1-0 shutout. His great effort was offset by a 9-3 shellacking handed to the Red Sox the next day. Old friend Earl Wilson went the distance to add insult to injury. More than one player thought about how good Wilson, who was traded to Detroit by the Red Sox in June 1966 for journey-man Don Demeter, would look in a Boston uniform again. Still, two out of three in Bengal territory wasn't shabby.

The next stop for the Red Sox was Baltimore's Memorial Stadium. After the Oriole's 20-run bombardment a week and one-half earlier, their pitching staff must have been quaking. The Friday night opener wasn't a bomb shell, but it didn't make the 4-3 loss any easier to take. Billy Rohr had to be relieved in the fourth inning adding to Dick Williams' pitching concern. The O's bats really came to life on Saturday. Frank Robinson's two home runs set the tone of a 10-0 drubbing. In the Sunday wrap-up, Jim Lonborg put his finger in the dike once more. Jim served up the stopper and Reggie Smith, who was finally starting to hit, led the offense to a 4-3 win.

In spite of their erratic ways, the Red Sox drew 32,012 fans to Fenway for a Memorial Day doubleheader against the Angels. They hadn't found the key to consistency yet, but they had turned on Hub fans with their dynamic brand of ball. This near-sellout crowd was a dramatic change from 1966 when the Red Sox averaged only about 10,000 fans per game.

Doubleheaders seemed to be the Red Sox forte as they swept California 5-4 and 6-1. Dan Osinski took the win in game one. Nine different pitchers had shared in the first twenty Boston wins at that point. Pinch hitter Tony Horton chipped in with a key double in the eighth to drive in the winning run in the first game. Dennis Bennett kept up his winning ways with a five-hit complete game in the night cap. The Red Sox used a variety of offensive tactics including a suicide squeeze bunt to seal the win.

FIRST QUARTER REPORT CARD

Overall B+: The team had improved by five wins over '66 and they were in third place only four and one-half games off the pace of the league-leading Tigers.

Straight A's: Rico Petrocelli with a .325 averages and infield leadership, and Jim Lonborg at 6-1, including several key wins, go to the head of the class.

A-: Tony Conigliaro, at .304 and Carl Yastrzemski, showing renewed enthusiasm, at .299 with ten home runs and John Wyatt as a tower of strength in the bullpen, all deserve recognition.

Solid B's: Mike Andrews at second, the catching combination of Gibson/Ryan, Tony Horton as a six-for-thirteen pinch hitter and Dennis Bennett with three wins and a 3.12 ERA are all contributing.

Needs Improvement: Reggie Smith must continue to improve his .204 average, plus Lee Stange with only one win and Jose Santiago with a 6.30 ERA must round into form if the Red Sox are going to truly make a run at it.

F for Weight: George Scott and Joe Foy continue to battle the scales and Dick Williams. The battle is tougher for Foy who is hitting about 20 points under his weight at 192 .

Selected Red Sox Hitters as of May 31, 1967

Player	H	R	HR	BA
Petrocelli	50	23	6	.325
Conigliaro	28	13	2	.304
Yastrzemski	46	30	10	.299
Andrews	36	16	2	.290
Jones	17	10	2	.283
Scott	39	18	3	.271
Gibson	14	4	0	.250
Smith	31	22	2	.212
Foy	23	17	4	.192

Next into Fenway were the heavy-weight Minnesota Twins for a two-game series. The Red Sox picked up their fourth straight win on Wednesday, May 31, behind Yaz's two home runs and Bucky Brandon's good effort with relief from John Wyatt. The Twins earned a split the next day as Dean Chance threw a four-hit shutout. Billy Rohr suffered his third straight loss.

The Red Sox then took their act on the road for six games. This Midwestern swing brought them to Cleveland for three games and on to Chicago for three more. They were counting on Jim Lonborg to get them off on the right foot and the 6' 5" right-hander came through again. His three-hitter gave the Red Sox a 2-1 win in the opener on June 2, before just 8,800 fans at cavernous Municipal Stadium.

Dennis Bennett was beginning to look like a potential number three starter as he improved his record to 4-1 on Saturday. Boston came up empty on Sunday as Steve Hargan blanked them 3-0.

The Red Sox made their first major player move on that fateful Sunday on June 4th in Cleveland. General Manager Dick O'Connell announced the trade of Tony Horton and outfielder Don Demeter to the Indians for veteran starting pitcher Gary Bell. The big right-hander was 30 years old, and in his 10th big league season, all of them with the Indians. Bell was originally a starter for the Tribe and averaged 12 wins a year for them in his first 5 years. Cleveland then used him in relief for a number of seasons and returned him to his starters' role in 1966 with a resulting 14 victories. The Red Sox projected him as a much needed number-two starter.

Just three days earlier, O'Connell had dealt veteran reliever Don McMahon to the Chicago White Sox for the versatile utility infielder Jerry Adair. Adair had played for nine seasons in Baltimore before his trade to the White Sox in June 1966. Jerry had been a teammate of manager Dick Williams on the Orioles in 1962 and 1963, and Williams told the media, "Adair is the consummate professional," when Jerry was acquired by the Red Sox on June 1, 1967. Williams was particularly impressed that Adair had once played the second game of a doubleheader for the Orioles after taking 11 stitches in the first game when he was hit in the face by an errant throw.

Clearly, the Red Sox front office was going to go for it. General Manager O'Connell told the *Boston Globe*, "This is one of those years when it looks like the pennant is up for grabs. I think we can win it." O'Connell was in his 20th season with the Red Sox when owner Tom Yawkey promoted Dick to the position of general manager in September 1965.

O'Connell was a local guy with a master's degree from Boston College, and he became the business manager of the Red Sox farm club in Lynn, MA, in 1946. When the Lynn franchise was dropped in 1949, Yawkey personally hired O'Connell for the Red Sox front office. O'Connell was the first non-baseball person to serve as the Red Sox general manager during Tom Yawkey's ownership and he was the first general manager that wasn't a crony of Yawkey's.

The newly bolstered Red Sox set off from Cleveland to Chicago and venerable Comiskey Park. If White Sox fans had shown up for the opener on Tuesday, they would have seen a highly embarrassed Boston team. The Red Sox blew a 3-0 lead and watched their teammate of a week earlier, Don McMahon; contribute in relief to a 5-3 White Sox victory. Following a rainout on Wednesday, and a 5-2 loss in the opener of Thursday's doubleheader, the Red Sox came back to life. The first bright spot was the complete game victory by Gary Bell: just what they had picked him up to do. The second ray of hope was Carl Yastrzemski. Yaz went four for five in the nightcap, including a home run, to cap an eight-hit evening. His recent tear had brought his average up 23 points in a week to .322 and raised his home run output to 12. The 27-year-old veteran was on fire.

The Red Sox were looking forward to their upcoming nine-game home stand and to the arrival of the Washington Senators for a four-game set. Washington had edged out the '66 Red Sox for eighth place by a game and one-half. The Red Sox knew they had progressed tremendously but the Solons had done little to improve themselves.

The Red Sox jumped out to a good start with an 8-7 win in the Friday night, June 9 opener. Joe Foy showed signs of coming to life with two key, late-innings, home runs. Foy had been benched a few days earlier for newcomer Adair. His Friday night performance let Dick Williams know that his proud third baseman had gotten the message. The bigger American League story that day was the Minnesota Twins firing manager Sam Mele. Mele had led Minnesota to the World Series in 1965 and to a second place finish in 1966, but Twins' owner Calvin Griffith was disappointed with his team's 25-25 start. Mele was replaced by Cal Ermer who was a long-time manager in the Twins' minor league system.

On Saturday the Senator's behemoth Frank Howard, 6' 7" with 260 pounds of muscle, did the Red Sox in with two towering four-baggers in a 7-3 Washington win. The Red Sox had to settle for a doubleheader split on Sunday: a 4-3 win and a tough 8-7 loss. Rico Petrocelli had the winning hit in the opener and Foy continued hot with a key double. Tony Conigliaro's three-run homer was the Red Sox highlight in game two.

When the Senators left town, the Red Sox had played all nine of their American League opponents at least once at home and once away. Many of the veterans of the 1967 Red Sox saw this as a turning point. Russ Gibson remembered, "We had seen them all a couple of times and we hadn't seen anyone who was noticeably better than us." Mike Andrews remembered it similarly, "Nobody scared us. We knew at that point that we had an even shot every time we took the field."

The arrival of the Yankees for a two-game stay lacked some of the luster of visits of earlier years. The former Bronx Bombers had finished a desultory tenth in 1966, and showed no signs of improving markedly on that in 1967. But a Red Sox-Yankees contest was still an event and the almost 19,000 fans on hand for the first game weren't disappointed. Gary Bell came through for the second straight time and the home team had a 3-1 victory. Russ Gibson hit his first 1967 (and what turned out to be his only) home run. The Red Sox lost 5-3 on Wednesday night but Tony C. homered again and Joe Foy continued his torrid streak with a home run of his own.

The three-game series with the visiting White Sox proved to be another turning point in the year. After splitting a doubleheader on Wednesday, the Red Sox showed that they were a team that wouldn't quit in the "rubber" game on June 15.

Rookie Gary Waslewski and the White Sox' Bruce Howard hooked up in a classic pitcher's duel. Howard left for a pinch hitter in the top of the eighth after putting seven shutout innings on the board, but Waslewski continued his string of zeroes through nine. The knuckleball specialist Hoyt Wilhelm kept Boston at bay through innings eight and nine. Dick Williams decided Waslewski had gone as far as he could at the end of nine. Red Sox iron-man John Wyatt continued the scoreless streak in the tenth and crafty veteran John Buzhardt matched him in relief of Wilhelm in the Red Sox' half of the tenth.

The White Sox finally squeezed out a run against Wyatt in the top of the 11th eleventh. In classic Go-Go-Chisox fashion, Walt "No Neck" Williams led off with a double, moved over to third on a Don Buford smash to Scott, and scored the go-ahead run on a Ken Berry single. That one run loomed very large in this evening of pitching dominance.

The White Sox sole run looked even bigger when the first two Red Sox hitters went down meekly in the last of the eleventh. More than a few of the 16,775 fans started for the exits as Joe Foy stepped in against Buzhardt.

This was a rejuvenated Joe Foy and he refused to say die, sending a ground ball single into left field. Tony C., who Mike Andrews calls "the greatest clutch hitter I've ever seen," stood in against the right-handed Buzhardt. The count ran to 2-2. Then Tony sent a Buzhardt fastball rocketing in the direction of the left field wall. Any fair weather fan who had made it to nearby Kenmore Square to catch the "T" must have thought a miracle had been performed judging from the roar of the remaining fans. Tony had snatched victory from the jaws of defeat with his game winning blast into the screen high above "the green monster."

If it failed to qualify as a miracle, the ensuing scene seemed to be a vision: every Red Sox player, led by Carl Yastrzemski, gathered at home plate to welcome the conquering hero. Veteran press box observers were hard-pressed to remember the last time this had occurred. This was another example of how different things were for the Boston Red Sox in 1967. And for the first time in the 1967 season long-time, cynical Red Sox fans began to wonder: could 1967 be different than all the disappointing years that came before?

At the time, the musical "Man of LaMancha," based on the legend of Don Quixote, was selling out every night on Broadway, and a road-show version was playing in Boston. The best-known song from the play, *The Impossible Dream*, had become a hugely popular hit. *The Boston Globe's* night editor Peter Stilla, Sr., had recently taken his wife to see Man of LaMancha, and on June 15 the musical offered him a bit of inspiration. So on June 16, the day following the Red Sox dramatic 11-inning victory,

The Boston Globe used "Impossible Dream" as their headline for the game story.

It was only one of hundreds of headlines about the 1967 team that year but it captured their unlikely quest for the American League pennant perfectly. The catchphrase "Impossible Dream" caught on immediately and it became their permanent theme. The ball club that had been commonly known as the "Red Flops" at the end of the 1966 season had morphed into the "Impossible Dream" team just 58 games into the 1967 season!

The Red Sox left home on a natural high. The win over the White Sox was one of the more dramatic comebacks in recent Red Sox history. They were in third place, only four games behind the just vanquished White Sox. And they were heading for Washington with new stopper Gary Bell slated for game one.

The 1967 Red Sox had something of a schizophrenic side and it showed in the series opening twi-night doubleheader in Washington. Gary Bell did everything that could be asked of him, going all the way and holding the Senators to one run. Unfortunately, his teammates came up with nine hits but could not score one runner. In game two, the Red Sox blew a three-run lead giving up four runs in the last of the ninth. Young teams, and the typical 1967 Red Sox starting lineup averaged 27-years of age, will have their ups and downs.

Jim Lonborg proved to be a legitimate stopper on Saturday as he pitched the Red Sox to a 5-1 victory. His win brought his record to 8-2 and his win total represented more than twenty-five percent of their wins to date. Unfortunately, the Red Sox dropped another tough one on Sunday to the Senators. Washington prevailed 4-3 in ten innings. Their record was back to .500: 31-31.

Joe Foy symbolized the Red Sox erratic performance more than any single player. Coming off of his excellent rookie year with the Red Sox, Foy expected to really shine in 1967. Playing for the ninth place 1966 Red Sox, he had still managed to score ninety-seven runs and put together a slugging average of .413. With old teammates Reggie Smith, Mike Andrews and Russ Gibson coming up from Toronto, he expected to play the role of the seasoned veteran and show them how the game was played in "the Bigs." Instead some of the rookies were outperforming him.

Joe also hadn't anticipated any problems with rookie manager Dick Williams. Foy had been Williams' star in his managing debut in Toronto in 1965. He had burned up the International League and led his team to the Calder Cup. His starry season was highlighted by *The Sporting News* designation as the Minor League Player of the Year. Then Foy became the first ballplayer that Dick Williams sent to the major leagues when Joe became the Red Sox regular third baseman in 1966.

Foy didn't have any illusions about Williams—he certainly didn't expect any special treatment. But he didn't expect to end up in Williams' doghouse within the first month of the season. Nor did he expect to be treated like another George Scott. Scott and Foy had been rookies together in 1966. Both were young African American infielders with enormous potential. But that was where the similarities ended. Joe was street-smart, having grown up in the Bronx. George was from rural Greenville, Mississippi, and the 23-year-old old was naive in the ways of dealing with the city. Foy had learned to use his mind and rapier wit to cope with his mostly white teammates and an all-white press corps. George had a tendency to say whatever was on his mind to whomever he was speaking. Scott's presence actually helped Foy as a rookie. The Boomer was such a lightening rod for attention that Foy was able to quietly establish himself.

Red Sox second baseman Mike Andrews, who was a teammate of Foy's in 1964 on the Red Sox farm club in Reading, PA, and again in 1965 at Toronto, remembered having a wonderful rapport with Joe. "Joe was the first black person I was close to," Andrews said, "and pretty soon he was my best friend. He was so special," Mike recalled, "and everyone felt the same way about Joe."

Foy was glad to be heading to New York for the scheduled three-game series with the Yankees. New York was home and it would give him a chance to visit with his parents and friends. It would also give him a chance to put his season into perspective. His season of high hopes had threatened to turn into a nightmare as he struggled to bring his batting average to .200.

Joseph Anthony Foy was born in New York City on February 21, 1943. Foy grew up in the Bronx and graduated from Evander Childs

JOE FOY

At 1967 Spring Training.

High School in 1960. He had played baseball throughout his youth and he excelled at catcher and all the infield positions. In spite of his versatility major league scouts were turned off by his weight—a weakness that would follow him throughout his baseball career. Foy continued to play sandlot baseball after graduation from high school and ultimately the Minnesota Twins signed him for a modest bonus.

Joe Foy began his professional baseball career in 1962, playing for the Twins' farm team at Eire in the New York-Pennsylvania League. He batted .285 and showed power in his first professional season but when the Twins failed to include him on their protected list for the minor league draft, the Red Sox claimed him for the bargain price of $8,000. Joe started his Red Sox career at Winston-Salem in the Carolina League in 1963, and three years later he was the starting third baseman for the Boston Red Sox.

Foy's parents lived within a mile or so of Yankee Stadium. He always looked forward to staying with them when the Red Sox came to New York. It was a big thrill for a kid growing up in the Bronx to journey from "home" to the ballpark he had only dreamed about playing in as a kid.

When Foy's cab pulled up in front of his parent's home, he almost went into shock: their house was in flames. He had the presence of mind to rush into the building, locate his parents and lead them to the safety of the street. There, they watched with neighbors as the three-story structure burned to the ground.

Foy's trophies and clippings heralding his starry New York schoolboy athletic career were all in the ashes. But his parents were fine and he knew they would start over.

Joe was relieved when the Monday night game with the Yankees was rained out. It gave him some time to help his parents to relocate and come to grips with the near tragedy. He was glad for the time but he was also anxious to get back to baseball to get his mind off the shock of the fire.

Foy was ready for the Tuesday night game against Yankee veteran Mel Stottlemyre. His parents had settled into temporary living quarters and he always looked forward to playing before his old home town crowd. Besides, he had raised his average almost 50 points since his benching and he was on a long-ball streak.

Just how ready he was would become apparent when he came to bat against the Yankees with the bases loaded in the fourth inning. Foy

Foy greeted by teammates and bat boy Ricky Williams.

got all of a Stottlemyre fastball and drove it into the distant left-field bleachers for a grand slam home run. Joe felt as if he was all of the way back. A Carl Yastrzemski homer was the frosting on the cake as the Red Sox eased into a 7-1 victory. Gary Bell showed once more why the Red Sox had been so anxious to acquire him as he picked up his third victory in two weeks.

On the morning of the second game against the Yankees Red Sox owner Tom Yawkey dropped a bombshell on Red Sox fans. The headline on the front page of *The Boston Globe* read: "Yawkey Will Move Red Sox If Stadium Not Built Soon." The story quoted Yawkey as saying, "This is not a threat it is simply a statement of fact." Asked if his club would still be playing in Fenway Park five years from then, Yawkey responded, "No."

Will McDonough of the Globe, who was granted this one-hour, exclusive interview, pointed out that Massachusetts politicians had been debating the merits of a new stadium for years but they weren't even close to action. Yawkey cited the small capacity of Fenway and the difficulty of parking nearby as impediments to a successful operation. Yawkey added, "I am losing money with the Red Sox and no one—unless he is a damn fool—likes to lose money."

Yawkey's dramatic statement didn't have any impact on the players and the Red Sox were sky-high as they took the field for the second game with the Yankees on Wednesday night. Their ace Jim Lonborg was on the mound and the prospect of facing twenty-six-year-old rookie pitcher Thad Tillotson didn't fill them with fear either.

The Red Sox jumped out ahead quickly. Tony C did most of the damage with a three-run homer and Boston led 4-0 when they took the field in the bottom of the first. Lonborg handled the Yankees with ease in their at bat and the Red Sox were sailing.

The Red Sox were back after it in the top of the second. Reggie Smith singled but was thrown out trying for second. After Lonborg struck out, Andrews walked bringing Joe Foy to the plate. Conscious of the previous night's grand slam, Tillotson worked Foy high and tight. His third pitch was so high and tight that it struck Joe flush on his left temple. Foy stood his ground—his batting helmet had taken the force of the pitch—and stared intently out at the mound. After registering his feelings, he trotted down to take his place at first. Yaz then singled in Andrews to put the Red Sox up 5-0.

When Thad Tillotson came to the plate in the last of the second, the whole ballpark was waiting to see what would happen. They didn't have to wait long as Lonborg nailed him between the shoulder blades with his first pitch. As Tillotson trotted to first, everyone watched for the spark that would ignite the blaze. Tillotson struck it by mentioning to Lonborg that he would get even.

Joe Foy didn't need a formal invitation to the festivities. He had plenty of pent-up emotion and Tillotson's body language brought him from third base to first base in record time. His words to Tillotson? "If you want to fight, fight me."

What happened next was a classic baseball brawl out of "This Week in Baseball," or in some ways, a re-run of "The Keystone Cops." Joe Pepitone, one of the most colorful Yankees of all-time, led his teammates' charge from the dugout. Rico Petrocelli, anxious to renew acquaintances with his old Brooklyn neighbor Pepitone, rushed to the scene from his position at short. Rico's brother Dave, a special policeman at Yankee Stadium, anticipating a neighborhood reunion, raced on to the field brandishing his night stick.

Both bullpens emptied. It's a long way from the pens in cavernous Yankee Stadium but the occupants were all at first base within moments of the start of the altercation. Tony Conigliaro was racing in from right field when one of the Yankees tackled him from behind. He told Ray Fitzgerald of the *Boston Globe*, "It definitely was an illegal block and a fifteen-yard penalty."

Reggie Smith finally got into it with Tillotson. Reggie was a student of karate and apparently saw this as an ideal opportunity to try out his skills. In Fitzgerald's words, Reggie "...gave it the old "Crusher Casey" treatment by picking Tillotson up, spinning him around and throwing him to the ground like an old candy wrapper."

But the real show was Pepitone and Petrocelli or the "Petrocelli's." After the game, they both claimed they were kidding. George Scott responded, "They said they were only kidding, but that was a helluva time to be kidding around, with everybody on the field."

Pepitone told the *Globe's* Cliff Keane, "I was having this session with Rico Petrocelli. I know Rico. We were kidding. All of a sudden somebody said something I didn't like. Maybe it was Rico. Pretty soon I was on the ground. I don't know who got me, but he was mussing up my hair and I don't like that. All I know is I grabbed some dirt and half tossed it at Rico to joke and the whole place was in a jam."

Yankee John Kennedy was angriest at Rico's brother. He told Keane, "I know the guy. He was out on the field. He's a special cop and he's out on the field yelling, 'I'll kill all you guys,' and that's a hell of a thing for anyone to be saying."

Rico Petrocelli was certain that Kennedy was mistaken. "I could hear my brother [Dave] and all he was saying was 'Where's my brother? Where's my brother…Pepitone, where's my brother?'"

Dick Williams was in the middle of the melee, and he told reporters later, "I had to look both ways to see if I was going to get whacked more from my own players than the Yankees."

One player stood apart and alone as the battle was pitched. Gentleman Jim Lonborg stood on the mound with his arms folded as the melee took place. "I didn't want to get hurt," is the way Jim remembers it.

Lonborg recalls, "Tillotson knew I was going to hit him. I didn't have any choice. I'm out to protect my teammates and to win the game." Jim had come a long way in overcoming his image as too nice to win.

A semblance of order was finally restored and the game was resumed. Actually the game was somewhat anticlimactic as most of the fireworks had already taken place. Scott homered in the third to put the Red Sox up 6-0 and now everyone waited for Lonborg's at-bat in the fourth. That proved somewhat anticlimactic as well. Tillotson came in tight to Lonborg but did not hit him. Whether his control wasn't good enough to nail him is unknown, but Lonborg eventually went down on strikes.

Joe Foy contributed a key single after Andrews had followed Lonborg's strikeout with a walk. Yaz brought in Andrews with a single to extend the lead. When the top of the fourth came to an end, Yankee manager Ralph Houk had been ejected for arguing a Bill Haller call at first and the Red Sox were up 8-0.

The balance of the game was largely uneventful. Lonborg did bean Dick Howser in the bottom of the fifth but the umpires said "enough is enough" and there were no further incidents. Lonborg recorded his ninth win of the year and the Red Sox prevailed 8-1. As a reminder that 1967 was a very different era than today, Lonborg threw 170 pitches to earn his complete game.

A baseball season consists of 162 games and a few critical incidents. These critical incidents indicate a team's character and its make-up. One such critical incident had occurred a week earlier when the Red Sox had come from behind to beat the White Sox 2-1 in 11 innings. The make-up of the team had been indicated when every Red Sox uniform had crowded around home plate to acknowledge Tony C's game-winning homer.

Another critical incident had occurred that evening in Yankee Stadium when Lonborg put the league on notice that Red Sox pitchers would protect their hitters. And the team had backed that up by showing they were ready to do battle. Dueling with fastballs would come back to haunt them on August 18 at Fenway Park, but this was not a Red Sox team of "twenty-five players and twenty-five taxi cabs."

Joe Foy would continue to play well for the next six or seven weeks. On July 15, in a game against the Baltimore Orioles that the Red Sox won 5-1, Foy started a triple play that contributed to the victory. By the end of July he was hitting a solid .240 with sixteen home runs. But he would fail to hit one home run in the final two months. On August 8, Foy was benched for Jerry Adair again and Adair got hot once more. For the rest of the season, Foy shared his third base spot with Adair and Dalton Jones. Foy ended the season with a batting average of .251, 11 points off his rookie mark of .262, and only 49 RBI after bringing in 63 in 1966.

Although Foy's performance tailed off, he remained one of the best-liked players on the team. Carl Yastrzemski was close to Joe Foy. "Joe was always up-beat and optimistic," Yaz recalled in an interview with *The Boston Globe*. "When the pressure built up, Joe was always the guy who kept us loose."

Dick Williams gave him a shot to redeem himself in the World Series against St. Louis. He started him at third in three games and used him as a pinch hitter in the other four, but the best he could manage was one single and one double in fifteen at bats. Foy's series batting average of .133 symbolized the personal disappointment that 1967 had turned out to be for Joe.

Foy was returned to his regular role at third for the Red Sox in 1968. After all, he was still only twenty-five-years old and he had a world of potential. But like many of his '67 teammates, he couldn't seem to get untracked. His average deteriorated further to .225 and his home run output declined to ten. A much-publicized off the field incident with itinerant Red Sox pitcher Juan Pizarro apparently exhausted the Red Sox' patience. During the off season, he was plucked from the Red Sox by the newly created Kansas City Royals in the expansion draft.

Kansas City represented a fresh start for the free-spirit Foy. He was one of the more talented players on that expansion team and he brought his average back up to the .262 mark. He led the team in at bats and RBI with 71. Demonstrating his athleticism, he appeared at every infield position and even played 16 games in the outfield.

The New York Mets were so impressed that they traded Amos Otis and Bob Johnson to get Foy. Otis went on to star for Kansas City in their outfield for 14 seasons. The trade appeared to be just the second chance that Foy needed.

The 1969 Mets had been the amazing Mets who had defeated the Baltimore Orioles four games to one for the World Championship. They appeared to be a dynasty in the making with only one weakness: a solid third baseman. At age 27, Foy seemed made to order to fill that role. Best of all, Joe was coming back to his native New York.

Things just didn't work out for the Mets or for Foy in 1970. Their pitching collapsed and they finished in third place, six games behind the Pittsburgh Pirates in the National League East. Foy's average fell off to .236 and he managed only six home runs. Worst of all, he committed 18 errors in only 97 seven games at third base. To round it all out, the ebullient Foy and taciturn Mets manager Gill Hodges never saw eye-to-eye. It was clear to all observers that Foy did not always make the best choices off the field.

Joe's next stop was with a terrible Washington team under manager Ted Williams. This Williams knew that Foy still had some talent left and he was willing to give him a shot. But Foy's skills were largely dissipated and he managed only 30 hits in limited action and produced no home runs in 128 at bats.

Washington turned out to be his last stop. At age 28 Foy left baseball never to return. The promising career which had begun only five years earlier was over.

Foy was not only out of baseball, but generally out of the public eye. While he stayed in touch with some of his 1967 teammates, he was little more than an answer to a trivia question for the Boston Red Sox fans.

Later in his life Joe Foy was able to overcome the substance abuse challenges that had plagued him for many years. He became a counselor to young people, sharing the importance of good choices and he was attending Lehman College in the Bronx. But on October 12, 1989, at the age of 46, Foy died of a heart attack. His death occurred on the 22nd anniversary of Game Seven of the 1967 World Series. Like teammates Tony Conigliaro, Jerry Adair, Elston Howard and Don McMahon, and nine other teammates from the Impossible Dream team, Joe was gone too soon.

Foy's son, Joe, Jr., was the starting guard on the Holy Cross football team at the time of his father's death. He played for the Purple on the very next day. After the game, he said "My father played on the day right after a tragedy [referring to the fire at his grandparent's house in June 1967], and I wanted to play too."

Before his death, Joe, Sr., was extremely proud of his son. The first thing he said to former Red Sox' public relations director, Bill Crowley at the twentieth reunion of the '67 Red Sox was, "Will you tell all these guys that my son is at Holy Cross on an **academic** scholarship!"

Joe Foy had to deal with a fair amount of adversity in his life after baseball. And deal with it he did. There is every reason to believe that Joe Foy had turned his life around before his untimely death.

It is often said that an abundance of talent is the greatest curse of all. In Joe Foy's case, there was a lot of truth in this quotation. He was certainly gone too soon. May he rest in peace.

Chapter 5

Ding Dong! The Arrival of Gary Bell

Boston Red Sox vs. Cleveland Indians, Sunday, July 23, 1967

When *Gary Bell* took the mound for game two of the doubleheader in Cleveland, he had been a member of the Boston Red Sox for seven weeks. Before then he had spent nine and one-half years wearing the uniform of his opponents, the Cleveland Indians. The thirty-year-old veteran pitcher was determined to show the raucous home crowd that he was still in his prime and that he could add to the Red Sox streak of nine straight wins. Bell had started strongly during his first weeks with the Red Sox but he had faltered of late. Gary Bell was arguably the funniest man on the Red Sox. When Bell and manager Williams attended a function where Gary was the featured speaker, a questioner asked Bell what kind of hitter Williams was when the two played against one another. Without missing a beat, Bell replied, "Without a doubt, the toughest hitter I ever faced."

After their "main event" in the melee at Yankee Stadium, the Red Sox returned home for a three-game series against the Cleveland Indians beginning on June 23. Tom Yawkey might have been concerned about the adequacy of parking around Fenway Park but 30,233 fans made their way to welcome home their new-found heroes. There hadn't been any "Pennant Fever Grips Hub" headlines yet, but their long-suffering fans recognized that something was different about the 1967 Red Sox. And with box seats at $3, grandstand seats at $2, and bleacher seats at $1, Red Sox tickets were within reach for all fans.

Home cooking seemed to agree with them as they took two-out-of-three from the Tribe. In the series opener Lee "Stinger" Stange won his second game of the season with an 8-4 complete-game and Joe Foy continued his hot streak with four hits and four RBI. On Saturday, the Red Sox lost 3-2 before 30,027 fans celebrating Family Day at Fenway Park. Their last four loses were all by one run, a disturbing trend. Carl Yastrzemski and Joe Foy homered on Sunday to set the tone for an 8-3 win. Gary Bell prevailed over his former club achieving his 100th major league victory.

A total of about 84,000 fans had watched the three-game weekend series, bringing the attendance to date to almost 500,000. Their attendance through the same date in 1966 was less than on-half of this figure. Attendance projected to more than one million fans for the season. The Red Sox had not exceeded one million fans since Ted Williams retired in 1960.

As the Red Sox packed for a long 13-game road trip beginning on June 26, they were in 3rd place, 5 games out of first and 3 games over .500. Most Red Sox teams have been tailored for Fenway and the road has often been their downfall. Experts felt that the next two weeks would tell quite a bit about the Red Sox' prospects.

Their first stop was Minneapolis-St. Paul and veteran Jim Kaat brought them down to earth immediately. Kaat out-dueled Jim Lonborg 2-1 and the Red Sox had another frustrating one-run loss. The following evening the Red Sox proved they could win a close one, as Tony C's two-run home run sparked them to a 3-2 win. Rookie Gary Waslewski from Kensington, Connecticut, was the surprise starter and the even more unlikely winner. It was the twenty-five-year-old hurler's first major league victory. The following night, the Twins' starting pitcher, Dave Boswell, struck out 12 Red Sox batters in five innings and held on for a 3-2 win. Lee Stange was the hard-luck loser for Boston and his record fell to 2-5.

Kansas City proved particularly hospitable to the Red Sox as they swept a three-game series, which began on June 30. Gary Bell advanced his Boston record to 5-1 as Tony C's three-run homer powered the Red Sox to a 5-3 win. Looking back, Gary Bell said, "It was so easy to fit in with that Red Sox team. Within a couple of weeks I felt like I have been with the Red Sox all season. That was a great bunch of guys."

Saturday was a "laugher" as Jim Lonborg coasted to his tenth win, 10-2. Conigliaro continued to set the offensive pace with three hits including his eleventh home run. Rookie Waslewski continued his imitation of Christy Mathewson as he held the A's to three hits on Sunday. Joe Foy's mammoth home run in the eighth proved to be the winner as reliever John Wyatt preserved a 2-1 victory, for his third save in five games.

At age 32, Wyatt was one of the older players on this young team. In fact, his professional baseball career had begun 14 years earlier with the Indianapolis Clowns in the Negro Leagues. Three years later he was sold to the Kansas City Athletics and he began a long climb through their minor league system. Kansas City called him up to the majors in 1960, and he remained with the A's until he was traded to the Red Sox in 1966. Wyatt was reported to use Vaseline to make the ball do magic in tight spots. When asked about it, he would only smile.

Selected Red Sox Hitters As of June 30, 1967

Player	H	R	HR	BA
Yastrzemski	84	47	18	.331
Conigliaro	60	32	11	.308
Petrocelli	66	29	8	.296
Scott	74	31	10	.289
Andrews	58	33	2	.259
Foy	57	41	10	.248
Gibson	22	6	1	.232
Jones	18	10	2	.231
Smith	48	29	4	.204

It was a happy band of players that enplaned to Los Angeles from Kansas City. The calendar had flipped to July and they were very much in the hunt. Best of all, they were 4-2 on their current road trip.

Game one against the Angels continued on a positive note. Starter Lee Stange pitched well to pick up the 9-3 win. Three players under the age of twenty-five: Mike Andrews, Reggie Smith and Tony C all homered in the game. The Red Sox juggernaut finally ran out of gas as they dropped the second game of the series, played on the fourth of July, by a score of 4-3.

That Fourth of July game was marked by the major league debut of Albert "Sparky" Lyle who pitched scoreless seventh and eighth innings for the Red Sox. Sparky's debut went unnoticed by the media, but he went on to pitch five strong seasons with the Red Sox before being traded to the Yankees for the immortal Danny Cater. During his seven seasons in New York he was a three-time All-Star and he won the American League Cy Young award in 1977.

Things deteriorated the next day as they lost by the identical score of 4-3. This rubber game loss was even tougher because super-sub George Thomas had put them up 3-2 in the top of the ninth with a two-run homer only to be outdone by Don Mincher's two-run game-winning home run in the bottom of the ninth. The Red Sox were now 5-4 on their road trip.

The team moved onto Detroit recognizing that the Tigers were a formidable foe but remembering their own doubleheader sweep at Fenway in mid-May, and taking two-out-of-three in Detroit one week later. This time the Tigers were anything but toothless as they bested the Red Sox 5-4 in eleven innings in the series opener. On Saturday, Denny McLain did a complete reversal of his Mother's Day form, when the Red Sox knocked him out of the game in the fifth inning, as he shut the Red Sox down 2-0. The Red Sox needed a doubleheader win on Sunday to resurrect their winning record for the road trip.

Things looked grim in game one as the Tigers hammered starter Gary Bell. Old friend Earl Wilson, who would go on to win twenty-two games for the year, took the 10-4 decision. Enter Jim Lonborg in game two. Lonborg fought off oppressive heat and humidity as the Red Sox earned a split with a 3-0 victory. Once more, Lonborg, who was 5-1 in games started after a Red Sox loss, had come through with an important win and the Red Sox concluded their road trip with a respectable 6-7 record.

Looking back years later manager Williams said, "Lonborg's performance that day may have produced our most important win of the season. Think about it: we had lost five straight and we were heading into the All-Star break. A loss would have broken our momentum and undone a lot of what we had accomplished. Instead we got a win, a lift going into the break and we went on a real tear after the break. Lonborg's win that day was absolutely critical.

ALL STAR BREAK REPORT CARDS

Straight A's: Conigliaro, Yastrzemski, Petrocelli and Lonborg. Go directly to California for the mid-season classic.

B's: Scott, Andrews, Foy, Wyatt and Bell. Go directly to some well-earned rest (watch the calories, George and Joe).

C's: Smith, Tillman, Santiago and Brandon. Go and concentrate on a second-half improvement.

The 1967 All-Star game was played in Anaheim Stadium on July 11. Red Sox representatives made up one-third of the American League starting lineup with Yaz and Tony C starting in the outfield and Rico Petrocelli at shortstop. Yaz had three hits in the fifteen-inning 2-1 National League victory, and Jim Lonborg, who had pitched two days before was the only Red Sox player not to get into the game.

The All-Star break is an important benchmark in the baseball season. It marks the approximate halfway point and patterns have begun to form. At this point, the Red Sox were in the middle of the pack. They were in fifth place, within striking distance at six games out of first. The team's offense looked solid, but the pitching was definitely suspect. Dick Williams continued to be bothered by those one-run game defeats.

The Boston Red Sox returned from the All-Star break with renewed enthusiasm. They recognized that they had as good a shot at the pennant as any of the contenders. When asked right after the break if the Red Sox

American League Standings at the All-Star Break in 1967

Team	Wins	Loses	Winning %	GB
Chicago	47	33	.588	-
Detroit	45	35	.563	2.0
Minnesota	45	36	.556	2.5
California	45	40	.529	4.5
BOSTON	**41**	**39**	**.513**	**6.0**
Cleveland	40	42	.488	8.0
Baltimore	39	43	.476	9.0
New York	36	45	.444	11.5
Washington	36	47	.434	12.5
Kansas City	30	49	.417	14.5

would finish in the first division, Joe Foy replied, "First division? That's fifth place. Forget that. Why not go all the way?"

The Red Sox drew the slumping Baltimore Orioles in the first series of baseball's "second season." The Birds had swept the Dodgers in the previous years' World Series, but their pitching staff had collapsed in 1967. They were not a factor in the race.

The Red Sox got off on the right foot as they won the opener of a Thursday doubleheader at Fenway Park on July 13th. Lee Stange appeared to be rounding into form as he picked up another win in a 4-2 victory. The Red Sox showed their schizophrenic side in game two, however. Gary Bell had absolutely nothing for the second start in a row and the home team was embarrassed by a score of 10-0.

The Red Sox shook that one off quickly as they came back Friday night with a resounding 11-5 win. Yaz and Tony C powered the offense with long home runs and Jim Lonborg picked up his sixth win immediately following a Red Sox loss. On Saturday, Jose Santiago earned his fifth win coming on to pitch six innings of long relief as the Red Sox had the edge 5-1, in a game highlighted by a rare Red Sox triple play.

The triple play happened in the first inning as the culmination of an unusual series of events. Gary Waslewski was the starting pitcher that day and when Russ Gibson caught his pre-game warm-up pitches he realized Waslewski had absolutely nothing. Gibson went to

Dick Williams to let him know and the brash manager had Jose Santiago warming up before Waslewski even threw his first pitch. After Waz walked the first two batters and went to 2-1 on the Orioles Paul Blair, Williams called Santiago in from the bullpen. On Santiago's third pitch Blair hit a screaming line drive to third and Joe Foy snagged it for the first out. Foy then threw it to Mike Andrews at second for out number two, and Andrews threw it to first baseman George Scott to complete a 5-4-3 triple play.

Next into town were the Tigers for an unusual Sunday-Monday, two-game series. The visitors quickly discovered that they preferred the confines of Tiger Stadium to friendly Fenway, as the home team held on for a 9-5 win in the series opener on July 16. Once again, homers by Yaz and Tony C set the tone. On Monday, Boston moved into third place with an easy 7-1 win. Lee Stange pitched well once more and Joe Foy joined Yaz in the home run parade.

General manager Dick O'Connell continued to wheel and deal for the Red Sox, purchasing veteran first baseman Norm Siebern from the San Francisco Giants on July 15. Siebern provided back-up for George Scott at first base but be was acquired mainly to give the Red Sox a credible left-handed pinch hitter.

"Looking back," manager Williams said about O'Connell, "whatever I asked for Dick went out and got. I told him we needed a utility infielder and he got us Jerry Adair. When we needed starting pitching he came up with Gary Bell," Williams marveled. "In my mind, Dick O'Connell was the unsung hero of the 1967 Red Sox."

Their brief home stand was over but the Hose were off to a great start. They were 5-1 since the break and Stange looked like he could really help in the pennant drive. Their 36 runs in 6 games showed that their offense hadn't missed a beat.

The Red Sox feasted on the Birds once more the following night in Baltimore. Jim Lonborg earned his thirteenth win in a 6-2 triumph and Boston moved within two and one half games of the league-leading Chisox. Six was the magic number again on Wednesday, July 19, at Memorial Stadium. The Red Sox came out on top by a 6-4 score as Mike Andrews launched a three-run homer to join "the hero of the day" brigade.

In the clubhouse after this sixth straight win Yaz told reporters, "Nothing can stop us now. The schedule is in our favor and our pitching will get better." Yaz added, "We have a lot of young players and they will stay strong through September, and a lot of them are making $13,000 to $15,000, so they are motivated."

Manager Dick Williams was more reserved than Yaz. He told the media, "I'd rather not comment. We will win more than we will lose," he added, repeating his spring training comment. Pressed further, he closed with, "We still have a long way to go."

The Red Sox made the front page of *The Boston Globe* the following morning under the headline, "Sox Win 6th in Row: 1 ½ off," referring to their distance from first place in the American League. Long-time Globe columnist Harold Kaese penned an article to help Bostonians to determine if they had pennant fever. One test was: "When somebody mentions Bell and you think of Gary instead of the telephone company." Even casual fans were starting to pay attention to the Red Sox' pennant hopes.

After the last game of the Orioles series was rained out, the Red Sox headed to Cleveland on July 19 having won eight of their last nine. And they were riding the crest of a six-game winning streak.

Ballplayers usually dread a four-game weekend series in Cleveland in late July. Cavernous Municipal Stadium usually featured 60,000 empty seats and the heat can be oppressive. But on this occasion, the red hot Red Sox couldn't wait for the Friday night game to begin.

As it turned out, their anticipation was for good reason. Bucky Brandon added his name to the list of rejuvenated Boston pitchers, going all the way to pick up a 6-2 win. Make it seven in a row! Almost everybody got into the act on Saturday. Carl Yastrzemski poled his twenty-third home run. Mike Andrews contributed three hits and Joe Foy pitched in with a pair. Best of all, the Boston bullpen got another much needed day of rest. Lee Stange was never in trouble as he won a 4-0 decision. Eight-in-a-row and counting!

Sunday was get-away day. Immediately after the second game of the doubleheader, the team would head to the airport for a return flight to Boston. Then they had a twelve-game home stand continuing into early August to look forward to. But all twenty-five ballplayers were totally focused on that afternoon's twin bill with the Tribe. They were hot and they wanted to stay hot.

The team's intensity was heightened by the fact that their ace, Jim Lonborg, would be on the mound in game one. Lonborg had been there when they needed him all year. With lanky number sixteen on the mound, the team felt almost unbeatable.

The Indians countered with 6' 4" portsider, John O'Donoghue, in the opener. O'Donoghue was only a journeyman hurler, but he was the best the Tribe had available that day.

The Red Sox touched up the Cleveland southpaw for two runs in the opening frame on a Tony C four-bagger. They really opened up in the second inning. The bases were filled with players in Boston uniforms as Joe Foy stepped to the plate. Foy promptly unloaded on O'Donoghue and deposited a fastball deep within the left-field bleachers. Jim Lonborg, who could nurse a one-run lead with the best of them, had been staked to a six-run cushion.

The outcome was generally predictable: Lonborg pitched as well as he had to for the win. Yaz added some frosting on the cake with his 24th home run and the Red Sox eased into an 8-5 win. The Red Sox had won their ninth straight and Tony Conigliaro had become the youngest player in American League history to total 100 career home runs. Sixth months shy of his twenty-third birthday he was on track to take his place among baseball immortals.

The Red Sox clubhouse was a frenzy of excitement between games. In a season of 162 games, momentum can be a great uplift and the Red Sox were on a roll. The Red Sox couldn't wait to get on the field for the second game.

The good-natured Bell was widely known as "Ding Dong." The public assumed it was a play on his last name, but that wasn't true. Early in his career with Cleveland, a batter hit a sharp line drive directly back at Bell, and the ball hit Gary in the protective cup. Municipal Stadium was practically empty and the sound of the ball ricocheting off Bell's cup resonated throughout the stadium. From that day forward Gary was known as Ding Dong throughout professional baseball.

The sparse crowd of 13,787 fans couldn't wait for Gary Bell to get to the pitcher's mound. During his almost ten seasons in Cleveland, the Indians had never won a pennant. The previous year Bell had lost fifteen games in a Tribe uniform. The Cleveland faithful were a frustrated lot and Gary Bell made a handy scapegoat.

Bell also made a ready target for the Cleveland brass that weekend. Stung by his comeback after getting off to a 1-5 start in Cleveland, "unnamed sources" were taking a shot at Gary in the local newspapers at every opportunity. Their theme was "Gary pitches just well enough to lose ball games."

"I felt some emotion when I was traded to Boston from Cleveland in June," Gary told me. "After all I had been in their organization my whole professional career. But playing in Cleveland had started to feel like a life sentence," he chuckled. "I was tired of looking up at 60,000 empty seats in old Municipal Stadium so I was happy to be traded to Boston. Of course I'd be lying if I told you I had any idea how it would turn out!"

Ironically, Bell would be opposed in the nightcap by a future Boston legend: Luis Tiante. El Tiante had been shelled by the Red Sox on Friday night but manager Joe Adcock decided to have another go with him on Sunday, mainly because no other pitcher was available.

This was Bell's first appearance in Cleveland wearing a visiting team's uniform. The fans' "welcome home" made it appear that Bell had single-handedly started the fire on Lake Erie. The cries of Bell's nickname "Ding Dong" didn't exactly resound with a thank you note.

Gary had some mixed feelings facing his former teammates. After all, he had spent more than twelve years in the Indians' system and he had dressed in the clubhouse across the way for almost ten years. Just six weeks earlier, he had been sharing beers and swapping lies with the batters he was about to face.

"It did feel funny," Gary told me, "standing on the mound in Municipal Stadium. I was really happy to get out of Cleveland but I still had friends on their team and in the city. I was worried I might walk into the wrong dugout!"

GARY BELL

Bell was a 12-game winner in 1967.

El Tiante held the Red Sox at bay in the top of the first. Bell prepared himself for the jeers that were about to rain down upon him.

Bell remembered going to spring training with the Indians as a twenty year old in 1957 and the going-over he received from Tribe pitchers Bob Lemon, Mike Garcia and Early Wynn. Anything the fans could dish out would seem tame compared to the barbs he endured from the grizzled veterans who saw Bell as a threat to their jobs. Then he thought about Cleveland general manager, Gabe Paul, and his parsimony when it came to negotiating players' contracts. These memories really made Bell want to concentrate and shut his old teammates down.

Gary had not been that strong in his last several outings and he was determined to get off to a good start. Unfortunately, lead-off hitter Lee Maye got hold of a fastball and drove it sharply into right field. By the time Tony Conigliaro tracked it down and got to it, Maye was safely encamped on second base. Bell looked in to second baseman, Vern Fuller, and forced himself to concentrate. He might have been putting too much intensity into it as his next effort was a wild pitch, advancing Maye to third.

The Cleveland crowd finally had something to get excited about and they were really enjoying Bell's misfortune. Bell got a serious scare when Fuller launched a long fly ball to left field but Yaz gathered it in and the only damage was Lee Mayes's tally after tagging at third. Gary breathed a sigh of relief when he got out of the inning without further damage.

For his part, Luis Tiant was proving as tough to hit on Sunday as he had been easy to hit on Friday. The Red Sox were retired meekly in the top of the second. Luis was in his fifth year with the Indians and he had won ten or more games each season, but it wouldn't be until 1968 that he blossomed into a premier major league pitcher.

Bell felt himself finding his rhythm in the second. Primarily, a fast-ball pitcher, it often took him a few batters to get into synch. He set the Cleveland batters down without incident in the second and Gary felt as if he was settling in.

Tiant continued to twirl and whirl and generally confuse the Red Sox hitters in the third. Luis frequently had the reverse experience from Bell. It often took at least one turn through the batting order for hitters to adjust to his corkscrew motion. When Luis shut the Red Sox down in the third without a run, Boston had gone seven straight innings (since the fifth inning of the first game) without scoring.

Gary Bell was born in San Antonio TX, on November 17, 1936, and he has spent most of his life in the Alamo City. Ironically, the Gary Bell who took the mound for Boston in the third inning could have spent his entire career in the Red Sox system if things had turned out differently. A superb all-around athlete in high school, Bell was actually better known around San Antonio, Texas as a football and basketball star. "My high school had football, basketball and golf, but no baseball. The only reason I got noticed at all," Gary recalled, "was from American Legion baseball. The Red Sox area scout, Hank Severeid, followed me around and I really got to like him. I was thinking of signing with him."

But Bell's big break in professional baseball came when he was selected to represent the *San Antonio Light* in the Hearst Schoolboy All-Star game in New York City. The game was played in the old Polo Grounds, home of the New York Giants, and scouts from every major league team attended the game to evaluate prospects.

"That was a big deal for me," Gary told me. "It was a chance to play in a big league stadium against the best young players in front of scouts that wouldn't have seen me otherwise. I ended up signing with the Cleveland Indians because they convinced me that their pitching staff was aging and they offered the quickest trip to the majors." As it turned out, he probably would have made it to "The Show" by age twenty-one as well with the pitching-poor Red Sox. Bell handled the Indians with ease in the bottom of the third frame and the game was beginning to take the look of a pitcher's duel.

The Indians came apart a little bit at the seams in the top of the fourth. Third baseman Max Alvis started things off by throwing high to former Red Sox first baseman Tony Horton, giving George Scott safe passage to first base. After Jerry Adair singled, Reggie Smith lined one safely into right field. Scott scored and Smith took second when Lee Maye's outfield throw was high to third. Next Luis Tiant threw one in the dirt, but Adair was too aggressive when he tried to score on the play. While Adair was being tagged out at the plate, Reggie Smith managed to advance to third. Mike Ryan drew a walk and proceeded to surprise his team, and more importantly, the Indians, with his base-running skills. Ryan took off for second to the astonishment of catcher Joe Azcue, who authored a weak toss to shortstop Chico Salmon. Smith was off for the plate as soon as Azcue drew back to throw and Reggie easily outran Salmon's return throw to put the Red Sox up 2-1. The Red Sox had done more running in one inning than many previous Red Sox teams had done in a week!

Gary Bell was really feeling confident now. He was in his groove with a one-run lead to work with. He also knew the strengths and weaknesses of the Cleveland hitters better than any other team and he set about exploiting his knowledge. Bell added another "0" to the total in the bottom of the fourth inning.

Yaz got things going again in the top of the fifth with a single. Then Tony Conigliaro stepped to the plate. Bell remembers Tony C as the most aggressive hitter he ever saw. Conig stood so close to the plate that "you could hit him with a strike," is the way Gary remembers it. The only hitting going on in this at-bat was Tony's smash that easily cleared the left field wall. The Red Sox dugout was ecstatic.

Gary Bell sailed through the Indians' lineup in the last of the fifth: he was in total control at this point. After Mike Ryan chipped in with an RBI double for an insurance run in the top of the sixth, the Red Sox were up 5-1. If the Indians were to make a counter-strike, it would have to come soon.

Bill Crowley, the Red Sox public relations director, was watching the game on television in his Needham home. When the customary announcement of the team's travel plans was made as a courtesy to the player's families, Crowley began to worry about a mob scene at the airport. He called the State Police at Logan Airport to apprise them of his concern. Crowley was told by the State Police that they had handled Presidents and The Beatles and that he was probably overreacting anyway. A cheering mob at the airport to welcome the Red Sox home seemed far-fetched to the State Police. Still, Crowley continued to worry about a crowd of fans descending upon Logan.

The Indians opened the last of the sixth by sending the left-handed Vic Davalillo up to pinch hit for Tiant. At 5' 7" and 150 pounds, Vic was no power threat, but he was a pesky little singles hitter who usually hit around .280. When he successfully retired Victor for the second out on a routine fly ball to Yaz in left field, Bell felt he had the game in hand. When he retired the ever-dangerous Rocky Colavito on another routine fly to Yaz, Gary walked off the mound at the end of six with a solid 5-1 lead.

At this point, the Red Sox bats went silent. It was almost as if they had complete confidence in Bell and they were anxious to celebrate in the clubhouse and start heading home. George Culver, in for relief of Luis Tiant, dispatched them easily in the seventh and the eighth innings. Gary matched Culver's scoreless frames in both innings. Bob Allen came in for Cleveland in the ninth and he breezed through the Red Sox in the top of the ninth. Now it was all up to Gary Bell.

It was a confident Bell that headed for the mound with Red Sox win-streak resting on his shoulders. Today, when he looks back, Gary marvels at just how strong this young team was. "You think about Yaz as the oldest guy on the field other than me and then you realize that he went on to play another sixteen years. Reggie Smith played another fifteen years and Tony might have played longer than either of them if he hadn't got hurt" And Gary added, "Scott and Rico were two more great players. They all were really. It was far and away the strongest team I ever played for!"

Gary Bell really wanted this one. He had been a serious baseball fan as a youngster and the thought of finally playing on a pennant winner really excited him. Wilbur Gary Bell was born in San Antonio, TX, on November 17, 1936. Asked about the name "Wilbur" Gary laughs and responds, "Most people don't even know my legal first name is Wilbur!" He grew up a short walk from the home park of the San Antonio Missions, the St. Louis Browns' double-A affiliate, and he spent every minute he could either inside the park or outside shagging foul balls. Bell remembers, "They got so tired of running me out of the ballpark that they finally gave me a job!" Not all ballplayers grow up as fans, but the ones who do have a special passion for the game.

Rocky Colavito and Max Alvis touched him for hits in the ninth, but Bell was determined to finish the game. He had played for serf's wages in

Cleveland, but he was aware of the Red Sox generosity and he knew that complete games translated into contract dollars. After almost 100 career wins, Cleveland had rewarded him with a contract of $26,000 in his last year. Bell was determined to upgrade his pay.

Old friend Tony Horton stepped to the plate with two men on and two men out. Bell remembers the moment well. "I knew that Horton was Mr. Yawkey's [Red Sox long-time millionaire owner] favorite ball-player and he was traded to Cleveland for me. I knew I had better get him out!" When Horton turned on a Bell fastball, Gary had a momentary sinking feeling in his stomach, but that feeling quickly receded as he watched Reggie Smith settle under the long fly for the final out. The next thing he knew, Gary was engulfed by his onrushing teammates. Ten straight!

The Red Sox clubhouse was awash in celebration following the second game. While few, if any, of the Red Sox players realized it, the ten-game winning streak was Boston's longest since 1951. Another plus was that the overworked bullpen finally got some rest as the starting pitchers excelled, going deep into ball games.

The plane ride home provided a chance for relaxation and celebration. The players were mildly amused and pleased by the announcement en route that there was a large group of fans waiting at Boston's Logan Airport. The announcement put the Red Sox entourage on notice, but hardly prepared them for the scene to follow.

Spontaneous crowds are always difficult to estimate. This crowd was very spontaneous. No media personality had urged the Red Sox faithful to turn out at Logan for Red Sox pride. There had only been that brief mention of their itinerary on the television during the second game, but nothing more. Boston fans had been starved for a pennant contender for so long that it seemed like the thing to do. The spontaneous turnout was variously estimated as anywhere from 5,000 to 15,000 people. State Police were certain of one fact: it was a bigger crowd than had turned out to greet the Beatles one year earlier. Bill Crowley had been right!

The players were generally overwhelmed by the turnout. Team members like Yaz and Tony C that had been flying into Logan for many years were used to welcoming parties of fifty to sixty family members and friends. They couldn't believe their eyes. Their only worry was how they would find their families among this mob scene.

There was one safety problem to deal with. The fans were so eager to get a look at their conquering heroes that they spilled out of the terminal and onto the actual landing area. Airport officials diverted the Red Sox plane to the far western extreme of Logan, the general aviation area. Players were escorted to a waiting bus that took them to the American Airlines terminal. Fans still managed to surround the bus and Tony Conigliaro was heard to utter, "How can you lose with people like this behind us?"

The American Airlines reception area was bedlam. When the team's bus was surrounded by the crowd and unable to move, an unidentified player shouted, "Maybe if we give them Conig as a sacrifice they'll let us go." Mike Andrews and Rico Petrocelli remember being a little bit frightened by the mob scene but mostly excited by the outpouring of support. Rico told me, "When they announced on the plane that there was a crowd waiting for us, we all thought that meant 500 fans, maybe as many as 1,000. When we got there the crowd was at least 10,000. We couldn't believe it!" Dick Williams told Kevin Walsh of the *Boston Globe*, "They told us on the plane that there would be fans at the airport. But I never expected anything like this. It's really something." Gary Bell told me, "I know one thing for a fact: there were more people at the airport than there were at Municipal Stadium for the game that day."

It is fair to say that if the Red Sox hadn't picked up Gary Bell, they would not have won the pennant in 1967. Gary would earn six more wins over the next two months and he gave Boston a solid number-two starter. His overall record after being obtained by the Red Sox on June 4 was 12-8 and he appeared in twenty-nine games, mostly in a starting role. Gary wasn't much of a factor in the World Series but 1967 still represents his fondest memory from a twelve-year big league career.

Gary parlayed his great 1967 season into a $40,000 contract in 1968. He figured that it would have taken five more good seasons for the Indians to get that amount from Cleveland general manager, Gabe Paul. Gary got off to a great start in 1968 and was named to the All-Star game in Houston, Texas. He tailed off in the second half but still managed a 3.12 ERA to go with his 11-11 record.

Red Sox general manager Dick O'Connell had originally offered Bell a 1968 contract at $35,000. Bell figured, "Why not go for it?" He asked for $40,000. O'Connell agreed saying, "As long as you'll go out and win twenty games." Although Gary only got about halfway to that total, there is no record of his having returned any of the Red Sox' money.

Bell's lackluster second half caused Red Sox officials to re-evaluate his future with the team. The combination of his age and the earlier acquisition of Ray Culp and Dick Ellsworth, led them to leave Gary unprotected in the expansion draft. The new franchise in Seattle was delighted to select a proven major league starter.

Bell's honeymoon with Pilot's manager, Joe Schultz, was short-lived. Gary was traded to the Chicago White Sox on June 8, 1969, for Bob Locker after compiling a 2-6 record and an ERA of 4.70. His most significant accomplishment in Seattle was rooming with former Yankee pitcher Jim Bouton author of the baseball tell-all book *Ball Four*. Bouton was sufficiently impressed with Gary's nocturnal activities that Bell was featured prominently in Bouton's book. Bouton wrote that Bell's former wife Nan called Gary's room at 4:30 AM and his roommate at the time, Woody Held, answered. When she asked to speak to her husband Held told her that he was out playing golf.

Asked about Bouton, Bell says, "I'm one of the one-and-one-half friends Jim has in baseball. Mike Marshall is half a friend of his and I'm his one whole friend. I've always gotten along with everyone."

Gary appeared in twenty-three games for the White Sox, mostly in relief. Gary's record for his last major league team was 0-0. At age thirty-two, a little over a year since his All Star selection, Bell's big league days were over.

During his 12-year major league career Gary played for four teams and earned 121 wins. His best year was 1959, when he won 16 games for the Cleveland Indians, and he was selected to three American League All-Star teams. "Texas is such a football state," Gary says, "That nobody here [San Antonio] thinks of me as a former ballplayer. My only chance of being recognized is if I go back east," he chuckles.

Bell spent the first six months after his release in Hawaii. His next stop was Arizona, first in Tucson then in Phoenix. Gary recalls, "Most of us weren't trained to do anything except play baseball. Back in the 1950s, very few baseball players went to college at all. I had to figure out a way to make a living."

Given his affable nature and ability to get along with people, Gary gravitated naturally to sales. Eventually he headed back to his boyhood home of San Antonio, Texas, where he presently resides. Gary operates a sporting goods business which keeps him involved in the game and gets him around to the schools and teams in the area.

When asked what the 1967 season meant to him, Bell told me, "It was the most exciting season of my major league career. When the 1967 season started with me in Cleveland I thought the only way I could get to the World Series was if I bought a ticket.

"That 1967 Red Sox team was the most united team in baseball history. We were all firmly united in our hatred of Dick Williams…kidding," Bell adds but not completely convincingly. "They really were a great bunch of guys. And it seemed like we had a different hero every day."

And how did Gary enjoy the city of Boston? "I was only there for a short time, but Boston was my favorite city out of all the cities I played in. And the team treated me very well." And what about Red Sox fans: did he enjoy playing in front of them in Fenway Park? "The Red Sox fans were great," he remembers. "Red Sox fans are the best fans in all of baseball."

Chapter 6

Mike Andrews: Class, Charity, and the Perfect Teammate

Boston Red Sox vs. Kansas City A's, Thursday, August 3, 1967

Mike Andrews took his familiar position at second base as the Red Sox began their 104th game of the season—two-thirds of the way through their 162 game schedule—against the last-place A's. Three weeks earlier during the celebrated sweep over Cleveland, the Indian's general manager, Al Rosen, had said of the twenty-four-year-old southern California native, "Without that guy (Andrews) you Red Sox would be nothing." Pretty heady praise for a rookie surrounded by stars like Yaz, Lonborg, and Tony C. Andrews appeared to be a likely candidate to give the Red Sox a steady all-around second baseman for the first time since Bobby Doerr had retired in 1951. Having Hall-of-Famer Doerr around as a coach that season was a real plus for Mike. Doerr was calm and positive in contrast to Dick Williams' volcanic and acerbic style. Andrews looked at the afternoon's game against the A's as just one more contest in a very long season. The previous day the native of Torrance, California, and former football star, had hit his first Fenway homer. But Andrews was the consummate team player and the home run had been in a losing cause as the A's won 6-4. His game was giving himself up to advance a runner to third and taking the hard slide while turning the double play at second. That's what he was prepared for on August 3.

When the Red Sox won game two of the doubleheader in Cleveland to extend their winning streak to ten-straight games, the Impossible Dream truly began to take shape. The season was more than half over, first place was within shouting distance and the club had momentum. Pennant fever was abroad and alive in the Hub.

Mike Andrews remembers this as the first time he really thought concretely about winning the pennant. Mike had been brought up to the Red Sox in the waning weeks of September of 1966, and in his words, "I didn't like what I saw. Guys like Gibby [Russ Gibson] and Reggie [Smith], who were rookies in 1967, had played for Dick Williams," Mike recalled, "And we won the International League championship both years. We didn't expect to lose, we didn't like losing, and we knew Dick Williams didn't like to lose!

"We never thought of ourselves as a second-division club," Mike emphasized, "and I didn't like the atmosphere of losing, and I didn't want to be any part of it. I had always been in a winning environment and I wanted to do everything I could to make the Red Sox a winning team."

There was every reason to be optimistic about the two weeks following the Red Sox' triumphant return from Cleveland on July 23. The Red Sox had thirteen games scheduled in their cozy bandbox and some home cooking was likely to help their position in the standings. The club was in second place in the American League and they were only one-half game behind the first-place Chicago White Sox.

The fans felt that the Red Sox were about to make a serious move. The demand for tickets was the highest it had been since the contending teams of 1946-49. After years of frustration, Bostonians were finally willing to wear their hearts on their sleeves.

The home stand began on an upbeat note. The contending California Angels came in for a three-game series that could determine who was a contender and who was a pretender. The teams split the first two games, setting the stage for a crucial "rubber game." Pennant fever had reached such a height in Boston that *The Boston Globe* began a feature entitled "Meet the Red Sox." On the morning of the third game of the Angels series The Globe ran a flattering story of George Scott's route to the major leagues. And to feed the fans' hunger for information about the upstart Red Sox, the Globe added another feature, ""Meet the Red Sox Wives."

Mike Andrews' wife Marilyn was featured on July 31, and readers learned that she was "just under 5'5" with lively brown eyes and a neat figure."

Fenway Park was nearly full for the Thursday afternoon game with against California, with a crowd of 34,193, the largest in Fenway Park since 1958, on hand. The Angels held the upper hand as all-star pitcher, Jim McGlothlin, brought them into the last of the ninth with a 5-2 lead. At this point, the Red Sox mounted a comeback which was typical of the style that had earned them the title: "Cardiac Kids."

Second sacker, Mike Andrews.

Mike Andrews led off with a single. Joe Foy followed with a blast into the left-field screen, which brought them within one run. One batter later, Tony Conigliaro matched Foy's feat and the game was tied at five and on its way into extra innings.

Yaz made two outstanding defensive plays in the top of the tenth to preserve the tie. Reggie Smith tripled to open the bottom half, and the nearly-capacity crowd knew he would score. They were not disappointed. Super-sub Jerry Adair bounced a ground ball by A's third baseman, Paul Schaal, and the Red Sox had come from behind once again.

The Red Sox won the series but it would be almost six weeks before California, an expansion team created in 1961, playing in only their seventh season would prove to be pretenders. The 1967 season was not a year of knockout punches.

The Minnesota Twins were next to step into the Fenway ring with the local heroes. The Twins were truly heavyweights led by the burly Harmon Killebrew and the equally burly, Bob Allison.

After four games over the next three days, the Boston pitching staff knew just how formidable this opponent was. In these four games, the

Twins had pushed 29 runs across the plate against the beleaguered Red Sox hurlers. Only Dalton Jones' clutch hitting and strong relief from iron man John Wyatt had allowed the Red Sox a 6-3 win in the first game of a Saturday doubleheader.

Lee Stange came through with a shutout in an unusual Monday wrap-up of the five-game series. This coupled with a Yaz three-run homer allowed the Red Sox to salvage two games from the series. As the calendar turned into August, the Red Sox were in second place two games behind the league-leading Chicago White Sox.

American League Standings July 31, 1967

Team	Wins	Loses	Winning %	GB
Chicago	58	42	.580	-
BOSTON	**56**	**44**	**.560**	**2.0**
Detroit	53	45	.541	4.0
Minnesota	53	47	.530	5.0
California	55	49	.529	5.0
Washington	51	53	.490	9.0
Baltimore	45	54	.455	12.5
Cleveland	46	56	.451	13.0
New York	44	56	.440	14.0
Kansas City	44	59	.427	15.5

The powerful Red Sox offense included three players—Yaz, Tony C, and George Scott—in the American League top ten in batting at the end of July. Yaz and Tony C were also in the top five in the America League for home runs and RBI. And Jim Lonborg's winning percentage of .778—14 wins and four losses—ranked third in the American League.

With last-place Kansas City heading into town for a three-game series, the Red Sox appeared poised to make up some ground. Someone forgot to tell the lowly A's that the home team was about to make its move. The best the Red Sox could manage in an August 1 doubleheader was a split. They lost to a Chuck Dobson five-hitter in the opener and rallied for an 8-3 victory in the nightcap. Jim Lonborg was credited with the win in the second game, improving his record to 15-4.

Selected Red Sox Hitters as of July 31, 1967

Player	H	R	HR	BA
Yastrzemski	115	63	26	.322
Conigliaro	89	53	19	.303
Scott	101	49	13	.289
Petrocelli	73	32	9	.267
Andrews	83	55	5	.266
Smith	86	43	6	.251
Foy	87	57	17	.247
Jones	21	11	2	.241
Gibson	24	6	1	.211

To make matters worse, the Red Sox dropped the third game of the series by a score of 8-6. Gary Bell pitched fairly well—six innings with only one earned run—and John Wyatt was brought in to protect a 5-4 Red Sox lead. Wyatt simply didn't have it that day and the A's rallied to take an 8-5 lead. About the only bright spot of the game was Mike Andrews' sixth home run.

The home stand that had opened with such optimism was slipping away. The momentum which had been gained was slowly receding.

August 3 is awfully early to call one single game a crucial one. After all, there were still 59 games to play. And, as it would turn out, the standings would have more ups and downs than a see-saw on a kindergarten playground.

If the game wasn't crucial to the Red Sox, it was certainly important. They had come home from Cleveland only one-half game out of first place. They had hopes of using the home stand to vault into the lead. Now they were in danger of leaving town with a losing record for the stay and falling three games out of first. A win in this wrap-up was very important.

Mike Andrews was always a player who took games one at a time. He was a distance runner, not a sprinter. He recalls of his school days, "Lots of guys had better numbers than I had. I might hit a couple of home runs while someone else had 15-17. But I was consistent and I always did what it took to win." Thursday's game was important to Mike Andrews. Every game was important to the rangy—6' 3"—second baseman.

The pitching-poor Red Sox started 24-year-old lefthander Bill Landis on this Thursday afternoon. Landis was to win only one game all year for Boston and August 3 would not be the day. The A's climbed all over Dick Williams' latest starter candidate, tallying three runs before they were retired in the first. The biggest damage was a two-run homer from Ken "Hawk" Harrelson.

Mike Andrews was the leadoff hitter as his team set about to work their way out of a three-run hole. Throughout his career, he was always one to make things happen. "I was always ready to throw my body at a ground ball or drop down a surprise bunt. I concentrated as hard as I could on every play," Mike recalled.

Make things happen was exactly what he did as he sent a Jim "Catfish" Hunter fastball in the direction of the Green Monster in left field. Andrews thought double as soon as he took off down the first base line. To this day, he can't remember if first base coach Bobby Doerr waved him on to second or not. Green light or no, Mike was going to get things going. But the weak-armed Danny Cater in left field for the A's threw the sliding Andrews out by ten feet at second base.

It can be a long way from second base to the home team dugout if you've just run your team out of a rally and Dick Williams is there waiting for you. When asked if Williams had a nice sense of humor about base running blunders, Andrews responded, "Dick didn't have a sense of humor about anything that went on around the ballpark. He had a great sense of humor away from the park but he was deadly serious about everything to do with the game. You didn't want to make him mad."

If Andrews was a little bit down as he headed out to his second base position to start the second inning, it certainly wasn't the low spot of his professional baseball career. That might have come in Olean, New York, when he made 70 errors in his rookie year. Sometimes he even wondered why they kept him. Or it might have been the following year when he was demoted in mid-season from the Winston-Salem ball club. The front office told him that Winston-Salem was a bad ball club and they didn't want him in that environment. The 19-year-old Andrews wasn't too sure he believed that.

Andrews at Chain-O-Lakes Park in Winter Haven, Florida.

The home team squeaked in a run against Hunter in the bottom of the second and Dick Williams summoned Dave Morehead in from the bullpen with instructions to keep it close. Morehead was another in a long-line of high potential, low-achievement Red Sox pitchers. For some unknown reason, the franchise had always produced hitters but had failed to develop pitchers.

113

Morehead was a southern Californian like Mike Andrews and he was gifted with a great right arm. Two months younger than Andrews, he had actually broken in with the Red Sox four years earlier as a nineteen-year old. Morehead won ten games as a rookie and displayed great promise. He fell off to eight wins in 1964 but he was still young and he was pitching for a poor ball club. Then in 1965 it all came together for him on one magical day. Pitching against the Cleveland Indians on September 16—just eleven days following his twenty-second birthday—Morehead pitched a no-hitter. His was the first no-hitter pitched in the American League in over three years.

Although he had only matched his rookie output of ten wins, the no-hitter seemed to signify the beginning of a great career. It was not to be. Plagued by arm trouble and the sizeable burden of a "can't miss" label, Dave won only one game in 1966 and began to shuttle back and forth between the parent club and their Triple-A affiliate in Toronto.

Dick Williams believed in Morehead and he had recently recalled him from exile in Toronto. He had started the first game of the Kansas City doubleheader on August 1, and he had been horrible. But Williams had a hunch that Morehead would hold the A's this time and Dick always went with his hunches.

Looking in from second base, Andrews saw a more confident Dave Morehead this time out. Mike was able to make a nice running catch of a Danny Cater fly into shallow right field to help the cause. Andrews had played with Morehead in Toronto in 1966, and he wanted to see him make it back.

Andrews worked Hunter for a walk in the third inning. Andrews didn't come around to score but the Red Sox managed to put another run on the board. The A's lead had been cut to 3-2.

Mike Andrews was born in Los Angeles, CA, on July 9, 1943, and he grew up in neighboring Torrance, CA. In many ways, it was a surprise that Andrews was out there at second base at all. He had grown up a mile from the Pacific Ocean and had spent as much time at the beach as he could. In his formative baseball years—ages fifteen to seventeen—surfing had just become the rage and the Beach Boys were singing their song. While Andrews toiled on the diamond, most of his buddies were "hanging ten."

But Andrews came from an athletic family and he had excelled at all sports as a youngster. Mike's father, Lloyd, played football and basketball at the University of Montana, and his younger brother, Rob, played second base in the majors with the Astros and Giants between 1975 and 1980. "Rob was nine years younger," Andrews said, "so we never really played together. But it was neat to have a brother who also made it to the big leagues."

Mike starred in football, basketball and baseball at South Torrance High School. But football was his first love. "You have to remember, the Dodgers didn't move to LA until 1958, and the Angels have only been around since 1961," Mike remembered. "So growing up, big-time sports meant UCLA and USC football. We were aware of the major leagues as kids because of the Game of The Week, but our dream was to play college football."

Mike was more highly touted as a football player than for his baseball prowess at South Torrance High. A sure-handed pass catcher, he was headed for UCLA on a football scholarship. He played football at El Camino Junior College to fulfill UCLA's language requirements and as kind of a warm-up for his big-time debut.

From time-to-time, as he toiled in the Red Sox farm system, Andrews would ponder the road not taken. Red Sox scout Joe Stephenson—father of future Red Sox teammate Jerry Stephenson—had convinced him to sign a pro contract at age eighteen holding out the lure of being the Red Sox shortstop of the future. Each year, as he looked at the depth chart with Rico Petrocelli slotted one level above him, Andrews would grow discouraged. Since Rico was only twelve days his senior it didn't seem likely that Mike would outlast him.

Years later Mike told me, "The other reason I signed with the Red Sox was that I wanted to marry my childhood sweetheart, Marilyn Flynn. If I went to UCLA that wasn't going to happen for what seemed like a long time. The Red Sox gave me a small bonus, we got engaged, and I married Marilyn after my first minor league season." Looking back on more than 50 years of marriage, Mike offered, "That was probably the best decision I ever made."

Dave Morehead continued to pitch well, holding the A's in check during the top of the fourth inning. When the game reached its halfway point it had evolved into a tight, one-run ball game.

Switching positions was probably the best option for Andrews as he tried to climb the ladder to "The Show." But third base was not a natural position for him and if he made it as a 6' 3" big league second baseman, it would make him the tallest regular second baseman in major league history. It seemed like kind of a long shot. The traditional second baseman was a 5' 10" Nellie Fox or 5' 9" Bobby Richardson, and baseball decision-makers were traditionalists of the highest order.

If the Red Sox hoped to salvage the home stand they had to make their move and fast. Hunter was the ace of the A's staff and Jack Aker was no slouch coming out of their bullpen.

Hunter continued his mastery over the Red Sox in the last of the fifth. When Petrocelli was retired to end the inning, Hunter had to feel good knowing that the seventh, eighth and ninth hitters would be coming up in the last of the sixth inning.

Morehead had held the A's hitless during his first three innings but he faded a little as the hitters got their second look at him. With Mike Hershberger on second base third baseman Dick Green sent a groan through the crowd when he singled sharply into left field. The third base coach waved him on and it looked as if the Red Sox would be down by two runs.

But this was the year of the Yaz and he rose to one more occasion. Hershberger had good speed but Carl charged the ball and let it fly. It was another perfect strike from Yastrzemski and when catcher Mike Ryan put on the tag, the Red Sox were out of the inning unharmed.

Center fielder George Thomas, playing in place of Reggie Smith, who had jammed his thumb up against the center-field wall the day before, led off the sixth. Thomas was one of the genuinely funny men in baseball. Andrews remembers that he was a good man to have around to offset Dick Williams' stern demeanor, and George had a knack for picking just the right moment to lighten things. George Thomas was also versatile: he could handle almost any fielding position and he would probably pitch credibly if Dick Williams asked him to.

To win a pennant a ball club needs a George Thomas-like player. In 1967, George only played in 65 games for the Red Sox, filling in at all three outfield positions, first base, and catcher. He was a guy that could spend a week on the bench, never complain, and come into the game on a moment's notice. Thomas could also run some and he got things going by beating out a ground ball down the third base line. Catcher Mike Ryan was up next. Ryan was a local boy from Haverhill, Massachusetts.

Ryan did the sensible thing and dropped a bunt down the third-base line. Hunter pounced on the ball and threw down to second to keep the tying run out of scoring position. Unfortunately for the A's, but fortunately for the Red Sox, his throw pulled shortstop Bert Campaneris off the bag and both runners were safe.

Now Dick Williams had to make a decision that American League managers don't have to make anymore (unless they are playing in a National League park). Should he let Morehead hit for himself or send up a pinch hitter? Sparky Lyle and John Wyatt were both ready in the bullpen. The situation screamed for a bunt and Williams elected to have Morehead execute it.

Morehead did his job perfectly, laying a soft bunt down the third base line. The Red Sox had the tying run on third and the lead run on second.

Now A's manager, Alvin Dark had his decision to make. The former star of the Boston Braves and New York Giants could walk Andrews and set up a force at any base. Or he could take his chances against the .268 hitter. Dark elected to take his chances with Andrews.

Dark had some solid reasons for his choice but it was a little bit insulting to Mike. He dug in a little deeper, determined to make things happen.

Catfish got a one strike edge on his first pitch, a nasty slider. He came back with the same pitch and Mike was in an 0-2 hole: a bad place for a hitter to be. Andrews shortened up on the bat as Bobby Doerr had taught him, to protect the plate.

Catfish got a little too cute with his next pitch and Andrews jumped on it. He lined it cleanly into left field setting both runners in motion. Thomas scored easily to tie it and Ryan steamed around third, heading for home, with the lead run. Ryan was no speedster but Cater's throw was off the mark and the Red Sox were up 4-3.

Standing happily on first, Andrews must have felt a long way from Waterloo, Iowa. Playing there in 1963 for the Red Sox farm team, he had broken his ankle sliding into second base in the next to the last game of the season. Andrews can still remember the sight of the bone sticking through his sanitary hose. The Waterloo fans felt so badly they took up a collection and gave him $130. The nasty bump on his left ankle is a lasting reminder of Waterloo, Iowa.

Morehead continued to hold the A's at bay. When he retired the side in the top of the seventh, he had given up only three hits and had shut out the A's during his five inning stint. The fans gave him a nice hand as they rose for the traditional seventh inning stretch.

The "lucky seventh" was of no help to the Red Sox and they took their positions in the field for the eighth inning nursing a one-run lead. The big question now was: how much longer could Morehead continue his mastery?

That question was answered quickly as the A's shortstop, Campy Campaneris, opened the inning with a double off the left-field wall. The ball was still in the air when Williams left the dugout to summon left-hander Sparky Lyle from the bullpen. Morehead had given everything that could be expected of him and he had earned the standing ovation from the 18,920 patrons gathered at Fenway Park.

Sparky, who would go on to fame and some fortune as a colorful member of the hated Yankees, had been brought in specifically to retire the left-handed Ted Kubiak. Kubiak showed bunt all the way and Lyle gave him heat inside. Down two strikes to Lyle, he finally grounded to Rico at short and Lyle's day at the office was over.

Williams semaphored to the bullpen for his right-handed relief ace, John Wyatt, to take the mound and face the right-handed Cater. Wyatt may well be the unsung hero of the 1967 Red Sox. They had picked him up during the 1966 season after spending almost six years with the non-contending A's. Not only did the Red Sox rescue Wyatt from oblivion, they probably saved him from having his arm blown out. Kansas City had used him in 81 games in 1964.

In 1967 Wyatt had a direct impact on 30 of the Red Sox ninety-two victories: 10 wins and 20 saves. Of course, the Red Sox starting rotation consisted of Jim Lonborg and whichever three starters were currently hot and not in Dick Williams' dog house. That insured Wyatt of a lot of work. He appeared in a total of 60 games that year for Boston, all of them in relief.

Wyatt wasn't on the mound for very long before Campaneris easily stole third base. The Red Sox infield edged toward the inner grass of the diamond to position themselves to cut off the tying run at the plate. Cater hit a ground ball to Rico Petrocelli's right and he was up and firing to Mike Ryan covering the plate. Rico's hurried throw sailed towards the first base line but Ryan gloved it and applied a sweep tag to Campaneris all in one motion. Campaneris was out by an eyelash and the Red Sox' one-run lead was preserved.

A one-run lead is never safe in Fenway. The eccentric dimensions invite offensive mischief and in August, the prevailing winds are generally towards the inviting left-field wall. To a man, the Red Sox dugout was hoping for a cushion to hold their lead.

John Wyatt made the first out of the eighth inning. Dick Williams was going to go all the way with his bullpen stopper. Mike Andrews stepped to the plate with the bases empty to face A's starter/reliever, Lew Krausse. Krausse was a solid journeyman pitcher who would ultimately spend 12 years in the major leagues with 5 teams. He was also from solid baseball stock: his father had pitched for the *Philadelphia* Athletics in the early 1930s.

Andrews was anxious to make something happen, to get something going. He turned on a Krausse fastball and drove it sharply towards left field. Mike went down the line with the same all-out intensity as he had on his ball that struck the wall in the first inning. This time he could relax; the ball had landed in the left field net to increase the Red Sox' lead to two.

The wise-guys in the press box calculated that Andrews, with his home-run-a-day pace started the previous day, would tie Roger Maris' season home run record on September 23 and pass him on September 24 against Baltimore. Andrews wasn't thinking about his home run pace. His focus was always on winning and doing whatever it took to achieve that end.

Andrews batting at an Old Timer's game.

Andrews felt comfortable at his position as he set himself near second base. It had taken him some time after years of playing shortstop. He had worked hard at his new position in Toronto and Bobby Doerr had been a great help in Boston. His one disappointment at the position had come in spring training in 1966 when he had been promised a shot that never materialized. He confronted then manager, Billy Herman, who replied, to Andrew's amazement, "I pushed for the trade (with Detroit) to get George Smith to play second and I'm going to make sure it works."

Wyatt retired the first two Kansas City batters without a problem but gave the crowd a little excitement by giving up a double to ex-Red Soxer, Jim Gosger. When Wyatt bore down to force a groundout the Red Sox had salvaged the home stand 7-6 and kept their winning attitude alive. When they arrived in Minnesota the next day to start their road trip, they would be in second place, only two games behind the Chicago White Sox.

Andrews had put together quite a day: three hits, one home run and three RBI, including the game winner. But Andrews was never the lead character in the game story. Although he rated the headline ("Red Sox Come From Behind Again, Topple A's, 5-3, on Andrews Hit," *Boston Globe*, August 4, 1967), his only media quote was on his base running blunder in the first inning. What were his words to Cliff Keane of *The Boston Globe*? "That was awful."

It was truly an outstanding day for Andrews but he was the type to look ahead to the next series with Minnesota. Looking back all these years later he is hard-pressed to remember even one detail about his big game on August 3, 1967.

Mike Andrews was an important part of the Red Sox drive for the pennant in 1967. But when he looks back on that memorable season, he focuses on an off-the-field experience. "I will always remember Bill Koster, who was the original Executive Director of the Jimmy Fund, asking me to speak to a 12-year-old patient just before one late-season game. I was happy to do it, all the players did what they could, but I have to admit I was a little distracted. We had a nice chat...the youngster told me how he was looking forward to playing ball the next season, and I wished him well.

"Later, Bill Koster took me aside and said, 'I really appreciate you helping out at the last minute. We have to send that young man home. There's nothing more we can do for him. I know your visit meant a lot to him.' All of a sudden, whether I batted .250 or .260 didn't seem to matter that much. It put a lot of things in perspective for me."

And what did Mike's teammates think about the contribution Mike Andrews made to the Impossible Dream team? When I posed that question to catcher Russ Gibson, he replied, "Mike was the ultimate team guy." Gibson went on to say, "He did the important things that don't show up in the box score.

"When you think of '67, of course you think of Yaz, and Lonnie [Cy Young Award-winner Jim Lonborg]," Gibson continued. "But you have to realize that first, and foremost, we were a real team. And Mike Andrews personified that team. He was the ideal teammate."

Asked to choose one memory of 1967 that stands out for him, Andrews answered, "I'll always remember beating Minnesota on the final day of the season with the crowd coming on the field after the last out. That was a once in a lifetime experience" he insisted. "We really shared the experience with the fans that day."

Andrews went on to provide the Red Sox with leadership throughout the 1967 season. He is still slightly distressed that he didn't start the first two World Series games at Fenway Park after doing the job all year. But in typical, generous fashion, he counters, "I'm glad that Jerry Adair got his chance to see if he could make a contribution."

Andrews returned to his native California after that season. His objective was to get a job to make some money and to stay in shape.

When his teammates who had remained in the Boston area convinced him that New Englanders couldn't get enough of the 1967 Boston Red Sox, he packed his young family in their car and headed back east. Peabody, Massachusetts, was their home for many years.

Mike played a total of four full seasons for the Boston Red Sox. His best year was probably 1969 when he batted .293, swatted fifteen home runs and made the American League All-Star team. But the highest the Red Sox finished over the next three years was third place.

Andrews would have been very content to play his entire career in Boston. It was his home, his family loved the area, and he had a great rapport with the fans. Baseball generally doesn't cooperate in these matters, however.

After the 1970 season came to an end, a hot rumor circulated in Boston and in Chicago that Andrews was going to be traded for the White Sox' outstanding shortstop, Luis Aparicio. When the rumor reached its height, Red Sox General Manager, Dick O'Connell, denied it saying Mike wasn't going anywhere. Days later, a few weeks before Christmas, Andrews was playing cards with a buddy when a bulletin came over the radio station they were listening to. He friend asked, "Did you hear what I just heard?" Mike would get new Sox for Christmas and they would be White.

Andrews put together a couple of good seasons in Chicago. He found easy-going Chuck Tanner to be a welcome antidote to the hard-nosed Dick Williams. He still wondered, though, if Williams didn't get a tad bit more out of him with his constant needling.

Andrews hit .282 for the White Sox in 1971 as the club finished third in the Western Division. Mike had a tough year in 1972, personally batting only .220 and being troubled all year by the wrist he had broken at the end of the '71 season. Always the team man though, Andrews remembers '72 as the year the White Sox, with the help of a rejuvenated Dick Allen's thirty-seven homers and 113 RBI, gave the Oakland A's a run for their money.

Andrews began the 1973 season in Chicago but the front office was in chaos. More than halfway through the season, Andrews still hadn't been signed to a new contract for the season. He went to Rollie Hemond in the White Sox front office and told him that he couldn't continue to play under those conditions. The White Sox obliged him with his outright release.

Free to sign with any major league team as the pennant races took shape, Mike contacted Dick Williams to get his advice. Williams allowed as how the division-leading A's could use him as a utility infielder and Andrews began a brief but eventful career in Oakland.

Andrews didn't play much—only 18 games—but he enjoyed the winning environment. And he was pleased to find himself in the World Series against the New York Mets.

Quite unexpectedly, Andrews was thrust into the national spotlight in Game Two. Mike was playing second base in the top of the twelfth inning with the score tied at six all. The Mets' John Milner hit a ball right at him. Unfortunately, the ball hit something, skidded through his legs, and two Mets runners came on to score. Jerry Grote, the Mets catcher, was next up and he also hit a ball directly at him. Mike fielded it cleanly but the replay shows clearly that first baseman, Gene Tenace, better known as a catcher, got his feet tangled and mishandled Andrew's throw. Unfortunately, the scorer gave Andrews his second error and the Mets were four runs up.

A's owner, Charlie Finley, went into one of his classic tantrums. He insisted that Andrews be placed on the disabled list and replaced by second baseman, Manny Trillo. Finley browbeat Andrews into signing a form saying that he was hurt and according to Dick Williams in his book, *No More Mr. Nice Guy*, both Andrews and Williams ended up in tears.

Ultimately, Commissioner Bowie Kuhn intervened to have Andrews reinstated.

He was vindicated, when, pinch hitting in game four at Shea Stadium, 55,000 Mets fans rose to give him a standing ovation. A partial winner's share in the World Series split didn't hurt either as Oakland defeated the Mets four-games-to-three. But Mike Andrews would never play major league baseball again.

Andrews attempted to get a "look see" from some major league team in 1974 but there were no takers. Even the San Diego Padres who had finished forty-two games off of the pace declined to give him a shot.

He was convinced that he had some more baseball left in him even if it meant packing up his young family and moving to Japan. Move to Japan for nine months they did, and Andrews finished his career not being able to read about his team in the sports pages. His strongest memory of his time in Japan is what an adventure it was for his family.

Back in the U.S., Mike thought briefly of returning to Japan for one more season. "I was ready to go back to Japan for another season," Mike recalled. "But my wife Marilyn put her foot down. She said, 'If you go back, you'll go back without me.'" That was the end of that idea and the end of baseball for Andrews.

At that point, Andrews did what, in his words all former ballplayers are duty-bound to do. "I tried my hand at broadcasting and I sold life insurance." Mike did well enough selling life insurance that he ended up working for five years for Mass Mutual.

In 1979 Ken Coleman, one of the great sports announcers of his generation, was part-time executive director of the Jimmy Fund. The Jimmy Fund has raised many millions of dollars to help find a cure for cancer in children and has enjoyed a long-standing relationship with the Red Sox. Ken asked Andrews to work part-time for the Jimmy Fund and Mike agreed. Shortly afterwards, Coleman accepted an offer to broadcast the Red Sox games and Andrews succeeded him as Executive Director of New England's favorite charity, the Jimmy Fund.

The Jimmy Fund is the fund-raising arm of the world-renowned Dana-Farber Clinic for treatment of children with cancer. If the odds against the Red Sox winning the pennant in 1967 were 100-1, the odds against Dr. Sidney Farber achieving his goal of eradicating cancer in children when he began his work in Boston in 1947, were even greater. Yet today, about 85%-90% walk away disease-free from Dana-Farber's Jimmy Fund Clinic, and from many other cancer treatment centers around the world.

The Jimmy Fund was established in 1948, and originally it was closely associated with the Boston Braves. When the Braves moved to Milwaukee in 1953, their owner Lou Perini asked Tom Yawkey and the Red Sox to spearhead the effort going forward. Mr. & Mrs. Yawkey enthusiastically embraced their role with the Jimmy Fund, and for almost 70 years the Jimmy Fund and the Boston Red Sox have been inexorably linked. The 1967 Red Sox voted to award the Jimmy Fund a full share of their World Series distribution.

When I interviewed Mike Andrews in his office at the Jimmy Fund in 2007, he had already served as the Executive Director of the charity for more than 25 years. Mike told me, "I am really proud of the fact that I played professional baseball for 13 years. And it was a thrill to play in two World Series and to make an All-Star team." And then he added, "But the sense of accomplishment I get as Executive Director of the Jimmy Fund far exceeds anything I ever got from baseball."

Chapter 7

Tony C: The Nightmare Within the Dream

Boston Red Sox vs. California Angels, Friday, August 18, 1967

Anthony Richard "Tony" Conigliaro. Born in Boston. Lived in Boston. Died in Boston. In many ways, Tony was the ultimate extension of all Red Sox fans. For nearly his entire life he lived within 20 miles of Fenway Park. He grew up a Red Sox fan, although he much preferred playing the game to watching. Two years after graduating from St. Mary's High School in nearby Lynn, Massachusetts, he was starting in center field for his home team. He had his glory years in a Red Sox uniform. For the last eight years of his life, he was always referred to as "the former Red Sox star." Tony Conigliaro had everything going for him when he stepped to the plate that Friday night before a full house at Fenway Park to face Angels' pitcher Jack Hamilton. Only twenty-two years old. Tall, dark and handsome. Sparkling brown eyes brought the girls running. And he could even sing to them in a fine baritone voice. In his fourth successful season with the Red Sox and clearly on a career track to baseball stardom and likely election to the Hall of Fame, Tony C already had a single off the fastball hurler and was looking for another hit when he came up in the fourth inning behind George Scott and Reggie Smith. Within moments, Hamilton's first pitched ball had rocketed like a spherical missile into Tony's left cheek, shattering it and sending shock waves reverberating within his skull. The Red Sox' right fielder whirled about and went down on his face like he had been poleaxed. "It was a fastball that got away," Hamilton said later. Many wondered whether the Angel pitcher deliberately tried to hit the Boston slugger. Dick Williams had complained to the umpires early in the game about Hamilton's spitballs. As for Tony, who would never play again for the "Impossible Dream" team, he graciously concluded that Hamilton didn't "have any good reason to go after me."

Their 5-3 win over the A's on Thursday afternoon placed the Red Sox in second only two games behind the first-place White Sox. They were disappointed with their 7-6 home stand which had begun with such promise, but they were still in the thick of the American League pennant race with 58 games remaining in the 1967 season. The surprising Red Sox had become the number one topic throughout New England.

Even *The Boston Globe*, which prided itself on its seriousness of purpose, had caught pennant fever. The August 4th edition of The Globe included an editorial entitled, "Those Wonderful Red Sox." The editorial said in part, "A man really ought to be a teenage girl to enjoy the wonderful Red Sox to the full. Then he could squeal the way the girls do." It went on to close, "Sports writers, a cold and calculating sort, insist it is too early to go lyric about these kids on the Red Sox. That may be. But there is no law against a slight paean, is there? So a slight paean it is and a falsetto squeal."

The upcoming nine-game road trip represented another important test. They would cover a lot of miles—Minnesota to Kansas City to California and then back home to Fenway Park to face Detroit—and two of the three of the opponents on the road would be contenders. They hoped for five wins and felt they needed at least three to even stay close.

The three-game series against Minnesota was a rude awakening. By the time they left town, they knew just how strong the Twins were.

About the only thing that went right in the opener was the arrival of veteran catcher Elston Howard who had been picked up from the Yankees. Twins' left-hander Jim Merritt handled the Red Sox with ease, limiting them to just five hits in the 3-0 loss.

The 38-year-old Howard had played 13 seasons with the Yankees and he initially balked at the trade to the Red Sox. But a phone call from Boston's owner Tom Yawkey convinced Elston that he was wanted in

Tony C. at Spring Training before the 1967 season.

Boston. Howard's addition gave the team a dose of pennant race experience that was badly needed by the young club.

The Red Sox got excellent pitching from Lee Stange in game two, but Dave Boswell was even tougher for the Twins. Tony Conigliaro lost a ball in the sun in the first inning resulting in a Twin double and a subsequent run. Zoilo Versalles' home run in the third proved to be the margin of victory as the Twins came out on top 2-1.

The Red Sox offense hit a new low on Sunday as Dean Chance shut them down with five innings of perfection. Lonborg pitched well, but not perfectly. When the rains came, Chance's name went into the record books with an asterisk and a 2-0 perfect game victory.

The Red Sox bats had nowhere to go but up, but they still couldn't come up with a win. In the first game of a doubleheader against the A's in Kansas City on Tuesday, Dave Morehead lasted only four and one-third innings and Boston lost their fourth straight, 5-3.

By game two of the doubleheader, Dick Williams felt that he had seen enough. Joe Foy was pulled at third in favor of Jerry Adair, Reggie Smith was sat down, Yastrzemski moved over to center and Norm Siebern was inserted in left field. For six innings, it looked as if all of this activity was for naught. Gary Bell had been shelled and the Red Sox were down 4-1 at this point.

In the seventh, the Red Sox bats came to life. They finally caught up with Kansas City pitcher Johnny Lee "Blue Moon" Odom and pushed across three runs. This uprising was led by Tony C's double, which tied the game at 4-4.

The Red Sox put it away in the ninth. The key hit was delivered by Norm Siebern with the bases loaded; another Williams' hunch had paid off. Bucky Brandon got the 7-5 win in relief.

Anthony Richard Conigliaro was born in Revere MA, on January 15, 1945. It almost seemed that Tony Conigliaro was born to play with and star for the Boston Red Sox. Tony spent his earliest years in Revere, he learned to play baseball in East Boston, and the Conigliaro family moved to Swampscott on the north shore of Boston when he was a teenager.

In his autobiography *Seeing it Through*, Tony wrote, recalling his early days on the diamond, "I'd get up every day, put on my sneakers, ask my mother to tie the laces for me and run out the door to the ball field across the street from my house. That's all I wanted to do." He added, "I was there so much that the other mothers in the neighborhood began saying my mother wasn't a very good one because she let me stay out there all that time."

After five hits in the doubleheader in Kansas City, Tony's batting average for the season was .302. Like so many gifted athletes, Tony made it look easy. But Tony's younger brother Billy, who spent three seasons with the Boston Red Sox, two of them playing in the same outfield with his big brother, told me, "I don't think people realized how hard Tony worked to get to the big leagues and how hard he worked to stay there. He would spend hours swinging a lead bat or squeezing a ball."

Tony's youngest brother, Richie, added, "The three of us would be watching television and I would look over and Tony would be using some of contraption that he put together to strengthen his wrists. He was always doing something to improve his batting skills. It's hard to believe any ballplayer ever worked harder."

The Red Sox showed signs of returning to life in the rubber game of the three-game series with Kansas City. Jim Lonborg interrupted two weeks of active duty with the Army Reserves to fly in from Atlanta to pitch a 5-1 victory. Jerry Adair paced the offense with three hits and the Boston pennant express appeared to be back on track.

Another derailing took place in Anaheim, California, over the next weekend. The Red Sox got excellent pitching on Friday night from Lee Stange, but they just could not mount any run production. Boston managed only three hits and George Scott was benched by Williams for being over his weight limit.

On Saturday, Scott was still in the steam bath and the Red Sox bats were still in the deep freeze. Gary Bell pitched well and managed to hold California to two runs. But Boston produced only one run and dropped their sixth game out of eight on the road. Now the Angels were nipping at their heels, trailing the slumping Red Sox by one percentage point.

Sunday was more of the same. Even Lonborg couldn't save the day. California prevailed 3-2 as the Red Sox saved their only runs until their last at bat.

The Red Sox had a 3,000-mile airplane ride to ponder their fate. As they returned to Boston, there was some evidence that they had "peaked." Two out of nine on a road trip was not pennant contending ball. To make matters worse, they had managed only a total of seven runs in the seven losses.

Detroit came into Fenway to kick off a twelve-game home stand with a three-game series starting on August 14. Dave Morehead carried the evening for Boston in the series opener. Pitching his first complete game since his September 16, 1965 no-hitter, Morehead shut out the Tigers 4-0. George Scott celebrated his return to the lineup by launching a first inning home run while Yaz and Smith added four-baggers of their own.

The Wednesday night game against the Tigers attracted 32,501 to Fenway. George Scott used his newly-svelte body to power two home runs and Boston never looked back in an 8-3 trouncing of the Tigers. Bucky Brandon pitched seven shutout innings in relief and picked up the win.

A crowd of 28,653 was thinking "sweep" on Thursday as the game moved into the tenth, tied at four. But Sparky Lyle gave up three runs in the tenth and the Red Sox fell, 7-4. Still, two out of three from the Tigers wasn't bad, and with nine games remaining in the home stand, the Red Sox were only three and a half games behind the league-leading White Sox.

The Red Sox were prominently featured on the front page of The Boston Globe on Friday morning August 18. There was a large picture above the fold of Jerry Adair and George Thomas arguing with home plate umpire Frank Umont after Adair was thrown out attempting to score in the eighth inning of the previous day's 7-4 loss to the Tigers.

The other big front page Red Sox mention came in a story, also above the fold, that was headlined "$60 Million Stadium Hailed." Massachusetts Governor John Volpe had filed a bill with the state legislature for the construction of a "domed or retractable roof stadium," to be funded using the full faith of the Commonwealth for the financing bonds with any annual deficit assumed by the general funds of the state. Obviously the politicians had been listening when Red Sox owner Tom Yawkey threatened in June to move the Red Sox out of town unless a new stadium was built.

Friday August 18, 1967, was a lovely summer day, the fourth consecutive day of full sun and daytime temperatures in the mid-80s. By game time the temperature would drop into the 70s, making it a perfect day to play and watch baseball. The crowd of just over 31,000 fans streamed into Fenway Park anticipating a great evening. Despite their disappointing play in August, the Red Sox were still only three games out of first place and it had been a long time since a Red Sox team had been in contention for the pennant in mid-August.

Tony C had been in a bit of a slump lately with only one hit in his last six games. But after four seasons in the big leagues he realized that a six month season will have a number of personal ups and downs. Earlier in the season Tony had served two weeks with his Army Reserve unit at Camp Drum in upstate New York. The conflict in Vietnam had picked up and most major league clubs helped their young single players to sign up with a reserve unit rather than face the draft. Jim Lonborg and Rico Petrocelli had nearly been sent to Vietnam when their Seattle reserve unit was almost activated in 1964. Dalton Jones and pitcher Bill Landis were two other Red Sox players who had to juggle baseball and military service.

When Tony returned from Camp Drum on June 4, he had found it difficult to regain his timing. Then three days later he had to fly back from Chicago for a meeting with his reserve unit in Lynn. But all of the Red Sox' "weekend warriors" recognized how fortunate they were and Tony got his timing back on track quickly. Then he was red-hot for the rest of June and all of July, and he knew he would be red-hot again. It was just a matter of time.

Tony Conigliaro watched his pal George Scott try to stretch a single into a double as the first man up in the fourth inning. George could stroke the ball but he was no track star when it came to running the bases. It was inevitable that George was nailed at second.

Tony and George went back to Wellsville, NY, at the Red Sox Class-A minor league team in 1963. The two teenagers from very different backgrounds bonded immediately and demonstrated their future promise. The following spring Tony C took the Red Sox training camp in Scottsdale, AZ, by storm and he was in the Red Sox starting lineup on Opening Day. Scotty took a little longer to make it to Boston, but in 1966, Tony C led the Red Sox with 28 home runs and Scott was right behind him with 27 "taters."

Tony knew that George liked to talk to his bats before he decided which one to take up to the plate. Sometimes he'd do it for an hour or more, endlessly asking, "You got any hits in you? You got a hit? You got a big hit for me tonight?" It seemed likely that Dick Williams was all over Scott for not holding up at first. Tony and Scott had made a number of visits to the manager's doghouse.

He put George and the manager out of his mind and swung several of his own bats as centerfielder Reggie Smith started for the plate. He shouted his encouragement. It was another big crowd that night, which was a lot better than looking out at 25,000, empty seats. It would be great to get another hit or two in front of them, especially since his parents and brothers, Billy and Richie, were among them.

Tony could reflect on the fact that he had been only one year old back in 1946 when Boston had won its last American League pennant. He knew personally the frustrations that the Red Sox loyalists felt. The fans were coming out in droves and they were the talk of the town. Only the day before, the Red Sox had a crowd of 28,653 to put them over the one million mark in attendance for the first time in seven years.

Reggie hadn't even gotten to the plate when an idiot fan tossed a smoke bomb into left field. Reggie and Tony looked at each other and shook their heads while the crowd shouted in a mixture of irritation and good humor. Even though Tony himself could have been sitting up in those very same stands just five short years earlier, he was constantly amazed by the antics of the Fenway crowds.

Still, it was ten minutes before the black smoke—which turned slowly to white as it hovered above the ground—completely dissipated. As he waited, Tony didn't consider it an evil omen, a sign of impending tragedy.

Finally, all traces of the smoke had blown away and the game was resumed with Reggie at the plate to face the battery of pitcher Jack Hamilton and catcher Bob Rodgers. Rodgers gave Hamilton the sign and the pitcher hurled the ball. Reggie came around quickly and drove the ball deep to center where it was caught easily by Jose Cardenal.

There were two outs when Tony came to the plate. Since he had singled off a curve ball his first time up, he took his stance in the right-handed batter's box expecting a fastball. Ever the scrapper, who determined in his early childhood that he would never back off from anyone or anything, he dug in to try and smash the first pitch far into the night.

If Tony had a trademark, it was his aggressiveness. He stood in the batter's box crowding the plate as if he owned it. He seemed to almost dare the pitcher to throw it inside knowing that if the pitch was off by even a fraction of an inch, he could turn on it and drive it into the inviting left-field screen.

Ironically, earlier that day Tony had been told by his business manager, Ed Penney, that he had bumped into Ted Williams who told him to tell Tony "To stop crowding the plate." Ted said, "You should back up before one of those guys hits you." Tony recalled that his only reaction was to ask Penney, "The way I'm hitting, who'd want to hit me?"

Tony, alert as a rousted rabbit, wondered whether the ten minute delay had caused Hamilton's arm to stiffen up. He'd find out in a moment. Hamilton reared up and whipped a fastball toward the plate. It zoomed across the intervening space right toward Tony's head.

The youthful batter had always figured with his lion's heart that he would instinctively know when to pull back and duck any ball by a fraction, no matter how hard it was thrown—even if directly at him. Still, the batter only has 0.4 of a second from the time the pitcher releases a 90-miles-per-hour pitch and the ball reaches the plate.

Tony did duck as he saw the ball headed for his chin. Still the ball as though radio-directed and fixed on his head came right at him. "It seemed to follow me in," he would say later. "I know I didn't freeze, I made a move to get out of the way." As he threw up his hands to protect himself and began to turn away to his right, his helmet flew off.

Tony never went to the plate thinking he was going to get hit or beaned. But he realized then that there was no way he was going to escape the impact of Hamilton's pitched ball. The ball was only four feet from his head when he knew it was going to get him. Simultaneously, he knew it was going to hurt like hell because Hamilton had tossed it with enormous force.

Thousands of the fans to this day and all the players on both teams can recall the wicked cracking sound the ball made when it crashed full force into Tony's left cheekbone and ricocheted directly downward to bounce off home plate. A huge audible groan, mingled with female shrieks of dismay and disbelief, echoed about the park. This was followed by the eerie silence that can only be produced by the sound of 31,000 people standing totally still in shock.

Tony admitted later that he was "frightened. I threw my hands up in front of my face and saw the ball follow me back . . ." The ball crunched into his left cheek bone, just below the left eye socket.

When the ball struck him, Tony's legs collapsed and he continued to twist to his right as he hurtled toward the ground. "It felt as if the ball would go into my head and come out the other side . . . I went down like a sack of potatoes. Just before everything went dark I saw the ball bounce straight down on home plate."

Prostate on the playing field but still conscious, Tony had lost sight temporarily in both eyes. As his teammates rushed toward him, led by Rico Petrocelli who had been in the on-deck circle and Mike Ryan, Tony's best friend and roommate on the road, the right fielder laid without moving. Rico knelt and gently shook his shoulders. "Tony, Tony, are you all right? It's okay. You're gonna be okay." More Red Sox gathered. The club trainer, Buddy LeRoux, rolled Tony over. When he didn't move, they all began to fear the worst. Rico almost got sick looking at his crushed cheek and swollen shut eye. Rico told me later, "When I first got to Tony, I thought he was dead. He was just lying there motionless."

A call went out for a stretcher. Just then Tony stirred and kicked his feet in the dirt. Out on the mound, Jack Hamilton, his arms folded, stood motionlessly as he was roundly booed by the hometown fans. He was convinced that he hadn't thrown at Tony. He also knew that according to baseball etiquette, he would not be welcome at home plate.

Tony would contend that he "was never knocked out by the impact of the Angel pitcher's fastball." He admitted though that he wished he had been because of the pain. The blow from the baseball within minutes had sealed both eyes shut and turned them a reddish blue color. Blood streamed from his nose.

Tony began to roll around on the ground to try to stop the pain. He also had a huge swelling in his mouth that was fast filling up with fluids. Besides thinking he was blind and never going to see, he was convinced that the mass in his mouth was going to close up and keep him from breathing.

"I won't be able to breathe," he thought. "If this thing closes up on me, I'm gone." He said that it was at that point that he began to pray to God to keep him alive. In his mind, God could have taken him right then and there, if He wanted to. It was like a showdown between them: God would make the choice. Hopefully it would be in his favor although he never had been much of a true believer.

Tony was rushed on the stretcher into the clubhouse where LeRoux placed an ice pack against his head. Dr. Thomas M. Tierney, the team's physician, was in the stands when Tony went down and hurried to his side in the clubhouse. The physician was an old friend of the Conigliaro family but had no time then for small talk. He ordered an ambulance to be called and began testing Tony's blood pressure and reflexes.

The clubhouse was full of people, including Tony's father and two brothers, but to the young player "the room was deathly still." He remembered that several players came by to squeeze his arm and whisper encouragement. Coaches popped in and out. All were very reassuring. Strangely, Dick Williams "never came back," Tony would recall later, "and that's always bothered me. Maybe he was too busy at the time . . ." in managing the team to a 3-2 win over the Angels.

Tony was rushed by ambulance to Sancta Maria Hospital in Cambridge where he was examined by Dr. Joseph Dorsey, a neurosurgeon. The doctor would say later that Tony had suffered a fractured cheekbone, a scalp contusion and that it was too soon to determine the extent of the injury to his left eye. He acknowledged that Tony might have been killed if the ball had hit him an inch higher.

The Angels' battery stuck to their position that Hamilton had not thrown at Tony. "I've not struck anyone all year," the pitcher noted. "I certainly wasn't throwing at him. I was just trying to get the ball over the plate. Tony tends to hang over the plate as much as anyone in the league."

Similarly, Angel catcher Rodgers contended that the pitch "was about eight inches inside. It took off when it got near Tony. It was a fastball and it just sailed."

Bobby Doerr, a one-time Red Sox second baseman, Hall-of-Famer and then a coach under Williams, wrote in his diary then, "There was a real ironic, almost strange thing about the game tonight, especially in the light of Tony's injury, which looks like it is serious. Jack Hamilton has been accused all during the season by a lot of people of throwing spitters. Well, in the first part of the game tonight, Dick Williams complained to the umpires of this. Dick also voiced a protest early on (maybe the second inning) that we all thought Hamilton was throwing spitters. The ball was acting strangely. Dick said that he was afraid someone would get hurt. Unfortunately, he was right."

Part of the beauty and appeal of baseball is its continuity. Even if one team is trailing 14-2 in the ninth inning, each hitter strives for success and the opposing pitcher works diligently to frustrate the hitter's efforts. On the last day of the season when two opponents have long since been eliminated from the race, they both show up and go about the business of securing victory.

In the case of the August 18 Red Sox-Angels contest, the continuity was almost too much to bear. Every person in the park had a part of his mind on the game and a part remembering the sight of Tony sprawled lifelessly at home plate. Somehow Tony's close friend, Rico Petrocelli, who had been on deck at the time of the dreadful beaning, found the concentration to drill a base hit off the rattled Hamilton. Somehow the Red Sox were able to dig down deep and put together two runs in that fateful fourth inning. The close of that inning will be forever recorded as 2-0 Boston. Jose Tartabull took Tony's place at first base and scored what proved to be a very important run.

The game lasted for nearly an hour and one-half after Tony's tragedy. Almost incredibly it featured near flawless baseball and intense pressure. If anyone ever doubted the professionalism of major league ballplayers, this game was the proof. The Red Sox got up 3-0 after six innings and hung tough for a 3-2 victory. Gary Bell pitched a gutsy four-hitter and helped his own cause with two hits and an RBI. Such is the continuity of baseball.

Gary Bell recalled how difficult it was to focus on the game that evening. "All I could think of was the terrible sound of the ball when it hit Tony. We weren't really sure how he was doing and it was difficult to put the incident out of our minds. But we were in the middle of a pennant race and concentrating on the game was our only way to cope with Tony's misfortune."

Jack Hamilton was taken out for a pinch hitter after five innings and took the loss. The official scorebook shows that he gave up four hits, two runs—both of them earned—struck out five batters, walked one man and hit one batter.

No matter what some people might think about his pitch, Jack Hamilton demonstrated his class by being among the first arrivals at the hospital in the morning to try to visit Tony. Except for his family, Tom Yawkey and Mike Ryan who sneaked in, Tony was forbidden visitors but was apprised that Hamilton had attempted to see him.

Tony was a big fan of Yawkey and was surprised when he was awoken the next morning by a voice saying, "Wake up, Tony. It's me, Tom Yawkey." The Red Sox owner had always been kind and patient with his young outfielder and often listened to his personal problems. "Now as busy as he was, he was sitting in my room, holding my hand, and telling me not to worry about anything."

After a few days in the hospital, Tony's head pain began to subside and he began to see out of his right eye. Still he was confined mostly to his bed and could do little but think about his situation. Once he realized that he wasn't going to die and that he was out of danger, he began to think about how he was hit.

Tony kept asking himself whether Jack Hamilton had intended to hit him. It didn't figure. "I had been in a slump going into the series with the Angels. Pitchers usually don't stir up guys who are in a hitting slump. If I had been hot at the bat, I could see where he might."

Tony decided to give Hamilton the benefit of the doubt even though he knew the pitcher had a tendency to hit players occasionally. "I figured he had no good reason to go after me." Ultimately, he figured, only one person in the world knew whether Hamilton was trying to hit him that night and that person was Jack Hamilton.

One of the things that bothered Tony the most during his weeks in the hospital was the fact that he never heard from Dick Williams at any time. "He never came up to the hospital and he never dropped me a line or anything." This particularly upset Tony because he felt he had made a contribution to the team's "Impossible Dream" drive to the pennant and had given Williams everything he had. "I had been hit in the face by a baseball and nearly lost my life. I felt the least Dick could do was show he knew I existed."

In his heart, Tony acknowledged that he and Williams had never hit it off from the time they first met in 1964. Tony was a rookie invited to spring training, only nineteen, trying to do the nearly impossible, to make the Red Sox club after that one year in the minors at Wellsville, New York, and Williams was a thirty-four-year-old utility player trying to save his pro career. Williams called Tony "Bush" in the condescending manner of the veteran.

Quick to fly off the handle and ready to fight anyone, Tony never forgot the ball that Williams threw at him as he came out of the dugout during his first spring training with the Red Sox in Scottsdale, Arizona. The very next day, Tony retaliated by brushing off Williams with a thrown ball as he came up from the dugout. When he picked himself up and wiped away the dust, the enraged Williams came after Tony, but he was warned off by Dick Stuart. "We just never hit it off after that incident," Tony recalled afterwards.

Neither Tony nor Williams realized it but they had a lot of personality traits in common. Both had a confidence level that was on the cusp of arrogance. Neither of them would back down from anyone. Tony was once shown a video of himself being interviewed after hitting a homer as a rookie on Opening Day in 1964, after hitting a home run in his first at-bat in Fenway Park. When asked what pitch he had hit for the homer, he had replied with supreme confidence, "Oh, a spitter." When asked several years later to critique his performance on the video, he responded, "pretty cocky."

This game against the Angels on August 18 was the last one for Tony Conigliaro in 1967. Vision problems with his left eye ruled out any possibility of his returning to the Red Sox. The blind spot in the eye just wouldn't get any better. Moreover, he still had a lot of swelling in and around the eye and he was told that "your distant vision is so bad that it might be dangerous for you to play anymore this year. You just can't be ready to play in the World Series if the Red Sox make it."

Tony, of course, was crushed by the news. He was always hopeful that the eye would improve and he'd get back with the team to make a bigger contribution to the race for the pennant. He went back to his apartment near Fenway and cried. "For the first time I realized how much I loved it all . . . I missed the games, the competition, especially now with the ball club fighting for the pennant. There was nothing else I wanted to do except play baseball."

Tony did drop by the Red Sox clubhouse a number of times following his injury and even sat on the bench in uniform on a few occasions. His teammates went out of their way to make him feel welcome but Tony was never truly comfortable because he wasn't contributing. He was in the Red Sox clubhouse after their win on the last day of the season and he could be seen sobbing quietly with owner Tom Yawkey's arm around him to provide comfort.

Although he was to be out of baseball until 1969, Tony had already chalked up a commendable record in the game, beginning with 1963 when he hit .363 with Wellsville and was named MVP of the New York-Penn League.

Tony moved up to the Red Sox in 1964 at the call of manager Johnny Pesky. When I asked Johnny if he had considered sending Tony down for more seasoning in the minor leagues after his outstanding performance in spring training, Pesky said, "Not for a minute. And if I hadn't brought him back to Boston the fans would have killed me!" As a nineteen-year-old rookie, hit .290 with twenty-four home runs—the most by a teenager in baseball history. On June 3 of that year, he hit a bases-loaded homer off Dan Osinski then of the Angels, and later a teammate of Tony's on the 1967 Red Sox, to earn the distinction of being the youngest player in he majors ever to hit a grand slam.

In 1965, Tony led the American League in home runs with thirty-two; at twenty years of age, he was the youngest player ever to lead the league in four-baggers. All told, he was at bat 521 times and got 140 hits for 82 RBI.

Johnny Pesky was fired as manager that year and replaced by Billy Herman, a man that Tony claimed was on "different wavelengths" than him. Tony was to say that 1966 was the year that "a lot of things happened to me that pretty much established my baseball image: I proved myself as a home-run hitter. I got myself into a lot of hot water with the baseball writers. I couldn't get along with Billy Herman."

Tony came to discover that his candid and outspoken views did not play well in the papers or in the front office. For the most part, he was a guileless local boy who spoke his mind. He never claimed that he was a rocket scientist and it took him a while to realize he was living in a fish bowl. Before he caught on he had made almost as many trips to general manager Dick O'Connell's office as he had made to the principal's office at St. Mary's of Lynn.

Tony managed, however, to achieve another exemplary year in 1966 by hitting .265 and rapping out 28 homers. He was at bat 558 times and got 148 hits with 93 RBI.

While Tony seldom had a good word for Williams, he did note after the "Impossible Dream" year that the manager "did an incredible job, taking a ball club that finished ninth two years straight and managing it to a pennant. If Williams ever was likable, it was in 1967 because he was up there fighting all the time and personalities never were a factor. We were a happy club and showed up every day believing we were going to win."

Until he was hit by Jack Hamilton's pitch, Tony was enjoying a 20-homer season and batting .287. He had been up to the plate 349 times and collected an even 100 hits and 67 RBI. He was obviously a young man on a path to a likely induction into baseball's Hall of Fame in Cooperstown, New York.

After missing the entire 1968 season, Tony was back with his beloved Red Sox for opening day 1969 against the Orioles in Baltimore. Everybody thought that Jack Hamilton's pitch had finished him, but he was determined to prove everyone wrong. He did it by hitting a tenth inning homer that tied up the game which the Red Sox eventually won 5-4.

All in all, he came back big in 1969, slamming out twenty homers and winning the Hutch Award for being the player "who best exemplified the fighting spirit and burning desire of the late (pitcher and manager) Fred Hutchinson." He was also voted Comeback Player of the Year.

The next year, 1970, was even more of a banner year for Tony as he batted a career-high thirty-six homers and hammered out 116 RBI. Incredibly, the Red Sox traded him in October to the California Angels,

Conigliaro poised to unleash his "Fenway swing."

partly because the Red Sox didn't want Tony and his younger brother, Billy, who had joined the Red Sox, to be playing on the same team. Red Sox general manager Dick O'Connell, perhaps Tony's best front office friend on the ball club over the years, said, "Frankly, we considered Billy a better ballplayer under the circumstances." For serious Red Sox fans the move was akin to trading the U.S.S. Constitution to Baltimore in return for the U.S.S. Constellation.

The Red Sox apparently made the right decision because Tony's eyesight began to fail when he went to the Angels and he only played seventy-four games total for them in 1971 before calling a middle-of-the-night news conference in June to announce his retirement.

Four years later in 1975, he asked the Red Sox to invite him to spring training where he made the Red Sox as a designated hitter. He played in twenty-one games that season but hit only two homers and .123 and finally decided to call it quits. It should be remembered, however, that Tony had burned up the Grapefruit League and astounded everyone with his hitting prowess. This may have been one of the most amazing feats in the history of baseball. The man had been out of baseball for nearly three and one-half years and there is some evidence to suggest that he was hitting literally from memory. Billy and Richie Conigliaro were continually throwing him batting practice during the years he was out of the game. "He clearly had a blind spot in his left eye," Billy told me. "I know that because if I threw the ball to a certain spot he would miss it entirely. I could tell that he hadn't really seen the ball."

Red Sox infielder and pinch hitter extraordinaire, Dalton Jones, came up to the Red Sox with Tony in 1964 and they were good friends during their six years together on the team. I asked Dalton what he thought Tony C might have achieved if he had never been injured, and he said, "First he would have hit over 600 home runs and been elected to the Hall of Fame. Then he would have gone to Hollywood and become a famous movie star. After that he would have come back home and been elected Governor of Massachusetts." And Dalton added, smiling, "And I'm only half-kidding!"

The years passed and Tony got into sports broadcasting as an announcer and a color man. After being interviewed by the Red Sox for a broadcasting job, Tony was being driven to Boston's Logan International Airport on January 9, 1982, by his brother Billy when he suffered a massive heart attack. The vicious blow disabled him completely, requiring his mother, Teresa, and his brothers, Billy and Richie, as well as nurses, to provide constant care.

During the week of February 19, 1990, Tony C, the local boy who shone as a star outfielder for the Red Sox from 1964 through 1975, was admitted to a hospital in Salem, Massachusetts. He developed a lung infection and kidney failure and died peacefully in his sleep at 4:30 p.m., Saturday, February 24, 1990. He was forty-five years old.

Tony Conigliaro was born in Revere, Massachusetts, in 1945. He played his first baseball on East Boston sandlots and then he was a three-letter athlete at St. Mary's in Lynn. After only a year in the minors, he was called up to the Red Sox.

He made his debut with the Bostonians at the age of nineteen. The date was April 16, 1964, and the site was Yankee Stadium. He hit a home run in his first at-bat in Fenway Park the next day.

Johnny Pesky, who was associated with the Red Sox for almost 70 years, called the death of Tony Conigliaro "so sad and a damn shame. He was the best young hitter I ever saw other than Ted Williams. He was six foot, three inches tall, and weighed about 190 pounds. A good-looking player with a lot of ability. A great hustler who could do a lot of things—run, hit and throw. Ted Williams always thought he could be another Joe DiMaggio. Remember, he was the youngest guy to hit 100 home runs in the American League."

On a cold, crisp winter morning in Revere, Tony's funeral mass was celebrated at St. Anthony's Church, a big and truly beautiful edifice, the Yankee Stadiums of churches. He had been baptized, taken his first Communion and confirmed in the same church.

Bishop John Mulcahy told the nearly 1,000 mourners, "Tony did what God wanted him to do. God gives special talents to many people, and it's obvious that He gave Tony a singular, unique talent of being able to hit a baseball. God gives those talents to people so they can make other people happy."

The Reverend Dominic Menna went on to tell the congregation, "Tony taught his fans that a runner who looks back never wins the race and he looked ahead to a successful career and did all he could to make it a success."

Among the mourners at the funeral were former Governor John Volpe, a host of former Red Sox players and Dave Cowens of the Celtics. Tony C was buried at Holy Cross Cemetery in nearby Malden.

It is hard to believe that Tony C has been gone for over 25 years now. But for as long as New England kids play baseball with snow shoveled to the sidelines, and dream of someday starring for the Boston Red Sox, the spirit of Tony C will always be among us.

Chapter 8

Dalton Jones: The Sweet-Swinging Gentleman of the South

Boston Red Sox vs. California Angels, Sunday, August 20, 1967

Dalton Jones was only 23 years-old in 1967 but he was already in his fourth full season with the Boston Red Sox. His picture-perfect swing at home plate had earned him the nickname of "The sweet swinger from Baton Rouge, Louisiana." When his boyhood idol Ted Williams had watched Dalton at bat in spring training in 1963, he told Jones, "Don't mess with that swing." Dalton Jones spent the 1963 season with Seattle, the Red Sox Triple-A minor league team, and he was switched from his life-long position at shortstop to second base because Rico Petrocelli was clearly Boston's shortstop of the future. Dalton had an outstanding spring training camp in 1964 and the Red Sox brought the twenty-year-old to Boston where he quickly showed that he had a big league bat. His only frustration in 1967 was that he had bounced around between second base and third base during his time with the team and he was still searching for a permanent position where he could start every day. But as the season went on and the Red Sox continued as serious contenders for the American League pennant, it became clear that every player's contribution really mattered. And by the time the crucial doubleheader with the Angels on August 20 came to an exciting end, a number of heroes would emerge.

Baseball fans all over New England awoke with a collective hangover the day after Tony C's tragic beaning. Saturday, August 19, was another pleasant late summer's day but the only thing Red Sox fans cared about was Tony's condition. They asked one another: how is Tony? Have you heard anything?

Media reports focused on Tony's fractured cheekbone with hardly a mention of the condition of his left eye. The morning newspapers repeated the statements by Dr. Dorsey, the attending neurosurgeon at Sancta Maria Hospital, that X-rays showed a broken cheekbone and a scalp contusion as his primary injuries. The initial medical forecasts suggested that Tony would be out for three weeks, while acknowledging that his absence could certainly be longer.

The Conigliaro family put out a statement saying that Tony was resting fairly comfortably and thanking fans for their well wishes. They also said that Tony appreciated Tom Yawkey's visit that morning and that visits were generally limited to family members. Finally, they confirmed that Tony would be watching the Red Sox-Angels game on national television Saturday afternoon.

It was difficult for Tony's teammates to go about the business of chasing a pennant while worrying about their teammate's condition. But the team was only three games out of first place, trailing the Twins and White Sox, and the Angels were only two games behind the Red Sox. Every game from here on in would be important. Somehow they were able to play flawlessly after Tony was hit in the fourth inning the night before, and they were going to have to come up with another strong performance that afternoon if they were to remain in contention. When Dalton Jones checked the lineup card for the afternoon he learned that he would start the game on the bench. That wasn't very surprising since he had only started one game in the last two months.

James Dalton Jones was born in McComb, Mississippi, on December 10, 1943, and he grew up in Baton Rouge, Louisiana. He was named for an uncle but he was called Dalton his whole life. Baseball played an important role in Dalton's life for as long as he could recall. "Family and faith comes first," he emphasized, "but I used to wait on the front steps until my dad would come home from work so we could play pepper."

When his fourth grade teacher asked everyone to say what they were going to be when they grew up, Dalton answered confidently, "a major league baseball player." When the teacher suggested that he should think about being a lawyer or a doctor, he said, "No m'am, I'm going to be a ballplayer."

Growing up in Baton Rouge, Dalton was more than 600 miles from the nearest major league city. But his parents arranged family trips to St. Louis, MO, where Dalton got to watch the Cardinals, and even as far as Cleveland, OH, to see the Indians, and on at least on one occasion, the Red Sox versus the Indians. Growing up in the 1950s, it is no surprise that he chose Stan "The Man" Musial as his favorite National League player, and Ted Williams as his American League hero. Dalton recalled, "We saw a game in Cleveland where Ted homered twice, catching and then passing Mel Ott as third on the all-time home run list. What a great thrill that was."

Jones excelled on the baseball diamond at every level from Little League to high school. And he is quick to credit his dad, Clinton Jones, for most of his success. "My dad gave up a lot of his free time to work with me, and he coached my Little League and other youth teams. He helped my skills, and more importantly he gave me confidence."

Long-time Red Sox scout George Digby, who would later sign Red Sox stars Wade Boggs and Mike Greenwell, spotted Dalton's sweet swing early in his high school career. Digby arrived in Baton Rougue shortly after Dalton's graduation from Istrouma High School in 1961. George showed up at the Jones home with the offer of a nice bonus and with Ted Williams, Dalton's boyhood idol, in tow! Dalton signed on the spot, with his parent's approval, and within a week he was in Texas playing professional baseball with Alpine Cowboys of the ClassD Sophomore League.

Jones moved quickly through the Red Sox minor league system reaching the Red Sox Triple-A team in Seattle, Washington, in just his third year of play

Spring training in 1963 had provided Dalton with one of his best compliments in baseball. "Ted Williams, my baseball idol as a youngster, watched me hit. And then he approached me and told me, 'I'm not going

Dalton Jones hit .407 over the last seven weeks of the season.

to say anything to you. Don't mess with that swing.' Wow! What a compliment that was coming from him."

There were two players at the Red Sox spring training camp in Scottsdale, AZ, in 1964 that stood out among all the younger players:

Tony Conigliaro and Dalton Jones. Both players, 19-year-old Tony C and 20-year-old Dalton Jones, went north with the Red Sox for the 1964 season. Tony was an immediate sensation and Jones played in more than 100 games in each Red Sox season from 1964 to 1966. After playing in a majority of the games for three seasons it was tough for Dalton to adjust to a back-up role under Dick Williams in 1967. And having his pal Tony C in the hospital with his future in baseball unknown made August 19, 1967 a particularly difficult day for Dalton.

Friday night's game featured good pitching, flawless fielding on defense, and a brisk pace. The quality of play was quite amazing considering the emotions felt by both teams after Tony was hit in the fourth inning. Saturday's game was nothing like that.

Maybe it was the emotional hangover that caused the pitchers on both sides to have trouble pitching and the fielders to have trouble fielding in a game eventually won by the Red Sox by a score of 12-11. It was as if someone had let the air out of a balloon and pitching and fielding drifted away for a day.

Jose Santiago, who had been used primarily as a reliever all season by Dick Williams, was given a spot start but he never found his rhythm. He was relieved by Sparky Lyle after giving up six earned runs over 4 2/3 innings. Lyle faced two batters who both produced RBI singles, and Sparky was out before he even broke a sweat. Veteran reliever Dan Osinski replaced Lyle and finally retired the side.

After holding the Angels scoreless in the top of the sixth, Osinski was scheduled to lead off the Red Sox half of the sixth inning with Boston trailing 6-5. But Dick Williams had already told Dalton Jones to grab a bat and to get something going. Get something going is exactly what Dalton did as he drove a line drive into center field for a single. Jones barely had time to nod to first base coach Bobby Doerr before pitcher Bill Landis came out to run for him.

Looking back on the 1967 season, Jones, who was the primary Red Sox pinch hitter that season, told me, "I found pinch hitting to be very difficult. Hitting is all about timing and you are coming up cold, often against a pitcher who has been brought in to face you." Jones added, "Don't get me wrong, I was always pleased when Dick Williams showed faith in me in a tough spot, but I can assure you that I swung at the first good pitch I saw when I was pinch hitting."

Dalton's single to lead off the sixth set the tone for a two-run inning which gave the Red Sox a 6-5 lead. Norm Sideburn's pinch hit triple with the bases loaded gave the Red Sox a seemingly comfortable 10-6 lead, but ultimately it took 12 runs for the Red Sox to defeat the Angels. The victory kept the Red Sox on the heels of the White Sox and three games behind the Tigers.

Sunday, August 20, was another warm summer day with temperatures reaching the low-80s. Fenway Park was filled with a near capacity crowd of 33,840 fans that were on hand to watch a single admission doubleheader beginning at 1 PM. Channel 5 in Boston televised the first game of the doubleheader but not the second. Fans at home would have to rely on Ken Coleman, Ned Martin, and Mel Parnell for a radio account on WHDH-AM.

The Sunday papers didn't have much new information on Tony C's condition. It was reported that his left eye was swollen completely shut. And there was more speculation that with only six weeks left in the season it was likely that Tony was done for the year.

Dalton Jones was not in the starting lineup for the first game. "I always came to the ballpark thinking I would be in the lineup and prepared to play," Dalton said. "You had to, because the one day you aren't prepared is the day you will start. If I wasn't in the lineup I did everything I could to keep my head in the game, watch the opposing pitchers. And I would be back and forth to the clubhouse to swing the bat to keep loose."

Friday night's game had been filled with emotion. First Tony was hit, and then the outcome of the game hung in the balance until the last Angel hitter was retired. And while Saturday's game had a sort of Keystone Cops flair to it, once again the Red Sox one-run margin was at risk until the final out. But a Red Sox win in game one of the Sunday doubleheader was a certainty before the home half of the sixth inning was complete.

Red Sox right-handed pitcher Lee Stange drew the start in the first game of the doubleheader. Stange's record for 1967 was only 7-8 at that point, but his ERA, was well under 3.00. "Stinger" had no problem with the Angels in the first inning, setting them down three straight with two groundouts and a strikeout.

Veteran left hander George Brunet, who was in his 12th major league season, was the Stinger's opponent. Brunet got into trouble almost immediately. Jerry Adair singled with one out and Yaz forced him at second on a groundball. After George Scott walked, center-fielder Reggie Smith hit a long drive into the left-field net to give the Red Sox a 3-0 lead. Following an Elston Howard single Rico Petrocelli drove another pitch over the left field wall and the Red Sox were up 5-0.

Lee Stange breezed through the next four innings and when George Scott doubled in Jerry Adair in the bottom of the fifth inning, Stange had a 6-0 lead to work with. At this point manager Dick Williams saw an opportunity to give Rico Petrocelli a chance to rest his sore wrist. He moved Mike Andrews over to shortstop and he sent Dalton Jones in to replace Andrews at second base.

First Mike Andrews drove in right-fielder George Thomas with a single, and following a Joe Foy single, Yaz drove his 30th home run into the right-field bleachers. The Sox were up 10-0 but the best was still ahead. Switch-hitter Reggie Smith, batting left-handed against Angel's right-hander Pete Cimino, with Jose Tartabull on first, drove a ball deep into the right-field bleachers. His blast gave the Red Sox a 12-0 lead but more importantly, he became the first Red Sox player to homer from both sides of the plate in the same game at home. He was only the second Red Sox player to homer from both sides of the plate in the same game, following Pumpsie Green who achieved the feat in 1961 against the Angels in Los Angeles.

With the score at 12-0 even the most diehard Angels fan would admit that it was a mountain too steep to climb. Lee Stange gave up two harmless runs on his way to a 12-2 victory. His complete game gave the Red Sox bullpen a much needed rest particularly with the second game still to play.

The Red Sox clubhouse was a happy place during the 20-minute break between games. And the easy win provided a little relief on the weekend of Tony C's beaning. Dalton Jones had singled in two at-bats after coming in the fifth inning of the first game so he felt a part of the good feelings. But when he checked the lineup card for the second game he saw that he would start that game on the bench as well.

Dalton Jones's Red Sox career started with a loud bang. The 20-year-old Jones was the starting second baseman in the home opener against the Chicago White Sox on April 17, 1964. A crowd of 20,213 fans at Fenway Park saw the rookie triple to right field in his second major league at-bat, driving in pitcher Jack Lamabe to give the Red Sox a 3-1 lead. When shortstop Eddie Bressoud singled, Jones scored to make it 4-1 Red Sox, which turned out to be the final score. It was quite a debut for rookies Jones and Conigliaro. Dalton tripled in his second major league at-bat and Tony C hit a home run in his first at-bat at Fenway Park!

The following day, in an afternoon game against the White Sox, Jones went one better. He homered in the ninth inning against 11-year major league veteran left-hander Don Mossi. This showed that the left-handed hitting Jones could handle left handed-pitching and that he wouldn't be intimidated by a crafty veteran.

Dalton still recalls that over the next several weeks he was used sparingly, and only as a pinch hitter. "Johnny Pesky was our manager," Jones said. "I loved Johnny, he was a wonderful man, but he was playing the veterans at the beginning of the season." But then on May 19 Dalton got a chance to show what he could do. "I remember that we were losing 3-0 to the Angels and I grabbed a bat and kept walking in front of Johnny to make sure he would notice me. Finally we got a few runners on and scored a run. Johnny sent me up to pinch hit with two outs and the bases loaded.

"I had wanted to get into the game in the worst way, but when he finally sent me up there I was half-scared out of my mind," Dalton chuckled. "With the count at 3-2, I managed to make contact and whistled a line drive by Don Lee's [Angels' reliever] ear. It went into the gap in center field scoring three runs for a 4-3 win. When we got to the clubhouse, Johnny [Pesky] and I called my dad in Baton Rouge to tell him all about it. I felt like I belonged in the big leagues after that."

In 1964, Dalton got into 118 games with the Red Sox , most of them as the starting second baseman. On a couple of road trips Jones roomed with veteran utility player Dick Williams, who was in his last major league season. And did Jones use this time to get some tips from this 13-year veteran? "I was young and I wasn't smart enough to do it," he chuckled. "I wish I had though!"

Dalton Jones played well in 1965, but he tore a hamstring muscle in May and that injury would bother him throughout his career. Despite the injury he made a successful transition from the right side of the infield to the left, playing 81 games at third base. "I was more comfortable at third base than second," Jones recalled. "I had been a shortstop my whole career until I was switched to second in 1963. Playing third base and moving back to the left side of the infield was a lot more comfortable after all those years at shortstop."

In 1966, he appeared in 115 games for the Red Sox, but he lost at-bats to rookie third baseman Joe Foy, who came on strong in the second half of the season. Jones played mostly at second base and his batting average dropped from .270 in 1965 to .234. At age 22 he had played in 345 big league games and had accumulated more than 1,000 official plate appearances. Dalton Jones was looking forward to the 1967 Red Sox season with hopeful anticipation.

The Red Sox started right-hander Dave Morehead, who had shutout the Detroit Tigers just five days earlier, in the second game. The Angels countered with Jim McGlothlin who had been selected for the American League All-Star team in July. McGlothlin featured a sparkling 2.44 ERA.

Morehead held the Angels scoreless in their half of the first inning despite a walk and a single and McGlothlin set the Red Sox down in the bottom of the first with only a walk to Yaz. But in the second inning California climbed all over Morehead. Dave gave up four runs and Dick Williams had seen enough. He lifted Morehead after 1 2/3 innings, replacing him with the winner of yesterday's ballgame, Dan Osinski. Osinski promptly gave up a two-run double to Rick Reichardt before retiring Bob Rodgers on a line drive to George Scott at first base.

With the score 6-0 in favor of California it looked like the Angels were turning the tables from the earlier game. The Red Sox went quietly in their half of the second and neither team scored in the third inning.

But in the top of the fourth inning Jimmie Hall singled and Don Mincher homered against Osinski to put the Angels in the lead 8-0.

A few of the 33,840 fans headed for the exits obviously feeling that not even the Cardiac Kids come overcome an eight-run deficit. But Dalton Jones insists that no one in the Red Sox dugout thought that way. "Yes, eight runs were a lot to make up but it was only the fourth inning and people had been counting us out all year," he pointed out. "Nobody took us seriously in spring training but we had a winning record in the second half of 1966, and we had a lot of young guys just coming into their own. We felt we could beat anybody."

As if to put an exclamation point behind Dalton's attitude, Reggie Smith homered in the fourth inning, his third round-tripper of the day, to make the score 8-1. Manager Williams wasn't waving the white flag but he decided to rest Rico in the second game as well, and Jerry Adair moved from third to shortstop and Dalton Jones took over at third base.

New pitcher Bill Landis retired the Angels 1-2-3 in their fifth and the Red Sox made some more noise in their half of the fifth inning. Dalton Jones started things off with a sharp single to right field, and with one out Jerry Adair drew a walk to put two runners on as Carl Yastrzemski stepped to the plate. Yaz came through, as he did throughout the 1967 season, and drove a McGlothlin pitch deep into the right-field bleachers. And just like that, the seemingly insurmountable eight-run lead had been quickly cut in half.

Dalton Jones was disappointed that Dick Williams hadn't given him more of a chance to win a regular job in 1967. But Jones is quick to credit Williams for changing a losing ball club into a winning one. "Williams was exactly what we needed at the right time. I remember that he called us all together at the beginning of training camp to go over the schedule. We all gathered around him in a semi-circle, and he said, 'You either play for me and win, or you are gone.' And believe me, we heard him loud and clear. We all got the message," Dalton Jones emphasized.

"The great thing about Dick was you always knew where you stood. You maybe didn't like it," Dalton laughed, "but you didn't have to waste any time wondering what Dick meant. Most of us found that refreshing."

Fate can take all sorts of twists and turns. After Bill Landis set the Angels down in order in the top of the sixth inning California brought in a new pitcher: It was Jack Hamilton, the villain of Friday night's beaning of Tony C, and Boston's public enemy number one. Not surprisingly, Red Sox fans responded with a chorus of boos and catcalls.

Mike Andrews, the first Red Sox hitter to face Hamilton, drew a walk to start things off. Then Joe Foy pinch hit for pitcher Landis and drove a Hamilton pitch into right field for a double. With no one out Andrews played it smart and stopped at third base. The next batter, catcher Mike Ryan, drew a walk and the bases were loaded for Dalton Jones. Angel's manager Bill Rigney had seen enough and called Minnie Rojas in from the bullpen to replace Hamilton.

Asked if he felt the pressure in this tight situation, Dalton said, "That year it seemed like we had a different hero every day and we just kept winning. You feel pressure on a losing team because there aren't many players to make it happen. In 1967, you felt that if you didn't get it done someone else would pick you up. So yes, I was pumped up but I didn't feel excessive pressure."

Jones launched a Rojas slider to straight-away centerfield, and at first it looked like it had the distance to reach the bleachers. "He threw me a high slider and I just let it rip! The wind was blowing in that direction so I thought it had a pretty good chance to reach the wall." Dalton's blast was up high enough on the center-field wall for a fan to reach over and touch it. What should have been a triple was turned into a ground rule double, but two runs scored and Dalton was perched on second with Mike Ryan on third and no one out.

The next batter, Jose Tartabull, hit a ball that was caught but it was deep enough for Mike Ryan to tag up and score and for Jones to tag and make it to third base. Jerry Adair followed Tartabull and he hit a soft liner into left field that landed safely and allowed Dalton to score the tying run. There was another walk and a chance for George Scott and Reggie Smith to play hero but Rojas got out of the inning without further damage. The Red Sox had scored four runs in the sixth inning and a game that looked hopelessly out of reach just two innings earlier was tied at 8-8.

The Red Sox top reliever, John Wyatt, came on to pitch the top of the seventh inning and he held the Angels scoreless. Rojas continued into the last of the seventh inning for California and managed to wiggle out of a first and third situation to end the inning with the score remaining at 8-8.

Dick Williams brought in Jose Santiago, who had pitched 4 2/3 innings the day before, to pitch the eighth inning. "My arm was tired," Santiago admitted to me almost 50 years later. "But when you are involved in that type of game, with us coming back from eight runs down, the adrenalin kicks in. Besides," he added, "we were running out of pitchers!" Jose retired the first two batters before Roger Repoz singled and Jim Fregosi reached on an error, but he got Bubba Morton to ground out to end the inning.

Minnie Rojas continued into the eighth inning for the Angels and the first batter he faced was Jerry Adair, who had been moved to short-stop to replace Rico Petrocelli. Red Sox general manager Dick O'Connell had traded reliever Don McMahon to the White Sox for 10-year veteran Jerry Adair in early June because Adair could play short, second base or third.

Jerry Adair hit only 57 home runs during his 13-year major league career but he picked the last of the eighth inning, with the scored tied at 8-8, to hit one of them. Adair's drive barely cleared the 37-foot left-field wall and landed safely in the net. Jerry told the media, "I never thought it was going to make it. I just let it fly out there, hoping it would hit the wall, anyway."

Carl Yastrzemski was the next batter and the cheering for Adair had barely died down when Rojas drilled Yaz in the elbow with a pitch. Yaz was okay, but emotions were still raw from the Tony C beaning and Dick Williams went ballistic. Accounts varied but most observers believed the manager was telling Yaz to get down to second base and "cut someone." First base umpire Bill Valentine told Williams to tone it down and Dick charged from the dugout towards Valentine. It wasn't clear if Williams spat on Valentine's shoes or spat on the field but it was clear that Dick had been tossed from the game. Third base coach Eddie "Pop" Popowski took over for Williams but the fiery manager could be seen yelling instructions to Pop from the tunnel leading to the Red Sox clubhouse.

Yaz did steal second base but there was no retaliation and Rojas got out of the inning without further damage. "I was really tired by then," Jose remembered, "but I was determined to finish the game. Then I gave up a single to Mincher and a double to Reichardt, and I was in big trouble. But Pop pulled the infield in and I got Bob Rodgers to ground to second with Andrews looking Mincher back to third and then I struck out Bobby Knoop. That was a big out. Then we walked Satriano (Tom) intentionally.

"With the bases loaded they sent Moose [Bill] Skowren up to hit," Santiago remembered. "Elston Howard had played with Moose on the Yankees, and he came out to the mound and said 'Jose, nothing but curve balls—and keep them down.' So that's what I did. He hit my first pitch to shortstop and we got a force-out. What a battle that game was!"

The game marked the Red Sox biggest comeback since they came from 10 runs down to beat the Indians in 1950. Boston had swept the four-game series from the Angels and moved to within one and one-half games of first place. Did that series eliminate the Angels from contention I asked Dalton Jones. "Not on paper," he told me. "But a sweep like that really sets a team back. And I have to believe the tragedy of Tony getting hit stayed in the back of their minds for a long time."

Dalton Jones saw the Red Sox amazing comeback that day as one of several turning points for the Impossible Dream team. "The Billy Rohr one-hitter in the Yankees' home opener was very special. Then we won a number of games after coming from behind in the late innings so we knew we could handle the pressure. But the lesson from this comeback was that we were never out of it. Regardless of how far back we were we felt we could overcome anything.

There was no way of knowing it but that weekend marked a personal turning point in Dalton's season. From August 19th through the end of the regular season Dalton batted .407 to lead all Red Sox hitters. Asked for an explanation, Dalton replied, "I got to play more in those last six or seven weeks for one thing. And if you are in the lineup on any kind of a regular basis your timing improves." And he points out, "The more trips you make to the plate the more chances you have for the ball to drop in or find a hole. And when you are going good it is like being a kid again; you can't wait to get to the ballpark!"

On September 18, in a crucial game in Detroit against the league-leading Tigers, Dalton had the kind of game that youngsters dream of having in the big leagues. Not only did he go four-for-five in the biggest game of the season to date, but he also hit the game-winning home run in the tenth inning off Mike Marshall, a premier relief pitcher. "That was the game of my life," Dalton acknowledges. "Mike threw me a slider right in my wheelhouse and I just turned on it and hit it into the second deck. I always saw the ball well in that park. It had a great background for a hitter."

It all came down to two games on the final weekend. And one thing was certain: the Red Sox had to win both games against the Twins to stay in the pennant race.

Dalton Jones was sent up to pinch hit for Russ Gibson in the Saturday game. It was the bottom of the fifth inning with no one out, Reggie Smith on second base, and the Red Sox trailing 1-0. Jones hit a soft ground ball towards Rod Carew at second base that took a bizarre bounce at the last minute, caroming off Carew's left shoulder for an infield hit. Jerry Adair scored Reggie Smith with a clutch base hit, and then Yaz came through, as he had all year, with a single that scored Jones with the go-ahead run. The Red Sox held on for a 6-4 win to tie the Twins for first-place.

"That was a fluke hit," Dalton insists. "I was just trying to hit the ball to the right side to advance Reggie to third and it took a crazy hop." Fluke hit or not, it was his 13th base hit as a pinch hitter, tops in the American League that season, and it kept a key rally alive.

Staff ace Jim Lonborg took the mound for Boston in the last game of the season with first place on the line.

Jim Lonborg surprised the Twins with a perfect bunt for a base hit, and Jerry Adair followed with a line single to start the Red Sox sixth inning. Dalton Jones fouled off two bunt attempts before he slapped a single down the third base line to load the bases for Carl Yastrzemski. Yaz delivered once again, this time with a two-run single, and when the inning ended the Red Sox were ahead 5-2.

The Red Sox lead was 5-3 with two out in the ninth inning as Twins pinch hitter Rich Rollins stepped into the batter's box. Moments later

Rollins hit a humpbacked line drive that Petrocelli gathered in, to clinch at least a tie for the American League pennant.

Dalton recalls the ensuing celebration on the field as one of his career highlights. "Pandemonium on the field," in the words of legendary announcer Ned Martin, was followed by a raucous clubhouse celebration after the Tigers lost, and the Red Sox had clinched the pennant outright. "That was an unbelievable day," Dalton remembers. "It was an unreal finish to an incredible season. I'll never forget it."

The 1967 World Series against the St. Louis Cardinals was Dalton Jones' time to shine. He started four games at third base, pinch hit in two others, and his .389 batting average was second only to Carl Yastrzemski among Red Sox players.

Dalton remembered that his mother and father got to attend all seven games and that was a highlight of the Series for him. And there is one vignette from the end of the 1967 World Series that he will never forget. "I had pinch hit and stayed in to play third base. We were down 7-2, and the way Bob Gibson was pitching you knew how it would probably turn out. At first I heard a cluster of fans applauding for us. Then I heard several other groups of fans. And the next thing I knew the whole ballpark was standing up and applauding us for our great year.

"I have to admit, I got tears in my eyes playing third base, it was so moving. And I have to tell you, I've got tears in my eyes right now, remembering and telling you that story," Dalton acknowledges.

In 1968 Dalton Jones appeared in 111 games with the Red Sox. During the second half of that season, he played 55 games at first base, logging more playing time there than regular first baseman George Scott., Dalton batted only .234 for the season, but contributed a sparkling .407 average as a pinch hitter.

In 1969 Dalton played 81 games at first base, but his batting average fell to .220 for the year. "I had changed my swing," he remembers, "because I knew they were looking for more power from a first baseman. But that wasn't me. I lost my confidence and I never really got it back."

Following the 1969 season he was traded to the Detroit Tigers. Dalton initially felt it would be a good move for him. "I had always hit very well at Tigers Stadium and I thought it would work out. But when I got over there [Detroit], I saw they really didn't have a spot for me. I think they picked me up just to get me out of their hair," he laughed referring to his history of feasting on Tiger pitching.

Jones played as a utility infielder and pinch hitter for the Tigers in 1970 and 1971. At the beginning of the 1972 season he was traded to the Texas Rangers, a team Dalton describes as "one of the worst teams in baseball history after the original Mets." When the Texas Rangers released him in January 1973, his major league baseball career had come to an end.

"It was time to go fishing," Jones mused, recalling his dad's words when Dalton was a youngster that if he got tired of baseball, there was always fishing and hunting. "Looking back, I probably could have been more of a student of the game. And I probably would have benefited from more time in the minors. But I had nine years in the big leagues to look back on."

When his baseball career was over Dalton Jones returned to Baton Rouge. He had several careers, working primarily in the financial-services sector. Dalton is quick to acknowledge that it was difficult to adjust to life after baseball.

"All I had ever wanted to do was to play baseball. And all I had ever done until then was to play baseball. It was hard to adjust. But faith and prayer have always been a comfort to me. And that helped me to accept that it was time to move on."

In 1989, at the age of 45, Dalton got a second chance at baseball. The Senior Professional Baseball Association, a winter league in Florida for players age 35 and over, had started up, and Dalton became a player-coach for the Winter Haven Super Sox. "It was patterned after the Senior PGA tour, which was very successful. But older baseball players are susceptible to injury," he points out.

"I would get a base hit, pull a hamstring, and then rehab. Then I would repeat the process," he chuckled. "The best part was that my wife, Barbara, got to see what life was like for a baseball player. She had been my childhood sweetheart; she was my best friend in the second grade. And she was my prom date, but when I signed with the Red Sox right after high school we lost touch."

"By the time the Senior League came around we had re-connected. In fact, we got married during that season in a double wedding with Butch and Krys Hobson. All of our teammates were at the wedding. It's a great memory."

Dalton and Barbara lived in New England for a period of time, and then moved to Charlotte, North Carolina The couple now resides in Liberty, Mississippi, which is about 20 miles west of McComb, where Dalton was born.

"We have a great spot here in the woods, with a pond. We get to play some golf and enjoy life. Best of all, we are about one hour from the Baton Rouge area where my son Darrin lives with his two children, Micah and Dalton. We get to see a lot of them and that is always fun. My son Brian lives in the Houston, Texas, area and he has three children: Lynley Nicole, Kayley, and Blake. Grandkids are special," Dalton adds.

Dalton Jones has fond memories of the fans at Fenway Park. "The crowd always helped us a lot," he recalls. "We would be behind but we could hear them pulling for us. No one wanted to be the one who made the last out. And we knew that they would be behind us whether we won or lost."

Like so many of his teammates Dalton feels like the 1967 season had almost a fairy tale quality to it. "It seems like another life—a lifetime ago. It had a dream-like quality. And I always marvel at these wonderful New England fans. Fifty years later they still can't get enough of us!

When he looks back on the 1967 Impossible Dream Red Sox, Dalton focuses on the camaraderie that surrounded that team. "We really were like a family having a great time together. And fans probably don't realize what a great job Gary Bell and George Thomas did of keeping us loose all year with their good humor.

"And it's important to point out that the 1967 team was made up of good guys. Not just fun guys, although there was plenty of that," Dalton laughs, "but really good and decent guys. Guys you could depend on."

Dalton Jones was one of those good and decent guys. He is a gentleman in the truest sense of the word.

Chapter 9

Rico Petrocelli: Captain of the Infield

Red Sox vs. Chicago White Sox, Saturday, August 26, 1967

Rico Petrocelli, a Yankee fan as a youngster growing up in the Sheepshead Bay section of Brooklyn, was the anchor of the Red Sox infield when the Red Sox moved into Chicago for a crucial series against the White Sox. There was a certain irony in Rico's de facto position as the Red Sox "captain" of the infield. In 1966, Manager Billy Herman had fined him $1,000 for leaving a game without permission and at that time Rico had developed a reputation as a sensitive sort for a ballplayer. But baseball was extremely important to Rico and he had matured rapidly. He had long been singled out as the Red Sox shortstop of the future, but on finally gaining the position, he had suffered with the Red Sox through 190 losses in his first two seasons, 1965-66. When Williams came to Rico on March 1, 1967, and told him that he was looking to him for leadership, it was the vote of confidence he needed. Rico felt that he had been empowered to pass on his baseball knowledge to the others, and more importantly, he felt accepted as a big leaguer for the first time. As the Red Sox got ready for the third game of the five game series, they were in a flatfooted tie for second with the White Sox, one-half game behind the league-leading Twins. Rico knew that his teammates were counting on him and it was leadership that he would provide.

The California Angels couldn't wait to leave Boston after their heart-breaking loss to the Red Sox in the second game of the Sunday, August 20th doubleheader. They had arrived in the city trailing the Red Sox by only one game and they were just four-and-one-half games out of first place in the American League. When the Angels left town they were five full games behind Boston and six-and-one-half games out of first place.

If the Angels were thankful to get out of town, the Washington Senators must have wished for almost any other destination. In their last series the Red Sox had won four straight and their red-hot hitters had rung up 33 runs in just three games. The Washington pitching staff must have shuddered at the prospect of five games in Fenway Park over four days. The Senators had only a remote shot at the .500 mark and the Red Sox were on a tear.

The Monday opener against the Senators was a see-saw affair. The teams traded runs and the lead. The Red Sox came up to bat in the last of the ninth with the score knotted at five. Jerry Adair, "Mr. Clutch" as he was starting to be known, opened up with a double. After Yaz grounded out and two were walked, Elston Howard became the hero of the day with a single to score Adair with the winning run. The "hero of the day" concept had become a recurring theme that would continue for the rest of the season.

In other baseball news the big story was that Kansas City A's owner Charlie Finley had fired first baseman/outfielder Ken "Hawk" Harrelson in a fit of pique. A's pitcher Lew Krausse had created an incident and Finley fired manager Alvin Dark because he didn't like the way Dark handled it. Harrelson told reporters that he thought Finley's actions were detrimental to the club and baseball. The next day's headline was, "Harrelson Says Finley Menace to Baseball," and Finley's response was to give Harrelson his outright release.

"I was scared to death," Harrelson told me. "I was making $12,000 per year, I owed about $20,000, and I was out of a job! I called the Commissioner's office and they said it had never happened before. After researching the matter they called back to tell me I was a free agent. Then my phone started ringing off the hook," Hawk laughed. Over the next several days Hawk heard from the White Sox, the Braves, and, of course, the Red Sox.

While the Harrelson drama was playing out, things got even better for the Red Sox when they swept a twin-bill from the Senators on August 22. In the first game, Dalton Jones was the man of the moment. His triple in the seventh inning brought in two runners and that was all John Wyatt would need to save the win for starter Jerry Stephenson. Gary Bell and Darrell Brandon teamed up to give the Red Sox a 5-3 win in game two. Reggie Smith continued his home run heroics and Yaz, Scott, Adair and Rico Petrocelli all contributed key hits. The Red Sox had moved within percentage points of the first place White Sox.

Boston fans' hopes for a pennant reached a fever pitch on August 23, 1967, when 33,680 fans crammed into Fenway Park hoping to be there when the Red Sox finally climbed into first place. Washington starter, Bob Priddy, had other ideas however, and he pitched a masterful complete game as the Red Sox fell 3-2. First place would have to wait.

On the final day of the home stand, the afternoon crowd of 31,283 included Boston's Cardinal Richard Cushing who was accompanied by 1,500 nuns from the Boston area. Dave Morehead pitched well into the seventh inning and three Red Sox home runs—Jerry Adair (of course), newcomer Jim Landis and a three-run blast by Elston Howard—gave the Red Sox a 7-2 lead going into the ninth. The Red Sox faltered in the ninth—nothing would be easy in 1967-- but they held on for a 7-5 win. The win moved the team into a virtual tie for first place with the White Sox.

"Nuns Day," and the visit of Cardinal Cushing, was a regular event at Fenway Park. Of course in prior years an afternoon game might have drawn about 4,000 other fans and 1,500 nuns. Rico had gotten used to the regular visit of the Sisters. "About once a month in the summer Cardinal Cushing would show up with a whole group on nuns. The Cardinal would be sitting right behind the Red Sox dugout and the nuns would fill in the rest of the section all the way to the last row—it was a pretty unusual sight! I remember one time I was reaching into the stands to catch a foul ball and one of the nuns was holding onto my arm so she could get the ball," Rico chuckled.

The twelve-game home stand had been very eventful for the Red Sox. They had come in with a 4-9 record for August, and a three-game losing streak. The club had turned it around with a 10-2 mark including several amazing comeback wins. More importantly, they had won when they had to.

Tony Conigliaro's tragic accident was the low point of the home stand and the season. It had shaken his teammates, but it hadn't slowed them down. Jose Tartabull and veteran utility man, George Thomas, had both filled in acceptably in right field in the near-term. They would miss Tony—he was clearly gone for the season—but his absence from the lineup would not defeat them.

The team received a lift on August 25, when the Red Sox announced they had signed Ken Harrelson to a contract for the balance of the 1967 season and for the 1968 season. Harrelson had been primarily a first baseman during his five years in the major leagues, but he had played enough in the outfield that general manager Dick O'Connell and manager Williams were confident that he could be their everyday right fielder. Ken told me he signed with the Red Sox for $150,000. "The Braves had offered me the most money. Then Red Sox GM Dick O'Connell called and asked how much money it would take to sign me. I just threw out the figure $150,000, and O'Connell said, 'Done.'"

The Red Sox told the media that Hawk signed for $80,000. That made him the highest paid player on the Red Sox by far.

The scene was set for a classic late-August pivotal series as the Red Sox flew to Chicago for a five-game showdown with manager Eddie Stanky and his White Sox. There was no love lost between the Red Sox and Stanky. Eddie had referred to Yaz as "an all-star from the neck down" earlier in the season. While everyone realized that he was just playing head games, they still wanted to beat the diminutive manager who was known as "The Brat."

The pennant race in the American League was as tight as it had been in years; no one could open up a lead of any significance. The Sox, Red and White, were in a virtual tie for first place. The Minnesota Twins and Detroit Tigers were hanging within a game of the two leaders. The season had only a little over a month to go and the contenders were running out of room to maneuver. The leaders only had about thirty-five games remaining to make their move.

For Rico Petrocelli, 1967 was the year he finally felt like a legitimate major leaguer. Even though he was in his third big league season, he was just starting to feel like he belonged. Baseball had been the most important thing in his life for as long as he could remember but he still had to battle insecurity.

Rico was the youngest of five brothers from a close-knit Italian family in Brooklyn, New York. His brothers were all fine ballplayers and big fans, but a job to provide some income for the family was a higher priority. It wasn't until Rico came along, that a Petrocelli could afford the luxury of concentrating on baseball. "When I was real young we were all Dodger fans, living in Brooklyn. But when the Dodgers moved to Los Angeles we became Yankee fans. We were all big Yankee fans but I got to see a lot of the Red Sox because one of my brothers loved to watch Ted [Williams] hit."

Rico was an outstanding young ballplayer on the Brooklyn sandlots and his brothers tutored him and cheered at his games. Throughout his career, they fulfilled their missed opportunities through his exploits. The bird-dogs first took note of his potential as a fifteen-year old performing for the Cadets at nearby Prospect Park. He continued to improve and earned the tagline "can't miss." As high school graduation loomed closer, veteran Red Sox scout, Bots Nekola, who had also signed Carl Yastrzemski, took over the pursuit of the young phenom personally.

Petrocelli was an All-Scholastic baseball and basketball player at Sheepshead Bay High School, and he was outfielder and pitcher for his team. At one point there were at least twelve big league teams scouting Rico and following him from game-to-game. But Rico injured his right elbow while pitching in the City Championship game and most of the scouts disappeared.

Nekola stuck with his injured prospect and he arranged for Rico to have a tryout at Fenway Park. Rico made the trip to Boston with his mother, father and one of his brothers. "I still remember walking up the ramp and seeing the field for the first time," Rico told me. "The grass was so beautifully kept that it looked like a carpet. I felt I could reach out and touch the left-field wall," he chuckled, "and it was the prettiest color green I had ever seen." The trip to Fenway helped convince Rico to join the Red Sox organization. While it was heresy in his neighborhood, and blasphemy to his brothers the Yankee fans, the Red Sox had kept faith

Rico looking to drive the ball to left field.

with the Petrocelli's after Rico's injury and he signed with the Red Sox before his eighteenth birthday.

Rico's first stop was Winston-Salem, North Carolina, in the Carolina league. It was a long way from Sheepshead Bay in Brooklyn. Rico recalls, "I was a city kid and I was used to a fast pace. I couldn't believe how slowly people moved down there. It was there that I saw my first cow. I remember going over to touch it like it was some kind of prehistoric animal like a dinosaur or something!"

The Red Sox had moved Rico to shortstop and he struggled to learn his new position. It was also his first taste of professional pitching and it caught him a little off guard. "When you're playing sandlot, you hit .400 something, but all of a sudden you're struggling to hit .280. It was a real adjustment. Sometimes it was discouraging."

While it might have been discouraging to Rico, the Red Sox had identified him as their shortstop of the future. No one has a good explanation for why it was so back in the day, but the major league parent typically had little to say to prospects about their futures. They would pass on some basic advice, "come to spring training in shape" and some platitudes, "keep up the good work and you'll continue to move up," but little else was said. Perhaps it was just the way that teams had always done it. Perhaps it was almost a macho initiation rite. Regardless, if Rico were on the fast track to Fenway, like all minor leaguers of his generation, the only way he would have known about it was to read about it in the newspapers.

Rico moved up the ladder to Reading, Pennsylvania, in the fast Eastern league. Rico continued to improve as a hitter as he moved through the Red Sox system. There never was any doubt about his fielding. When the Reading regular season came to an end in 1963, the twenty-year-old Rico was brought up to "the Bigs" to spend the last two weeks of the season with the major league club. For a minor leaguer, this was as close to becoming "anointed" as you could get.

"That was great," Rico recalled. "I got to take batting practice with the major leaguers and I learned a lot. I even got to play one game," he smiled. "In my first at-bat in the major leagues I doubled off the left-field wall in Fenway," earning Rico a standing-ovation from the 6,469 fans on hand. "I still remember standing on second base and thinking how great that felt."

Rico started the 1964 season with great optimism. At training camp in Scottsdale, Arizona, he felt that he was being singled out as a prospect. For the first time, he really believed he belonged with the Red Sox. Red Sox manager Johnny Pesky understood shortstops and that helped.

Rico was only twenty-years-old but he was assigned to the Red Sox top farm team in Seattle, Washington. He was in Triple-A ball, the last stop before the majors. He was in good company at Seattle. Jim Lonborg was honing his pitching craft and Russ Gibson was demonstrating to the brass on Jersey Street that he was ready for "The Show."

Rico's roommate was 36-year-old journeyman, Billy Gardner. Billy was coming off a ten-year major league career which encompassed six teams and experience at second, short and third base. Gardner had finished up his career in the majors with the Red Sox and he was determined to hold on for one more shot. Baseball was his life and he was just the mentor Rico needed.

Things got off to a good start for Rico in Seattle but then he pulled a hamstring and his batting average began to fall. Rico kept playing hurt, afraid he would lose his big opportunity if he sat down, and his average continued to deteriorate. Billy Gardner recognized the syndrome and told him to go to manager Edo Vanni and ask for some time to heal before he put his career in jeopardy.

Rico went to Vanni and explained the situation as best he could. Edo told him that he didn't want to hear about it and implied in baseball terms that Rico was "jaking it" i.e. malingering. Where Rico grew up, that was akin to questioning your manhood. In the tradition of his Brooklyn neighborhood, Rico responded by questioning Vanni's parentage. Things deteriorated from there.

This began a period of time when Rico developed a reputation as a moody ballplayer, in some eyes a prima donna. These labels come easily in baseball—a hard-nosed culture—but die hard. The Red Sox ended up bringing Petrocelli to Fenway for ten days to have their medical staff examine him. When Rico returned to the minors he was still so hampered by his injury that the Red Sox decided to try to convert him into a switch-hitter. Overnight, it seemed he had gone from a future superstar to a weak-hitting, good-fielding shortstop with a questionable disposition.

In spite of a dreadful '64 season, shortstop had his name on it at Fenway Park. He played ninety-three games at the position in 1965, but the grand experiment of Rico as a switch hitter was abandoned early in the season. He still remembers his few left-handed appearances in 1965. "I hit a sharp line-drive down the right field line in Fenway and it was just foul—that was the closest I came to a left-handed base hit in the majors," he laughed. As a rookie, he banged out thirteen home runs in only 323 at bats and it didn't make sense to have a guy with that power slapping 125-foot line drives from the left side. Asked when he first felt like a genuine big leaguer, Rico replied, "Not in 1965, that's for sure!"

Rico goes on to say, "There were several of us, myself, Lonnie, maybe Dalton Jones, who could have used another year in the minors, but the Red Sox didn't have anyone else. We were learning 'on the job,' so to speak. It was tough but we learned a lot quickly!"

The following year, Rico was installed as the regular shortstop right from Opening Day. While he batted only .238, he increased his home run output to 18 and he fielded his position brilliantly. But his relationship with Red Sox manager Billy Herman left something to be desired. The players respected Herman's baseball knowledge but he was not a great communicator or motivator. By his own admission the 23-year-old Petrocelli was still coming of age and he and Herman had their differences. It all came to a head when Rico was fined $1,000—one-sixth of his $6,000 salary— by the Red Sox for leaving a game early in 1966.

The 1965 and 1966 seasons were difficult for Red Sox players and fans alike. "In 1965, there wasn't much to be positive about," Rico admits. "We had some older players like Bressoud [shortstop Eddie] who had been good, and some younger players like Lonnie and me who were going to be good, but we still lost 100 ballgames and finished ninth. It was discouraging."

The 1965 Red Sox drew 662,051 fans to Fenway Park., for an average attendance of about 8,000 per game. Trying to picture Fenway Park with 25,000 to 30,000 empty seats must be difficult for younger Red Sox fans, but it was a day-to-day reality in 1965. "If there were only 3,000-4,000 fans there you could listen in on conversations in the stands," he laughs. "And the Red Sox were always hosting Boy Scouts Day or Little League Day trying to appeal to young fans. They [the Red Sox] would always stick them way out in right field where no one would ever buy a seat. With the empty ballpark they sure could make a racket.

"There was a group of men, maybe 30-40 of them, who would be at every home game sitting together down the line in right field. If there were only a few thousand fans, and no boy scouts," Rico smiled, "you could hear them talking constantly. It was so odd that I finally asked somebody who they were. The answer I got was 'You don't want to know.'"

Much has been written about the glorious history of Fenway Park, that "little lyric bandbox of a ballpark," in the words of John Updike. But very little, if anything, has been written about the gamblers who were a constant presence at Fenway Park from the 1950s through the Impossible Dream season. At each game there were anywhere from a couple of dozen to nearly 100 gamblers sitting clustered around what is now "Pesky's Pole" in right field. They would wager on every pitch and that was the chatter Rico picked up.

Rico remembered that the 1966 season was very different from 1965, even though the club finished in ninth place once again. "The year started out about the same." Rico remembered, "And at the half-way point we were in 10th place, headed for 100 losses. But then we started to play better baseball. Guys like Yaz and Tony were established, new guys like me and George Scott felt more comfortable, and the front office picked up some pitchers like Jose Santiago and Lee Stange that helped. We played very well in the second-half of 1966."

Rico's memory of the Red Sox performance for July through the end of September 1966 was very accurate. After losing the first game of a 4th of July doubleheader to the lowly Washington Senators, the club was in last place with a record of 28-51, and they were 25.5 games out of first place in the American League. For the rest of the season the team went 44-39, a record that was very competitive with the better American League clubs and a pace that set a tone for 1967.

Dick Williams recognized Rico's full potential from the very beginning. He knew his seriousness could be converted into leadership. He knew the emotionalism could be channeled into an intensity to win. He knew the histrionics were just a manifestation of Rico's frustration at losing. He was the right manager for Rico at the right time.

Williams was tough but he was also smart, and he recognized that Rico need special handling. Williams made sure that Rico's locker was next to coach Eddie Popowski, who had managed Rico in his first year as a professional baseball player at Winston-Salem and the following year at Reading.

Williams' demonstration of confidence helped get Rico off to a great start in 1967. By the end of June, he was batting .296 with eight home runs and thirty-two RBI. He was playing at a level that would earn him a position on the '67 All Star team. But injury struck again when the Indian's George Culver nailed him on the left wrist with a fastball.

Williams gave Rico the rest he needed. When Rico returned to the lineup, his average fell—he had dropped to .267 by the end of July—but he still fielded his position flawlessly, anchored the young infield, and got the job done. Rico's average stabilized in the .260s during August and he continued to do the small things that don't show up in the box score. He advanced the runner from second with a groundout to the right side. He took the extra base on a throwing mistake and he picked up an extra step by moving the Red Sox fielders around depending on the upcoming pitch. He was Dick Williams' kind of ballplayer.

White Sox manager Eddie Stanky was known as "The Brat" because he would do anything to rattle the opposition. He was all over the Red Sox before Friday night's series opening double header. His most outrageous quote was "...the City of Culture is crying about Conigliaro's injury. Big deal. We've had injuries all season, but we aren't crying." The Red Sox players resolved to ignore him.

Jim Lonborg did their talking for them in the opener with a seven-hit complete game. Once again, Gentleman Jim had been the stopper: winning a key game when it really counted. The Red Sox pounded out sixteen hits to help Lonborg to his seventeenth victory: 7-1. Rico contributed a key RBI single.

The nightcap turned out to be a nightmare for the Red Sox and for Rico Petrocelli. Boston starter Lee Stange pitched masterfully but White Sox rookie Cisco Carlos pitched even better. Incredibly, Carlos was pitching in his first major league game. Perhaps he didn't feel the pressure of the pennant race as much. Ken Berry's home run had given Carlos a 1-0 lead and Rico found himself on second with the potential tying run in the top of the seventh. He had a good shot at scoring on a Dalton Jones looper, and third base coach Popowski was urging Rico to head home. But Rico played it too cautiously and he was stuck on third with Norm Siebern coming to bat and only one away. Siebern took a big swing that produced only a nubber in the direction of the pitcher's mound. This time Rico elected to take a risk but he made the wrong decision once again. He was a dead duck at the plate. Dick Williams wouldn't even look at him when he returned to the dugout. The White Sox ultimately prevailed 2-1 and Rico was as low as you can feel.

Rico much preferred being at home to the long, lonely road trips. He was, and is, a family man. He had come from a close family and in 1967 he was married and the father of three children, including a set of twins. He missed them a lot when he was traveling with the team. "For me, one of the toughest parts of baseball was being away from your family," Rico recalled. "It's tough: especially when you have young kids."

Saturday, August 26 was a new day for the Red Sox. In a season of 162 games you can't get too high after a win or too low after a loss. When you split a doubleheader, you just put it out of your mind and focus on the next game. The Sox—White and Red—remained tied and they were both one-half game off the pace following a Twins' victory Friday night. It was going to be that kind of year.

Boston nominated Gerry Stephenson as their starter for the afternoon game. He had pitched well since his recall from Toronto, but he appeared overmatched in comparison to Chicago's starter, Joel Horlen.

Horlen was 13-5 going into the game and would end the season with an ERA of 2.06 to top American League pitchers. But funny things happen in a long season. Gerry Stephenson pitched like the reincarnation of Cy Young for the first five innings. Meanwhile, Red Sox batters were drilling out timely hits off Horlen. In the third inning, Jose Tartabull got things going with a triple that totally befuddled White Sox right-fielder Rocky Colavito. Adair, Yaz and Scotty all followed with singles and the Red Sox had jumped out to a 2-0 lead.

In the top of the fourth, with Mike Andrews at first after a walk, catcher Mike Ryan sent another triple in Colavito's direction to score Andrews. To some observers, Colavito, who was a fearsome slugger, appeared to be playing right field on roller skates. After five innings the Red Sox had a semi-comfortable 3-0 lead. More amazingly, Gerry Stephenson had a no-hitter going!

The Boston dugout was upbeat but they knew they had to get some more runs. Stephenson was likely to run out of gas any time now. And Horlen looked like he was up for grabs. Not even the greatest pitcher is outstanding in every start and Joel wasn't quite as sharp as usual.

Super-sub, Jerry Adair, got it rolling with a single. George Scott followed suit and Reggie Smith brought Adair home with a single of his own. Eddie Stanky had seen enough of Horlen and wig-wagged knuckle-baller Wilbur Wood in from the bullpen. In the on-deck circle, Rico Petrocelli tried to recall everything he knew about Wood. Wilbur was a Boston guy. He had made his mark as a schoolboy athlete growing up in nearby Belmont, Massachusetts. He had been signed originally by the Red Sox and spent parts of four seasons with them in the early 1960s. But Wilbur had never put it together with the Red Sox and he ended up in the Pirates' organization where he learned the knuckle ball.

There was a certain irony as Rico dug in against the left-handed Wood. Wilbur had grown up dreaming of playing for the Red Sox and here he was trying to pitch them out of the pennant. Rico had grown up as a die-hard Yankees fan and here he was trying to propel their most-hated rivals to the pennant. And both of them were playing for serious money a thousand or so miles from their boyhood homes.

Rico thought, "knuckleball," "contact," and "patience" as he waited for Wood's delivery. His patience was rewarded as he lined a knuckle ball into left center and he lit out in the direction of first. Scott was home easily as Rico picked up the sign from first base coach, Bobby Doerr, to leg it for second. Rico went in to second standing up since the White Sox were more interested in holding Reggie Smith at third. Rico's RBI had given Boston a five-run cushion and the Red Sox dugout relaxed a little.

In the last of the sixth, Stanky out-managed himself just a bit with a dose of over-managing. Stephenson was, predictably, losing it and he walked Don Buford and Pete Ward. Down by five runs, with a tiring pitcher on the mound, Stanky put on a double-steal. Mike Ryan's snap throw caught Buford at third base. While the White Sox went on to drive Stephenson from the mound with two runs, an opportunity for a "jumbo" inning had been missed. Darrell Brandon came in to relieve Stephenson and pitched shutout ball the rest of the way. A Red Sox run in the seventh was icing on the cake as they went on to a 6-2 victory.

For Rico Petrocelli, it was just another day at the ballpark. He had fielded flawlessly and kept the hyperactive Stephenson settled down. He felt that he had redeemed himself for the base running gaffe of the night before with his key double in the Saturday game. He was pleased with his day's work but it was just one more game in a 162-game season.

The Red Sox win, coupled with a Minnesota loss to Cleveland, gave Boston undisputed possession of first place. **This represented the latest point in the season that Boston had been in first place since 1949.** It was just another game for Rico but it was a landmark for Boston fans.

But the Red Sox-White Sox series was far from over. Their double-header the next day will long be remembered by Red Sox fans. And the outcome would set the tone for the balance of the 1967 season.

Gary Bell squared off against the White Sox Fred Klages in game one. All baseball fans remember the 1967 Chicago White Sox for their pitching. Few remember that Eddie Stanky started Cisco Carlos and Fred Klages in this crucial series.

Bell had his good stuff on Sunday and he went into the ninth inning with a 4-3 lead. His one-run lead was courtesy of two Carl Yastrzemski home runs. Bell began the final inning allowing a lead-off double to Red Sox nemesis, Ken Berry. After Berry was sacrificed to third, Dick Williams decided it was time for relief ace John Wyatt to face pinch hitter, Duane Josephson.

Wyatt would throw one pitch to Josephson. That one pitch would produce one of the more memorable plays in Red Sox history, and a play that was certainly a highlight of the 1967 season. Josephson lofted an average fly ball to Jose Tartabull in right field. Tartabull was known for his weak arm. Berry, tagging at third, was known for his speed. Jose got off the best throw he could, a rainbow in the air, to catcher Ellie Howard. Howard had to leap to catch the throw one-handed while Berry was barreling in on top of him. Howard somehow came down with his left foot blocking Berry's access to the plate and made the tag in one sweeping motion. A Red Sox fan can see that replay 100 times and still get excited every time. Berry was out, the ball game was over, and the Red Sox were still in first place. In a season of "once-in-a-lifetime" plays this would turn out to be the only runner Jose Tartabull threw out all season! For perhaps the first time it seemed that the Red Sox really could do it—they really could possibly win the American League pennant.

Looking back on this memorable play many years later, catcher Russ Gibson said, "Give Tartabull credit for getting the ball to home quickly. But his throw was really a lollypop. Elston Howard made that play. Getting up there to grab the ball, coming down at the one spot that would block Berry from reaching home, and then applying a sweep tag—absolutely amazing! That was an all-time highlight play."

The second game was almost as exciting, but it ended with a whimper, not with a bang. Jose Santiago pitched his heart out for nine and two-thirds innings. Jose remembers that game as one of his best efforts of 1967. Jose pitched into the tenth inning and didn't give up a single run. He had to come out of the game with two down in the tenth inning when he was injured in a collision with catcher Mike Ryan as they both attempted to field a bunt.

But the Red Sox had even more trouble with the crafty Gary Peters. Darrel "Bucky" Brandon was on the mound in the eleventh inning of this 0-0 game. With the bases loaded and a three and two count, Bucky walked in the winning run and went immediately into Dick Williams' doghouse. Williams was heard to utter, "I'd rather lose on a grand slam home run than a - bases-loaded walk." The pennant race would be like a roller coaster for the rest of the year.

Rico's distinguished Red Sox career covered thirteen years, including his brief stint as a twenty-year old at the end of the 1963 season. The 1967 season will always stand out as the year he came of age, the year he became a stable veteran. And what does Rico remember best about 1967?

"What I remember most is the way we meshed as a team that year. Nobody gave us a chance at the beginning of the year, but we believed in ourselves. Some of us had been around for a while, then we had a bunch of rookies, and we added players during the year and we all managed to come together. We had our share of laughs and pranks, but these were all classy guys, good people," he emphasized.

"And I have to mention the fans," he added. "Players will say that the fans cheering don't matter but they do, especially that year. In 1967, they started filling the ballpark and cheering us on. If you struck out you could almost hear them say, 'That's okay. You'll get them the next time.'"

Rico's peak years were probably 1969-1971. During those three years, he played in almost every game, averaged over thirty home runs and knocked in nearly an average of 100 runs each year. In fact he was tops on the Red Sox for home runs and RBI during that three-year period. In 1969, he socked forty home runs and batted .297. His 40 home runs stood as the American League record for shortstops until ARod hit 42 in 1998. Not too bad for a hitter who was considered so marginal that he tried switch-hitting!

In 1971, Rico was moved over to third base to make room for the newly acquired All-Star shortstop, Luis Aparicio. Petrocelli had been the regular shortstop for six years, but he made the move without a word and without missing a beat. If anything, he was an even better fielder at third than at short since the "hot corner" suited his range at that point in his career. In fact he established an American League record for errorless games by a third baseman, with 77 games.

The year 1972 was a disappointing one for the Red Sox and for Rico. The Red Sox finished one-half game behind the Detroit Tigers in that strike-abbreviated year. Rico saw his home run output cut in half to fifteen and his batting average fell to .240. Still, he was solid in the field and he led American League third basemen in double plays with 38.

Rico had become a role-player as he entered his thirties. He would start at third for 100 or so games each year, hit around .250 and serve as a good role model for the rookies. The days of thinking of Rico as temperamental were long forgotten.

When lightning struck again in 1975, Rico was the starting third baseman in 112 games. While his home run total declined to seven, he still managed to knock in fifty-nine runs in only 402 at bats. He was also a stabilizing force for twenty-four-year old Rick Burleson who had been installed as the regular Boston shortstop.

Rico had a great World Series against Cincinnati. He started all seven games and fielded magnificently at third. He rapped out eight hits and finished with a batting average of .308 as the Red Sox went down to a heart-breaking defeat at the hands of the Reds. He and Carl Yastrzemski go into the record books as the only Red Sox players to appear in the 1967 and 1975 World Series.

During his career with Boston, Rico hit 210 homers, knocked in 773 runs, and finished up with a batting average of .251. But statistics don't tell the Rico Petrocelli story. He went from the "itinerant shortstop" to a team leader. And he became such a fine hitter, that his solid fielding was sometimes overlooked. He set Red Sox fielding records at shortstop and then later at third base.

After his release from the Red Sox during spring training in 1977, Rico tried his hand at a number of things. He worked as a baseball correspondent for the *Boston Herald* for a while and did some broadcasting. He did his share of sales and promotional work and he managed in the minor leagues for the White Sox for three years. He then worked with Mike Andrews at the Jimmy Fund from 1989 to 1991.

In 1992, Rico re-joined the Red Sox, working in a number of capacities within their minor league system for the balance of the decade. I interviewed Rico several times in the late-1990s when he was the hitting coach in Pawtucket. My strongest memory of Rico in the Red Sox minor league organization is talking to him in the PawSox dugout when a middle-aged fan with two youngsters in tow leaned into the dugout and said, "Rico, I just want to thank you for your catch for the last out of the 1967 season!" Rico's response was, "Thank you for remembering,

I appreciate it." Rico, who was obviously used to these exchanges, told me, "That happens all the time. It was years ago, but a lot of fans still talk about it like it was yesterday. It's funny, I was a regular in 1975 and I had a nice World Series for the Red Sox but nobody ever mentions that. Long-time fans still focus on 1967," he marvels.

Rico was inducted into the Red Sox Hall of Fame in September, 1997. "I am really proud of that," he said. "There are some really great players in there including teammates like Yaz, Jim Lonborg and George Scott. It's an honor just to be included with all those great players.

Rico is currently enjoying retirement. He spends part of the year in southern New Hampshire and part of the year in Florida. Best of all, Rico and his wife Elsie, who celebrated their 50th wedding anniversary in 2015, get to spend lots of time with their four sons and their grandchildren.

He gets to Fenway Park on a fairly regular basis and he is impressed with all of the changes ownership has made to improve Fenway Park for the fans. "They have done a great job of updating Fenway while still preserving the sense of history. I can't believe how much room the players have in the clubhouse," he added. "We had these steel cages with a hook to hang your clothes on," he laughed, "and we had these old fashioned stools in front as the only place to sit. We were all crammed together. But you know, those close quarters kind of forced us to go over the game together. That was a real plus."

When asked to characterize what the 1967 season meant to him personally, Rico replied, "It really affected me. It has influenced where I live, what I do, who I am. It really is a part of me. When people think of me they say, 'you're the guy who played for the 1967 Red Sox.'

And I am."

Yes you are, Rico. Yes, you are!

Chapter 10

Reggie Smith: A Star is Born

Boston Red Sox vs. Detroit Tigers, Tuesday, September 19, 1967

At age twenty-two, *Carl "Reggie" Smith* was the finest all-around athlete on the 1967 Boston Red Sox team. He was strong, he was gifted with natural speed and he was an outstanding hitter from either side of the plate. Like Joe Foy, he was originally signed by the Twins and he was picked up by the Red Sox when Minnesota failed to protect him on their forty-man roster. Smith advanced swiftly through the Red Sox system with outstanding seasons at Pittsfield in 1965 and for Toronto in 1966. Dick Williams knew that he was ready for the big leagues and he probably exhibited more patience with Reggie than any other single Red Sox player in 1967. At the end of June, Reggie was still only hitting .204, but Williams stuck with him. In part, this reflected Smith's defensive contribution in center field and also the dimension that his speed provided offensively. Mostly it reflected the manager's conviction that Reggie would be a star. His faith was rewarded throughout the second half of the season as Reggie Smith finally came into his own.

The Red Sox left Chicago downcast over their tough loss in the second game of the doubleheader but just one percentage point out of first place. They flew to New York for an important four game series at Yankee Stadium. With thirty-two games remaining in the season, every series was critical and every game was important.

The Red Sox got off to a good start on Monday night, August 28, with a 3-0 victory. Dave Morehead pitched well for five innings and Sparky Lyle, who was emerging as a key factor coming out of the bullpen, earned his fourth save since he was called up from Toronto. Reggie Smith, who had been hot at the plate since the All-Star game, had the key hit as he deposited his thirteenth homer into the right field bleachers. In another important development, Ken "Hawk" Harrelson reported to the team to provide some much needed help in right field.

General Manager Dick O'Connell had been making player moves the way a great symphony conductor orchestrates his musicians. His only peer with a better record that year was Arthur Fiedler who was leading the Boston Pops to an undefeated season at the Esplanade on the banks of Boston's Charles River.

O'Connell had acquired Adair and Bell in June to provide infield depth and a number two starter. Ellie Howard's addition had shored up the catching and provided veteran leadership with a winning attitude. Harrelson was the "coup de grace."

Neil Mahoney and Ed Kenney, Sr. of the minor league system deserved a lot of credit as well. Sparky Lyle had been developed in the Red Sox system, and the shuttle between Toronto and Boston of starting pitchers Morehead, Stephenson, and Gary Waslewski was testament to the depth of the Red Sox farm system. And there were many games that season when every player who took a starting position had come up through the Red Sox system. Not many teams could say that, not even in 1967.

In Tuesday's doubleheader, Jim Lonborg came through once more pitching brilliantly and driving in the winning run with a single. Reggie Smith's speed, with two stolen bases, was the other offensive key to the first game, 2-1 victory. Game two went on for twenty innings and took over six hours to play. The score was tied 2-2 after nine innings and the Red Sox looked good when they took a 3-2 lead in the top of the eleventh.

REGGIE **SMITH**

Reggie Smith added the dimension of speed to the Sox, both on offense and in the field.

But Steve Whitaker homered in the bottom frame to knot it up for the Yankees. The weak-hitting Horace Clarke, of all people, won it for the Yanks in the 20th with a single against hard-luck loser Bucky Brandon.

Reggie steals second base.

The biggest surprise of the doubleheader was the crowd of 40,314 fans on hand at Yankee Stadium. The Yankees were entrenched in ninth place, 15.5 games out of first, and weeknight crowds of 10,000-15,000 had become the norm. The Boston and New York media agreed that at least one-half of the 40,314 fans were there to cheer on the Red Sox with more cheers for the visiting team than for the Yankees!

The Red Sox showed a lot of character the next day. Gerry Stephenson and Yankee southpaw, Al Downing, went toe-to-toe and matched pitch-for-pitch. At the end of regulation, the game was tied at one. Yaz had begun the game on the bench. The combination of the previous evening's marathon session of 29 total innings, and an 0-17 hitting drought, had convinced Yaz and Dick Williams that a rest was in order. Yaz was inserted in left in the eighth, and in the tenth inning he propelled a Downing serve into the right-center bleachers for his 35th home run of the season and a much-needed 2-1 victory. Since Yaz had only hit 16 home runs for the entire 1966 season, it was clear that he had advanced his game to a whole different level.

The Red Sox were heading home to Boston in first place by one game and one-half. The Chicago White Sox were coming to town for a four game series, trailing the Red Sox by two and a half games. The stage was set for the **knock-out punch**.

There was a standing-room-only crowd of 35,314 fans on-hand on Thursday night at chilly Fenway Park to watch their first-place Red Sox continue their winning ways. Unfortunately, the White Sox got a well-pitched game from rookie Cisco Carlos, Red Sox stalwart pitcher Gary Bell ran out of gas in the 8th inning, and the ChiSox prevailed 4-2. More than one fan was heard to mutter, "They look like the same old Red Sox to me!"

But despite the disappointing loss, the Red Sox remained in first place in the American League with a one-half game lead. As the calendar flipped to September the standings looked like this:

American League Standings August 31, 1967

Team	Wins	Loses	Winning %	GB
BOSTON	**76**	**59**	**.563**	-
Minnesota	74	58	.561	0.5
Detroit	74	59	.556	1.0
Chicago	73	59	.553	1.5
California	66	65	.504	8.0
Washington	64	70	.478	11.5
Cleveland	63	71	.470	12.5
Baltimore	59	71	.454	14.5
New York	59	75	.440	16.5
Kansas City	55	76	.420	19.0

Yaz (.308) and George Scott (.304) were a rather distant second and third in the American League to Frank Robinson's .331 for the AL batting lead. And with Tony C out of the lineup and likely lost for the season, Yaz was the main source of power for the Red Sox. At the end of August Yaz had one more home run than the Twin's Harmon Killebrew—35 to 34—and the MVP candidate topped the AL with 95 RBI, closely followed by Killebrew with 90. Jim Lonborg's winning percentage of .750—18 wins and six losses—was the best in the American League.

Selected Red Sox Hitters August 31, 1967

Player	H	R	HR	BV
Yastrzemski	149	88	35	.308
Scott	142	64	17	.304
Conigliaro	101	59	20	.289
Petrocelli	104	43	13	.263
Smith	120	64	13	.262
Jones	28	13	2	.255
Andrews	105	67	7	.249
Foy	106	64	17	.248
Ryan	43	19	2	.211

With more than 80% of the season completed, and only 27 games remaining for the Red Sox, the report cards looked like this

AUGUST 31 REPORT CARD

A+: Yaz (.308, 35 homers, 95 RBI)

A's: Scott (.304, 17 homers)

Lonborg (18-6, 3.26 ERA)

Wyatt (8-6, 2.39 ERA)

B's: Petrocelli (infield leader)

Adair (super-sub)

Smith (from .204 to .262 in two months)

Andrews (solid at second)

Foy (17 homers)

Santiago (starter & reliever)

Stange (8 wins, 2.64 ERA)

Disabled: Tony C.

On Friday evening, the Red Sox redeemed themselves before 34,054 loyalists. Hawk Harrelson finally earned some of the $100,000+ that Tom Yawkey had ponied up in the bidding war for Hawk's services with a double, triple and a home run. Boston won going away as Jose Santiago picked up his eighth win. Their hold on first place was down to one-half game over the second place Twins, one game above the White Sox and only one and one-half games above the Tigers.

Standings on August 31

Team	Games Behind
Minnesota	--
Boston	1/2
Chicago	1
Detroit	1 1/2

Jim Lonborg failed to rise to the occasion for one of the few times all season in the third game of the series on Saturday. The White Sox got to him for three runs in the opening frame and Joel Horlen pitched masterfully, holding the Red Sox to six hits for a 4-1 win. The defeat dropped Boston to second place, one-half game behind the Twins. The White Sox pitching carried the day in the Sunday finale as well. Twenty-four-year-old stylish southpaw Tommy John, who would pitch for 26 distinguished seasons in the majors, about half before the surgery that would famously take his name, shut them out 4-0. As Labor Day, 1967, dawned, the American League standings looked like this:

The four contenders were strung together like beads on a pearl necklace. Nothing would come easy in 1967. The California Angels were now 9 games out of first place, so it looked like a four-team race right down to the wire.

The Red Sox headed to Washington for a three-game series against the Senators who were twelve and one half games off the pace and going nowhere. The Red Sox knew they had to take at least two out of three in DC to stay in the hunt.

Labor Day is another benchmark in the six-month season. With only two dozen games remaining, every single game is important. Unfortunately, the Red Sox continued to struggle in game one of the doubleheader. Red Sox jinx Camilio Pascual, who always seemed to baffle Boston hitters, tantalized them with slow curves and the lowly Senators prevailed by a score of 5-2 despite Yaz' 36th home run.

If there was one single victory that Dick Williams could take credit for in 1967, it was probably the second game of this Labor Day doubleheader. His first move was to bench regulars Foy, Harrelson and Scott. After dropping three straight, and four of five crucial games, drastic measures were in order. Besides, the Boomer hadn't had an extra base hit in over fifteen games. Williams' next move was to "jury-rig" a pitching corps that produced five decent innings from Gerry Stephenson, three good innings from Sparky Lyle, and featured John Wyatt in his role as closer in the ninth. Every move worked including George Scott, who appeared in a cameo pinch-hitting role as the Boomer, and driving a key double in the eighth. The Red Sox held steady with the Twins, who also split, with their much needed 6-4 win.

Carl Yastrzemski assumed the leadership mantle in the deciding game of the series. Yaz rocketed home runs numbers thirty-seven and thirty-eight to take over the home run lead in the AL and help the Red Sox to coast to an 8-2 decision. Gary Bell picked up his tenth win in a Boston uniform.

Wednesday was the Red Sox's first day off in almost a month and it was a good time to reflect on the remainder of the season. There were only twenty-one games remaining and thirteen of them were scheduled in friendly Fenway. The Red Sox were positioned to control their own destiny, but they would have to "make hay" in the upcoming nine-game home stand against New York, Kansas City and Baltimore. Those were three teams they had handled easily all year. There were only two brief series left with any of the contending teams: a two-game series against the Tigers immediately after the home stand and a two-game set at home against the Twins on the last two days of the season. The season wrap-up against Minnesota was beginning to loom as awfully large.

The Red Sox needed a big home stand and the logical choice to get them off on the right foot was Gentleman Jim Lonborg. Once more Lonborg didn't disappoint as he three-hit the Yankees for his nineteenth win in front of the almost 29,000 fans crowding Fenway Park on a Thursday evening. Rico Petrocelli led the batting brigade with three hits and two RBI in the 3-1 opener of a four-game series. All season long Red Sox fans had been hoping for an American League pennant and the team's first trip to the World Series since 1946. That hope got a little closer to reality that day when the Major League Baseball Commissioner's Office gave the Red Sox permission to print World Series tickets. There was still an awfully long way to go, but the Commissioner's letter made it seem possible!

Former Red Sox pitching stalwart, Medford, MA, native Bill Monbouquette, turned the tables on his old mates on Friday night. Monbouquette bested Lee Stange 5-2 as the Yankees tied the series. Monbouquette, who had won 96 games over eight seasons with the Red Sox, said to the media, "I was just doing my job. But I certainly hope the Red Sox win the pennant." Mombo told me many years later, "I gave the writers what they wanted to hear, but I'll tell you, that was one of my sweetest wins! They traded me to the Tigers after all those years [12 in total] with the club, and then they [the Red Sox] didn't sign me when the Tigers released me. You bet I wanted to beat them!"

Spot starter Dave Morehead saved the day on Saturday as he gave the Red Sox seven quality innings. Carl Yastrzemski's thirty-ninth homer and Rico Petrocelli's fifteenth set the tone for the 7-1 decision. The Red Sox needed a victory on Sunday to stay within a half game of the Twins and they won in a "laugher" by a score of 9-1. Gary Bell came through with a four-hit complete game for his eleventh triumph for Boston. The Red Sox win was their 82nd of the season, making good on Dick Williams' spring training promise that they would, "win more that they would lose."

Monday September 11, was a much needed day-off for the Red Sox and especially their beleaguered pitching staff. With last-place Kansas City coming to town for two games, the Red Sox knew they had to demonstrate some killer instinct. Jim Lonborg went to the mound on Tuesday night determined to do whatever it took to secure his twentieth victory. Lonborg didn't have his best stuff—he had to work himself out of trouble in the second through the fifth innings—but he hung tough against the A's Catfish Hunter. He came to bat in the last of the eighth with pinch runner, Jose Tartabull, on first, locked in a 1-1 battle. Jim "showed" bunt and swung away to produce a towering drive to the right-center triangle. Lonborg's long legs propelled him to third from where he tagged up on a long Mike Andrews fly to ice a 3-1 win.

On the following afternoon, Rico Petrocelli provided all the fireworks the Red Sox needed as he drove in three runs. Lee Stange (seven innings) and John Wyatt (two innings and credit for the win) teamed up in the 4-2 decision. The Red Sox looked forward to a day off and the arrival of their "cousins," the Baltimore Orioles on Friday for a three-game series.

The O's seemed to be the ideal candidates for the Red Sox to improve their position in the standings. Although the teams hadn't met in almost two months, Boston had handled them easily in their two July series. Unfortunately, a poor effort by starter Dave Morehead—three wild pitches—and a number of fielding gaffes resulted in a 6-2 loss in Friday's opener. To make matters worse, the Red Sox bats went silent on Saturday. Red Sox hitters could only manage one run off Baltimore rookie, Jim Hardin, as Lonborg proved human by dropping a 4-1 decision. The Red Sox were fortunate to be holding on to second place at one game out of first.

With only twelve games remaining after Sunday, it seemed that the Red Sox had to have a win against the O's in the series wrap-up. Gary Bell drew the nod for this all-important game. But once again the Red Sox bats were somnolent and Bell was only mediocre. O's starter, Gene Brabender, picked up the win as the Red Sox were limited to only two runs. Baltimore's tally of five was more than enough and Bell absorbed the loss. As the crowd of 30,301 left Fenway Park there was the unspoken sense that the 1967 Red Sox may have already reached their peak.

The only salvation in the Red Sox three-game "swoon" to the Orioles was that the Tigers, the White Sox, and the Twins also failed to open up any daylight. The four contenders were all within one game of one another. Detroit was in first holding a half-game lead over the White Sox. The Red Sox, who had gone from first to second to third place during the three-game series with the Orioles, had gone only 5-4 in their home stand, but incredibly they were still very much in the running at only one game out of first place!

After the third loss of the series to the Orioles, Dick Williams was fairly calm with the media. "We were due for something like that, I guess," was about all he had to say. Gary Bell told me, "Just when you thought he [Williams] would lose it, he would surprise us and take it in stride. When we lost because of physical short-comings he could take it. It was the mental mistakes that drove him nuts."

Boston was heading off for a two-game series with the front-running Tigers and they recognized that they were flat out of reprieves. Dick Williams pledged to shake the team out of its lethargy. Williams inserted Jose Tartabull, Russ Gibson and Dalton Jones into the starting lineup. Jones was a calculated gamble since he hit like Ted Williams in Tiger Stadium. Dick Williams cracked, "Wouldn't it be something if I put Jose Tartabull up there in the cleanup spot? I just might."

The Red Sox clubhouse was loose before the game, as it had been all year. Dalton Jones, who would turn out to be the hero of the first game of the series, told me, "We had come back so many times that we never doubted ourselves. We knew how important the two games in Detroit were, but we were very confident."

The opening game on Monday night included everything that a game between two contenders in a tight pennant race should contain. The ten inning contest featured suspense, drama, disappointment, and heroics. If the game contained more offense than defense it was as it should be in this ballpark between these two teams.

The game unfolded like a classic heavyweight championship fight. The Red Sox drew first blood with three runs off Tiger starter Denny McLain in the first inning. Yaz doubled in Jose Tartabull to get things going and Reggie Smith's single moved Yaz to third. Reggie then stole second base, his 15th steal of the season, and George Scott's sacrifice fly plated Yaz. Reggie Smith used his speed to score on a Dalton Jones' single to give Red Sox starter Jerry Stephenson a three-run cushion to work with. The Tigers scored three runs of their own in the second inning, but Reggie Smith's deep fly to center in the third inning allowed Mike Andrews to tag and score putting the Red Sox up 4-3. Stephenson struggled with his control throughout the game, laboring gallantly through seven innings and holding Detroit to four runs to keep Boston in the game. The Red Sox threatened in the eighth inning with the contest knotted at four, but Dick McAuliffe's heads-up, unassisted double play killed that rally. Tiger-killer Dalton Jones' three hits were the Red Sox highlight at this point.

Stephenson gave way to John Wyatt as the game moved to the last of the eighth. Wyatt had been the Red Sox's most dependable reliever all year, but this was not to be his night. Jim Northrup doubled home Al Kaline and the Red Sox would enter the ninth trailing 5-4. More than one Red Sox fan wondered if the team was finally running out of gas.

Carl Yastrzemski wasn't out of gas by any means. In fact, beginning in the top of the ninth, Yaz would put in the high octane and he would keep it there for the next two weeks. He kicked off the best two-week stretch when every game counted of any hitter in major league history with a game-tying home run deep into the right field stands. The Red Sox's hopes were still very much alive.

Yaz's clutch blast seemed to be just the catalyst his teammates needed. John Wyatt held the Tigers scoreless in the bottom of the ninth to create an opportunity for Dalton Jones to seize the hero's mantle. The crown was a perfect fit as Jones drove rookie Mike Marshall's slider into the upper deck in right. Jones also made a nice defensive play on a Bill Freehan bullet to end the game proving that Dick Williams really was a genius. A disappointed capacity crowd of 42,674 Detroit fans filed quietly out of Tigers Stadium when the 10th inning and the game were over. The Red Sox had finally won a big one, and what a big one it was!

The morning of September 19 found three American League teams in a dead-heat for first place: the Red Sox, the Twins and the Tigers. Following a loss to the California Angels, Chicago was in fourth place, one-half game behind.

The story in the National League was very different. The morning papers recounted the St. Louis Cardinals' victory over Philadelphia by a score of 4-1 behind Bob Gibson. This victory clinched the National League pennant for the Cards. While they had no idea of who their opponents would be, they did know that games three, four and five would be played in Busch Stadium in St. Louis.

Reggie Smith went about his pre-game rituals in Detroit representing another in a starry history of Red Sox centerfielders. Much has been made of the Red Sox royalty in left field and rightfully so. A nearly unbroken string of stars from Ted Williams, to Yaz, through Jim Rice, and on to Manny Ramirez is unprecedented in baseball history. This group includes three Hall-of-Famers, and one legitimate Hall-of-Fame candidate.

While the continuity is not as pronounced, center field in Boston has been manned by some outstanding players as well. The first great star center fielder was Tris Speaker who patrolled the ground for the Red Sox from 1909 to 1915. Speaker hit .383 in 1912 and never hit less than .309 in his seven full years with the Red Sox. Dom DiMaggio held down center field with great distinction for the Red Sox from 1940 to 1952. While he always suffered from the long shadow cast by his big brother, Joe, Dom's lifetime average of .298 is testimony to his skills. Jimmy Piersall also played a number of spectacular seasons in center field for Boston in the mid-50s. Piersall overcame a nervous breakdown to achieve stardom and some of his great catches are still relived by long-time Red Sox fans.

While he couldn't have known it in 1967, Smith would ultimately be succeeded by Fred Lynn and the legacy would pass to Ellis Burks then to Jacoby Ellsbury and to Jackie Bradley, Jr. today. Not quite as spectacular as the left field tradition, but a formidable group nonetheless.

Carl Reginald Smith was born in Shreveport, LA, on April 2, 1945. He was the youngest of seven children and he grew up in the South Central section of Los Angeles. "I was always called by my middle name," Reggie remembered. "On my first day of school I told the teacher she hadn't called my name," Reggie laughed, "because I didn't know who Carl Smith was!"

Reggie's father Lonnie had been a catcher in the Negro American League and he played catch with Reggie whenever he could. Reggie also remembered helping out with the family egg delivery business and how that brought him to closer to his parents.

Smith starred at baseball and football at Centennial High School. He was voted "All-California" as a high school shortstop and a running back in football. Along the way he had taught himself to switch-hit but he thinks he was a better football player. "Football was my first love," he recalled.

Reggie wanted to go to college and play football and he had several scholarship offers but family came first for Reggie. "My father became very sick at that time," he said, "and the Twins were offering me bonus money to sign with them. I decided that was the right thing to do so I could help out my parents. I'm glad I did it."

The Minnesota Twins shipped him to Wytheville, North Carolina, in their lower minors where he played shortstop. He showed speed and power in his debut, but his forty-one errors in sixty-six games gave the Twins pause. When they left him unprotected in November of 1963, the Red Sox drafted him for the bargain price of $8,000. The Red Sox had also drafted Joe Foy from the Twins so two of the more important players on the 1967 Red Sox team had originally been signed by Minnesota.

He began the 1964 season with Waterloo (Iowa) in the Midwest League, and his fine play earned him a promotion to Reading (Pennsylvania) in the Eastern League that same year. He spent 1965 in Pitts-field (Massachusetts), also in the Eastern League, where he first met Red Sox minor league manager "Pop" Popowski. His next stop was the Red Sox top minor league club, Toronto, in the Triple-A International League, where he played for Dick Williams.

Smith got off to a slow start at the plate for Toronto, but he finished the season with a batting average of .320, good enough to lead the International League. He was called up to the Red Sox in September and his six late-season games with the Red Sox gave him a taste of life in the major leagues.

The Tigers felt they had to have a win on Tuesday night. To be swept in their own home park would be devastating to their chances and to their morale. Manager Mayo Smith went with veteran lefthander, Mickey Lolich, to combat Yaz and the left-handed hitting, Dalton Jones. Manager Williams countered by lifting Jones in favor of the right-handed hitting, Jerry Adair.

The Red Sox started right-hander Lee Stange who had a record of 8-10. The "Stinger" had pitched well of late and Williams was looking for six or seven good innings from him.

Tiger fans showed their loyalty by filling Tiger Stadium with another capacity crowd of 43,004.

Both pitchers got through the first inning without damage. Lolich put an exclamation point on his effort by striking out Adair, Yaz and Scott. In the top of the second, the Red Sox started a mild uprising.

Reggie Smith opened the second with a single to center. The one unique dimension Reggie brought to the Red Sox was his speed. The Red Sox have always featured power hitters and Smith was one of their few players who could manufacture runs with his speed. With Ken Harrelson at bat, Mickey Lolich uncorked a wild pitch and Reggie was on second in a flash. After Harrelson struck out, Reggie tagged and moved to third on a long fly ball by Rico Petrocelli. When Russ Gibson singled into center, Smith scampered home with the first Red Sox run and the first tally of the game.

Stange breezed through the last of the second and Lolich did the same in the top of the third. The Tigers came to bat in the last of the third trailing 1-0.

Stange got into a bit of a jam in the Tigers' third. With the bases loaded Mike Andrews then made a nice play on a Lumpe grounder by tagging McAuliffe and firing to Scott to turn the inning-ending double play.

Lolich retired the Red Sox in 1-2-3 order in the Boston half of the inning. Stange ran into a little more hot water in the Tigers' fourth. But Stange bore down and induced a pop out, struck out the dangerous Norm Cash and finally got out of the inning unscathed when a Bill Freehan grounder forced Horton at second.

Both pitchers held the line in the fifth inning. And after the Red Sox failed to score in the top of the sixth, Al Kaline got things going for the Tigers by sending a liner to left-center, which placed him on second. After Horton grounded out, Northrup picked on a Stange slider and put it into the third deck in right field. With one swing of the bat, the Tigers had earned a seemingly large 2-1 lead.

The Red Sox had no luck against Lolich in the top of seventh and the Tigers appeared poised for their knockout punch. Don Wert singled to open the seventh. When Lolich followed with a single of his own, Williams knew it was time to get Stange out of there. His choice was young reliever Al "Sparky" Lyle and he was the right choice. When Jerry Adair snagged a Ray Oyler line drive the Red Sox had wiggled out of another jam.

The Red Sox were down to six outs and they needed a rally fast. Lolich struck out Gibson to start the eighth. Joe Foy was sent up as a pinch hitter for Lyle. Lolich fanned him. When Andrews suffered the same fate to end the inning, Lolich had notched thirteen strikeouts over eight innings. Boston was running out of time.

As Reggie Smith took center field in the last of the eighth, he couldn't help looking ahead to the Boston ninth. Jerry Adair would lead off followed by Yaz. George Scott was next, and if any of them reached, it would bring him up with the tying run on base. He wondered if Mayo Smith would stick with Lolich. If he went with a right-hander, Reggie would cross over to bat lefty, with a shot at the inviting right field bleachers. Then he turned his full attention to the scene in front of him.

Jose Santiago came on to face the Tigers in the last half of the eighth inning. He was in trouble before he even got adjusted to the mound. First Kaline walked. Then the usually sure-handed Adair bobbled a Horton grounder for an error. When Santiago failed to handle a Northrup dribbler the bases were jammed with Tigers with no outs.

Jose took a deep breath. He breathed a little easier when he forced Norm Cash to foul out to Gibson. Then he breathed a huge sigh of relief when he got Bill Freehan to ground into a double play to end the inning. The Red Sox had pulled their Houdini act one more time and remained within striking distance.

The Red Sox needed a break as they entered the ninth. Dick Williams was not superstitious, but he had noticed an omen in centerfield before the game began. Someone had placed a red broom, a dozen roses and a red sign reading "sweep" in the deepest reaches of Tiger Stadium.

Jerry Adair set the spark with a leadoff single to right. Then Lolich walked Yaz on four straight pitches. George Scott fought off a number of tough pitches and rifled a single to center. Jerry Adair was running all the way and slid safely into home with the tying run.

This brought the switch-hitting Reggie Smith to the plate and manager Mayo Smith to the mound. Mayo Smith pulled out all the stops by bringing in twenty-game winner Earl Wilson for his first relief appearance of the year. Reggie showed his versatility by deftly dropping a bunt down the first base line. His sacrifice worked and the runners advanced to second and third.

Now all the wheels were turning. Manager Smith ordered pinch hitter Dalton Jones walked to load up the bases and set up a force play all around. Dick Williams countered by sending up lefty Norm Siebern to bat for Rico. All of this strategy went for naught when Wilson uncorked a wild pitch to score Yaz with the lead run. Gibson followed an intentional walk to Siebern by sending a drive to deep center to score the tagging Scott with an insurance run.

The Red Sox had a two-run lead as the Tigers came to bat in the ninth. Santiago retired Wert on a nice catch by Yastrzemski to start the inning. Then his control faltered. He walked Lenny Green and McAuliffe to put the tying run at first. Williams brought in lefty Bill Landis to face aging slugger Eddie Mathews. Landis eased the tension by striking out the Tigers' veteran pinch hitter. Williams wasn't taking any chances: he brought in Gary Bell to face the ever-dangerous Al Kaline.

Reggie Smith felt quite comfortable in center field as he watched Bell take his warm up pitches. With his speed and reflexes, he was confident in his ability to get to any ball hit in his direction. He had played second, short and third in the minors and he had started the 1967 season at second for the Red Sox, but center was his home.

Kaline didn't wait for the suspense to build. He smashed Bell's first pitch on a dead line into center field. Both base runners were in full motion as soon as bat met ball. Smith was charging in from center field, but the hard liner was sinking fast. If it got by him, both runs would probably score and the game would be tied. Reggie turned on every ounce of his speed and snared the drive on the run at his knees. The Red Sox had pulled off another thriller and they had swept the Tigers.

In the clubhouse after the game, Yaz said, "At first, I didn't think Reggie was going to get it." Manager Williams echoed the compliment. "Reggie got a terrific jump on the ball," he said.

Reggie credited Yaz with an assist on the play. "If I trap the ball, it's a single. If it gets by me, Yaz is there to back me up."

Reggie would go on to make many similar catches during his seven-year career in Boston. During that time he batted .282 with 149 home runs and he made two All-Star teams. But the Red Sox never made it back to the postseason during that time.

Reggie was traded to the St. Louis Cardinals after the 1973 season. Reggie looks back on his trade to the Cardinals with mixed emotions. "I had been with the [Red Sox] organization for ten years, and I had a lot of friends there. Yaz took me under his wing and he was my fishing buddy.

"It's funny. Boston was so different from Los Angeles it took my wife and I time to adjust. But once we adjusted, we liked it there and we made Boston our year-round home. But I think I was more suited to play in the National League," he reflected. "They played a more aggressive style of baseball, more hardnosed. I was able to use my speed more.

He played two full seasons with the Cardinals making the National League All-Star team in both 1974 and 1975. He had his first 100 RBI

Reggie, flanked by fellow outfielders Carl Yastrzemski and Tony Conigliaro.

season in 1974, and he batted over .300 in both years. On June 15, 1976, the Cardinals traded him to the Los Angeles Dodgers. Reggie Smith was headed home to southern California.

"It was like going home," Reggie agreed. "I didn't move my family from the Boston area until then. We had spent ten years there. And both of my boys were born there. But I was headed back to where I grew up, where my family was. I had come full circle. That part was nice."

Reggie's first full season with the Dodgers, 1977, was one of his finest in the big leagues. He set a personal best with 32 home runs, and he walked more than 100 times for the first time in his career. He was named to the National League All-Star team, and he made it back to the World Series for the first time in ten years.

Reggie Smith was a National League All-Star in 1978 and 1980. In 1981 he finally earned a World Championship ring, as the Dodgers reversed the outcome of the 1977 World Series, defeating the Yankees four-games-to-two. Reggie was hampered by injuries in 1981, and appeared in only 41 games during the regular season, but he still cherishes that World Championship. "It was a real team effort that year. And it felt good to be a part of a winning team."

The 1982 season was Reggie Smith's final season in the major leagues. He finished out his big league career playing for the San Francisco Giants.

When his playing career was over, Reggie joined the Dodgers organization, working with their minor league players. In 1993 he took over as field coordinator of the Dodgers minor league operations department. From 1994 to 1998 he was the major league hitting instructor and first base coach for the Los Angeles Dodger.

Today, Reggie's primary activity is the Reggie Smith Baseball Center (reggiesmithbaseball.com) located in Encino, California. Founded in 1998, the center provides individual and group instruction for players of all ages and skill levels. He has expanded his focus to include the Lakeland Baseball Academy, in Lakeland, Florida, which is intended to attract players on a worldwide basis.

Smith served as the hitting instructor for the United States baseball team for the 2000 Olympic Games in Sydney, Australia. That team was described as a "rag tag band of minor leaguers," before the games began, but they went on to upset Cuba 4-0 in the final game to win the Gold

Medal. He was also the hitting instructor for the US entry in the 2006 World Baseball Classic.

But Reggie's greatest challenge as a hitting instructor came when he was hired by Billy Crystal to be the technical advisor for the HBO movie, *61**. The movie portrayed the adventures of Roger Maris and Mickey Mantle of the 1961 New York Yankees, as they struggled to catch, and to pass, Babe Ruth's record of 60 home runs in a single season. Smith's task was to work with actor Thomas Jane to develop a swing that reminded viewers of Roger Maris' swing, and to do the same for Barry Pepper in his portrayal of Mantle.

"We had six weeks to work with them," Smith recalls, "and on the first day Thomas Jane admitted that he had never played baseball before. Barry Pepper was a little better. He had never played baseball, but he had played softball. I give Billy Crystal credit. As I was working with the two of them, they actually started getting competitive with one another. Billy saw that, and he used it in the movie to make it even better."

Reggie Smith and his wife Rose, live in the Los Angeles area. He has two grown children, both of whom were born in Boston, and he dotes on his three grandchildren.

Asked how much baseball means to him, Smith responds emphatically. "It is still a big part of my life today. An awful lot of good things have happened to me because of baseball. And I realize how fortunate I was to be able to play a little kid's game. I try to give back through my teaching. I believe I was meant to teach."

Reflecting on the storybook 1967 season, Smith offered, "It was one of my great thrills. I got to live out my childhood dream. I can remember sitting in class as a youngster, while the teacher let us listen to the World Series on the radio. Getting to play in a World Series was a dream come true for me."

Reggie Smith was a seven-time All-Star, and he is a member of the Red Sox Hall of Fame. He compares favorably with the elite, five-tool players who have performed in the major leagues over the years. He hit for average and with power, he was an outstanding fielder with a strong accurate arm, and he could run like a deer. He will always be remembered as the best athlete on the 1967 Boston Red Sox.

Chapter 11

Carl Yastrzemski:
Impossibly Good When
It Mattered Most
A Season for the Ages

Boston Red Sox vs. Tigers-Indians-Orioles-Indians-Twins, Monday,
September 18, through Sunday October 1, 1967

After six years of frustration, *Carl Michael Yastrzemski* and the Boston
Red Sox finally put it all together in 1967. Following two outstanding
years in the Red Sox' minor league system, Yaz arrived in Fenway Park
in 1961 as the twenty-one-year-old designated heir to Ted Williams in
left field. He played well as a rookie, but his .266 batting average and
eleven home runs didn't stir many memories of Williams. Although he
elevated his game each year, the Red Sox continued their dismal performance and Yaz had a few problems with managers Johnny Pesky
and Billy Herman. Things started to change for Yaz between the 1966
and 1967 seasons. Carl entered into a grueling physical regimen which
put him in top form when he arrived at spring training. Also, Dick
Williams relieved him of his duties as team captain, freeing him up to
concentrate on his game and to provide leadership in a more comfortable way. The 1967 season was to be the greatest year of his career and
in September he would have as good a month when the pennant was
on the line as any player in the history of the game.

When the Red Sox had arrived in Detroit on September 18th for that all-important two-game series with the Tigers, the standings for the four teams contending for the American League pennant looked like this:

Team	W	L	W-L%	GB	RS	RA
DET	85	65	.567	-	627	546
CHW	85	66	.563	0.5	503	463
BOS	84	66	.560	1.0	661	552
MIN	84	66	.560	1.0	615	546

It seemed clear that the battle to represent the American League in the World Series would come right down to the wire. Younger baseball fans that have gotten used to multiple postseason hurdles are sometimes surprised to learn that until 1968, the team that finished first in their league would go directly to the World Series. The 2013 Red Sox played ten games to win two series before they even reached Game One of the World Series. The 1967 Red Sox needed to win two more games than the Tigers and White Sox and one more game than the Twins in the twelve regular season games remaining for Boston in order to represent the American League in the World Series.

The statistically-inclined took comfort in the fact that the Red Sox run differential (generally a reliable predictor of future success) of 109 (661 runs scored vs. 552 runs allowed) was significantly higher than the run differential of their three rivals. On a more basic level, the Red Sox had a generally favorable schedule over the last two weeks. Of the twelve remaining games, eight of them—four each—were against the sub-.500 Indians and Orioles. The other four included the two upcoming games against the first-place Tigers and the last two in the final weekend of the season in Fenway against the Minnesota Twins.

The first-place Tigers were generally considered to be the strongest of the four contenders. They had a well-balanced lineup led by future Hall-of-Famer Al Kaline and solid pitching including starters Mickey Lolich and Earl Wilson. A sweep of the visiting Red Sox, who were reeling from three-straight losses to Baltimore, would go a long way towards opening up some daylight in the standings for Detroit.

Day	Date	Opponent	Where
Monday	18	Tigers	@Detroit
Tuesday	19	Tigers	@Detroit
Wednesday	20	Indians	@Cleveland
Thursday	21	Indians	@Cleveland
Friday (1)	22	Orioles	@Baltimore
Friday (2)	22	Orioles	@Baltimore
Saturday	23	Orioles	@Baltimore
Sunday	24	Orioles	@Baltimore
Monday	25	Off-Day	Off
Tuesday	26	Indians	Boston
Wednesday	27	Indians	Boston
Thursday	28	Off-Day	Off
Friday	29	Off-Day	Off
Saturday	30	Twins	Boston
Sunday	1	Twins	Boston

For once a critical game lived up to its hype. The two teams played at a level of quality in the series' opener that you would expect from two pennant-contending teams. The lead went back and forth until the Tigers jumped out ahead in the home half of the eighth inning when Jim Northrup singled in Al Kaline to give Detroit a 5-4 lead. Carl Yastrzemski came to the plate in the ninth inning with one out, the bases empty, and the fate of the Red Sox Impossible Dream season hanging in the balance. And then Yaz turned on a Fred Lasher fastball and drove it deep into the upper deck in right field to tie the game at 5-5.

One of the great themes of the 1967 Red Sox was, "a different hero every day." It started with Billy Rohr's one-hitter on Opening Day at Yankee Stadium; later it was Jerry Adair's home run to cap a Red Sox rally from 0-8 to a 9-8 win over the Angels one month earlier. On September 18, at Tiger Stadium the hero of the day would turn out to be utility man Dalton Jones who had only started two games during the past six weeks. Jones came to the plate in the top of the tenth inning and launched a Mike Marshall pitch deep into the right-field upper deck that landed near the spot where Yaz's ninth inning home run came to rest.

Jones, who had three singles to go with his game-winning home run, said, "That was my best game in the major leagues. I wanted to give the game ball to Jose Santiago because he was the winning pitcher, but Jose insisted that I keep it."

If Monday's game was a "must-win" contest for the Red Sox, Tuesday night's game fell into a similar category for the Tigers. The Tigers and Red Sox were tied with records of 85 wins and 66 losses, and the Twins had an identical record for a three-way tie for first place, while the White Sox were one-half game out of first. A sell-out crowd of over 43,000 Detroit fans jammed the ballpark to watch the two first-place teams.

The second game of the Tigers series was a pitching-duel. Red Sox starter Lee Stange didn't have his best stuff but he managed to hold the Tigers scoreless through five innings and a Russ Gibson RBI single in the second inning gave the Sox a 1-0 lead heading into the Tigers' sixth inning. A Jim Northrup home run in the last of the sixth with Al Kaline aboard put Detroit up 2-1, a lead they would take into the ninth inning. But Jerry Adair singled, Yaz was walked and George Scott singled to drive in Adair with the tying run. Earl Wilson was brought in for his first relief appearance all year and promptly uncorked a wild pitch scoring Yaz with the lead run. Russ Gibson's sacrifice fly brought the score to 4-2 and the Red Sox held on through a rocky Tigers ninth to pull off a two-game sweep.

The Red Sox clubhouse was jubilant after their decisive, late-game wins over the Tigers. Mike Andrews was yelling "Fabulous" And Rico was hollering "Beautiful," after the team stepped back from the precipice two nights in a row. Catcher Russ Gibson was the "hero of the day," with two RBI and Carl Yastrzemski continued to provide clutch hitting when it was needed the most. In the two most important games of the season to date, Yaz had been on base six times, scored the tying run in the ninth inning Monday night, and scored the winning run in the ninth inning Tuesday night.

Fans back in Boston were euphoric after the sweep of the Tigers. The Red Sox were the media story 24/7, and Channel-5, the TV home of the team, announced they were picking up three more road games to be telecast. It may be hard to believe fifty years later, but most Red Sox games **were not telecast**; all games were broadcast on the radio but baseball on TV was still the exception. Neither the Red Sox nor Channel-5 thought that the Red Sox would be in pennant contention after Labor Day! And the big fan news on September 20th was the Red Sox announcement that they would begin accepting applications for World Series tickets. Box seat prices were increased to $12 each and bleacher tickets were doubled from $1 to $2, but tickets were still within reach of the average fan.

The decisive sweep of the Tigers placed the Red Sox in a flat-footed tie with the Twins for first place with a record of 86-66. Chicago was even with the leaders in the win column, but had one more loss to trail by one-half game. Detroit now resided in fourth place, one game off the pace.

The Red Sox had 10 scheduled games remaining to be played over the next 13 days. The next six were road games in Cleveland and Baltimore. The final four games were scheduled at home against Cleveland and the Twins.

Boston came into Cleveland's Municipal Stadium Wednesday on a high and they continued their clutch play. Lonborg got the nod from Dick Williams and Sudden Sam McDowell took the mound for the Indians. Both teams played long ball as a shower of one-run homers rained on the bleachers. Ex-Red Soxer Tony Horton had one of three Cleveland homers and Yaz, Petrocelli and Andrews added four-baggers of their own.

When the home run barrage halted, the scoreboard read 4-4 after eight. George Culver had replaced McDowell for the Tribe and Yaz touched him for a single when two were gone in the eighth. After Scott had walked, the stage was set for more late-inning heroics. Reggie Smith came through with a sharp single to right field scoring Yaz with the go-ahead run. John Wyatt came on to close out the 5-4 win, picking up his tenth win in the process. Once again, Yaz had come through in the clutch with four hits, and his 41st home run gave him the AL lead in the Triple Crown categories of homers, batting average and RBI. The win was the team's 87th of the season, the most wins by a Red Sox team since 1951.

The pressure of continuous "must win" games may have gotten to the Red Sox the following night. Starter Gary Bell pitched well for

Yaz focused on the next pitch.

six innings and the Red Sox held a 6-1 lead based on timely hitting. Then things started to unravel a little—a misplay here, a miscue there—and the next thing anyone knew, it was a tight 6-5 game. One of their many unsung heroes— John Wyatt—rode to the rescue again and the Red Sox held on to their share of first place. Bell got credit for the win running his record in Boston to 12-7. Carl Yastrzemski continued his torrid offensive streak, reaching base on a walk, an error and a double deep to right field.

Things really unraveled in the first game of the doubleheader in Baltimore on Friday. Most people would certainly consider giving up ten runs and scoring none in the heat of a pennant race as unraveling. That's exactly what the Red Sox did. Gerry Stephenson gave up five earned runs and took the loss while Billy Rohr, who had recently been recalled from Toronto, gave up four runs. The Red Sox were flat out inept.

Dick Williams decided to really shake things up in the important second game. First, he elected to start Jose Santiago, who had been used primarily as a reliever for most of the season. Jose was making only his tenth start of the season, but he had come on strong in the second half to compile a record of 10-4. In addition, Williams shook up his lineup by putting Joe Foy at third base, installing Elston Howard behind the plate, and returning Ken Harrelson to right field.

Santiago was a wise choice as he went the distance in a 10-3 victory. Jose's complete game gave the Sox bullpen a much needed rest and the win was his third in five days. The offense was propelled by three hits each from Ken "Hawk" Harrelson and Joe Foy. The split of a double-header to the lowly Birds was disappointing, but the Red Sox were still only one-half game from the top rung of the American League ladder behind the Minnesota Twins.

The Red Sox were in danger of losing their tenuous grip on second place the next day with a 7-5 loss to the Orioles, but the Twins lost and the Tigers did not play so they remained one-half game out of first place. Baltimore jumped out to a 4-0 lead, but Boston came roaring back to take the lead at 5-4 as Yaz launched his forty-second home run. His three-week tear had now propelled him into the league lead in five offensive categories: batting average, hits, runs scored, RBI, and home runs.

Williams went to the John Wyatt-well one more time. Unfortunately, the well was empty as Brooks Robinson took Wyatt downtown for a two-run homer. The loss dropped the Red Sox to third place, but still one-half game behind the Twins and one-thousandth of a percentage point behind the Tigers. All four contending teams are now within one game of each other. The tight race sent researchers to the record books to find an earlier race that had been as tight as this one.

Jim Lonborg found himself in a familiar spot on Sunday in Baltimore: he was starting a must-win game for Boston. In fact, Jim was shooting for his twenty-first victory and if he was successful, it would be his ninth win immediately following a Red Sox loss. He was opposed by Tom Phoebus who was Baltimore's best pitcher.

Williams continued to search for the ideal combination as the team headed down the stretch. In this crucial game, he started Jerry Adair at second and he got Dalton Jones' left-handed bat into the lineup at third. His managerial Midas touch paid off again as both of them responded with four hits for the day, and Jones added five RBI for his season-high.

Lonborg pitched as well as he had pitched in any game all year. After six innings, he had given up only two hits and he had held the Orioles scoreless. With a safe 7-0 lead, Williams elected to pull him so he would have something extra for the last week of the season.

The Red Sox played the balance of the game like a racehorse with a twelve-length lead at the three quarters pole: they played just well enough to win. George Scott joined Adair and Jones in the four-hit club as Boston held on for an 11-7 victory. Manager Williams was less than enamored with the performance of his bullpen.

The Red Sox had passed their road trip test, coming home with a record of 6-2 for their trip through Detroit, Cleveland, and Baltimore. A number of Red Sox players had really stepped up with the season on the line. On the pitching staff, Jose Santiago had earned three of the six road trip wins, and John Wyatt and Gary Bell had each contributed one win and one save. George Scott was back in form raising his batting average to .303 and Dalton Jones had gone from a little used substitute to an offensive force.

But it was Carl Yastrzemski who came through with key hits time-and-time again. On the eight-game road trip Yaz batted .367, scored 13 runs, hit three home runs and stole his tenth base for good measure. And his hitting had been so productive all season that it overshadowed his Gold Glove-caliber defense in left field.

With four games left in the regular season Yaz had 42 home runs compared to 16 homers in the 1966 season. His batting average was 35 points above his 1966 average and he had driven in 30 more runs. When I asked Yaz how he accounted for the substantial differences year-to-year, he said, "The off-season between the 1966 season and 1967 was the first one that I wasn't going to college since I joined the Red Sox in 1961. I had signed with the Red Sox while I was a student at Notre Dame and I promised my parents I would get my degree. I attended Merrimack College [Andover, MA] in the off-season and I received my degree in 1966. Between school and my family I never had time to work out before spring training."

Before spring training in 1967, he entered into an intense physical training program at the Colonial Country Club in Wakefield, MA, not far from his home. "Gene Berde was the physical therapist there and when he first started working with me he said, 'I can't believe you are an athlete because you are in terrible shape!'" Yaz laughed. "But he worked with me all winter and when I got to Winter Haven I was my best shape ever."

In spite of being in the best condition of his career Yaz got off to a start that paralleled his earlier seasons. In the first 25 regular season games he had hit only two home runs and his batting average was hovering around .275. At that point he reached out to Bobby Doerr who was the Red Sox first base coach and hitting coach. "We went in early before a doubleheader (the May 14ᵗʰ doubleheader against the Tigers) and after an hour of hitting, Bobby suggested I hold my hands higher. I followed his advice and hit a home run in both games that day," he recalled. "Holding my hands higher gave me more power and helped me to pull the ball."

There had been almost no separation among the four teams during September: the Twins and White Sox had gone 16-9, while Boston and the Tigers had gone 14-9. But the Red Sox were heading home in good position. While they remained one-half game off the top, their four remaining games were all at home and they were nicely spaced over seven days. The fact that the next two games were against the eighth place Indians didn't hurt either.

Monday was an off day for the team, but when you're hot, you're hot. Boston moved back into a tie for first place without even lifting a bat as the pesky Angels defeated the Twins by a score of 9-2. Yaz took a little extra batting practice—as if he needed it—solidifying his reputation as the hardest-working player of the team.

As luck and the pitching rotation would have it, Gary Bell was on the mound to face his old teammates on Tuesday night. He drew Luis Tiant (11-8) as his opponent. Surprisingly, given the tight pennant race, only 16,652 fans showed up at Fenway Park on a clear night with temperatures in the 50s.

Perhaps the fans that would have filled the other half of the park had a premonition. Gary Bell just didn't have it that night and he was gone after four innings. El Tiante was a complete mystery to the Red Sox on the other hand, and he brought a 6-0 lead into the last of the seventh. At this point, Yaz produced the one bright note of the evening as he powered a three-run homer 450 feet into the center field bleachers. The blast was home run number forty-three which tied him with Ted Williams for the most home runs by a Red Sox left-handed hitter.

This highlight would have to suffice as Tiant dug a little deeper to hold on to the 6-3 win. The loss dropped the Red Sox back to third, one game behind the Twins and .001 behind the White Sox. Tomorrow would be another "must" game for Boston.

Dick Williams went with his ace Lonborg on just two days of rest. Lonborg had left with a 7-0 lead after only six innings on Sunday in Baltimore and the hope was that the relatively brief outing would allow him to be effective on short rest. In early August Jim had come back two days later after pitching four innings against the Twins and held the Kansas City A's to one run in seven-plus innings, but two days would prove inadequate in this case. He skated through the first, but the Indians jumped on him for four in the second and he was gone early, after only three innings of work.

The Red Sox couldn't seem to get anything going against starter Sonny Siebert. They showed signs of coming to life in the sixth. With the score 5-0, Jerry Adair led off with a single. Yaz kept things going with a single of his own. Reggie Smith ran the count to 2-0 and the 18,415 faithful started to get into it.

Major league baseball is played at a different level of intensity than other sports at the end of a season. In some sports, the clubs at the bottom of the pack seem to play as if a high draft choice is their top priority. In baseball, at least until very recently, the also-ran clubs challenge the contenders down to the last out. Cleveland manager Joe Adcock summoned reliever Bob Allen to complete the walk to Smith. Then he brought in his "horse," Stan Williams, who proceeded to strike out Jones, Scott and Petrocelli. The Boston bats went silent for the rest of the game. The final score was 6-0.

Many of the Red Sox players felt that the season was over for them following this disappointing loss. Although they were still just one game out of first place, the Twins only needed to win two out of their last three to win the whole thing and the White Sox were finishing up against the lowly A's and the Washington Senators.

Yastrzemski recalls wandering around the locker room to thank the other players for their efforts. He recounts the following conversation with Lonborg, "Way to go, Jimmy, you kept us in it."

"Thanks, Yaz, you did too."

But 1967 was a very unusual year. Shortly after the loss, the players remaining in the clubhouse learned that California had beaten the Twins. There was a faint glimmer of hope.

When Yaz returned to his home in Lynnfield, he told his wife, Carol, that the Red Sox were out of it. Still, he couldn't resist calling the Boston papers to check on the progress of the White Sox-A's doubleheader. After the A's won the first game, Carl began to rethink his position. When the A's won the second game, everyone had to rethink their positions.

Thursday turned out to be an off-day for all of the contenders. The Tigers were scheduled to play the Angels but they were rained out. The four teams stood in place with one and one half games separating the top club—Minnesota—and the fourth place White Sox. The Red Sox and Tigers were both only one game out, but the Red Sox led Detroit by percentage points because they had played two fewer games.

Yaz was so heartened by the A's sweep of the White Sox in Wednesday night's doubleheader that he came into Fenway for some more extra batting practice on the Thursday off day. "I thought we were dead after losing to the Indians Wednesday night," Yaz told the few reporters who were on hand for the impromptu work-out. "We were really lucky," he admitted, "But maybe this is just meant to be. I know we learned against the Indians that we have to be more aggressive!"

On Friday, the Red Sox were off again. The two off days served to build the tension surrounding the weekend showdown with the Twins who had already arrived in Boston to be well-rested for the next day. Jose Santiago was nominated to take his 11-4 record to the mound on Saturday.

There was some movement in the pennant race on Friday. The Chicago White Sox eliminated themselves by losing 1-0 to the seventh place Washington Senators. It rained in Detroit again and the Tigers faced back-to-back doubleheaders against the Angels on Saturday and Sunday.

The combinations of wins, losses and possible finishes among the three clubs seemed endless. One thing made it simple for the Red Sox: they had to win both games against the Twins.

No one felt this more strongly than Carl Yastrzemski. He had been preparing for this moment since childhood. Born August 22, 1939, in Southampton, New York, Carl Michael Yastrzemski came of age in nearby Bridgehampton, Long Island (population 3,000) where he often played alongside his father in local semipro games. Yaz's father Karol Yastrzemski (the name was Anglicized to Carl) and his uncle Tommy owned and worked a 70-acre potato farm.

A familiar sight: Yaz greeted at home.

Yaz's dad was a good local baseball player and he formed a semipro baseball team, the Bridgehampton White Eagles; he played shortstop and managed the team. It was almost entirely a family team, with Carl Sr.'s four brothers on the team, as well as two brothers-in-law and three cousins. The team played on Sundays and Yaz first played for the team at age 14 - young for a semipro player. Even at age 40, Carl's father was still "the guts of the ball club, a good shortstop and the best hitter of the team," Yaz recalled years later.

Some of Carl's teammates with the Boston Red Sox saw the influence of Carl's father in his son's drive for success. Former Red Sox catcher Russ Gibson remembered one time early on: "Yaz and myself, and two other guys, shared an apartment in Raleigh [North Carolina] when his dad came for a visit. We were all just starting out, but Yaz was hitting about .390 at the time. We all went off to play golf while Yaz visited with his father. When we got back, all his things were gone. When I asked Yaz what had happened, he said, 'My dad thinks I'm distracted living with you guys. He's moved me into an apartment by myself.'"

Things were just too hectic in Yaz's Lynnfield home on the Friday night before the first game against the Twins on Saturday afternoon. With the Yastrzemski home filled with relatives and visitors Yaz decided to check into a nearby hotel to see if he could get some sleep. Ironically, the hotel was adjacent to the facility where he worked out all winter to get in better shape. He tossed and turned for most of the night, retracing the path that led him to this point and anticipating game situations for the next day.

At about 6:00 a.m., Yaz gave up on sleep for the night and headed for the nearby golf course. As he walked the deserted links, he envisioned situations he might encounter and how he would respond. He had been on a tear for the whole month and the last ten games in particular. In these ten key games, Yaz had hit .444 and most of his sixteen hits had come at crucial times. He truly believed that he would get a hit every time he came to bat.

Yaz was in his seventh year with the Boston Rdd Sox, and his first six years had their ups and downs. Yaz batted .266 in his rookie year, with 11 homers and 80 RBI. There was no sophomore slump: The next year, Yastrzemski boosted his totals to .296, with 19 homers (and 43 doubles) and 94 RBI. His third year, he made the All-Star team for the first time, and improved dramatically again, winning the American League batting championship with a .321 mark. All the while, Yastrzemski was improving in left field, honing the solid defensive play that he is remembered for today.

He took a step back in 1964, but then he resumed adding to his totals, making the All-Star teams again in 1965 and 1966. Yaz's first six seasons in the major leagues had established him as one of the star players in the game. But his 1967 season would propel Carl Yastrzemski to a place among the elite players in the history of the game.

Yaz was relieved when he could finally go to the ballpark. On this particular day, he really talked it up in the clubhouse. Now that he was out from under the captaincy, he could be himself and let his natural emotions out. He made a special point to seek out starter Santiago. Jose promised to keep Harmon Killebrew—who was tied with Yaz for the home run lead in the American League—from hitting one out. Yaz promised he would hit one out for Santiago.

The game had the festive air of a World Series contest. Vice President Hubert Humphrey was there to cheer on his hometown Twins. Senators Ted Kennedy and Ed Brooke were both on hand. A total of 32,909 fans were ready to react to every pitch.

Yaz was nearly perfect at the plate in the two final games, the two most important games of the season. He singled in the first inning of the Saturday game, another of a long series of "must win" games for the Red Sox. In the third inning, Yaz struck out against Twins reliever Jim Perry, who had replaced the injured Jim Kaat. It would be the last time the Twins retired Yastrzemski that weekend.

In the fifth inning, with the game tied at one run apiece, Yaz singled, driving in Dalton Jones to put the Red Sox up 2-1. Then in the last of the seventh inning of this pivotal game Carl Yastrzemski landed the knock-out blow. George Scott had put the Red Sox up 3-2 with a sixth inning home run and there were two runners on with one out when Yaz stepped to the plate against Twins' lefthander Jim Merritt. When the count went to 3-1, Yaz drove a Merritt fastball into the Twins' bullpen to put Boston up 6-2, and Fenway Park erupted.

"When the count went to 3-1, I guessed he would throw me a high fastball," Yastrzemski told reporters after the game. "I knew it was gone as soon as I hit it," Yaz said. "I was out in front of the pitch good and [I] knew it would be gone." Years later Carl still remembered the fans reaction to his dramatic home run. "It started from the bleachers—those stands 380 feet away that I never thought I'd ever reach—and a roar started. It built as I circled each base, continued as the '3' went up in the scoreboard, to show we had a 6-2 lead, and the noise didn't end for three minutes. It continued long after I had gone into the dugout." It was his 44th home run of the season putting him one up on the Twins' Harmon Killebrew. The sellout crowd in Fenway Park gave Yaz a standing ovation as he trotted out to take his spot in left field to begin the eighth inning.

The Twins gave the Red Sox a bit of a scare in the top of the ninth inning when Harmon Killebrew hit his 44th home run to close the gap to 6-4 Red Sox, but Gary Bell, pitching in relief of starter Jose Santiago, got Tony Oliva to line out to third baseman Jerry Adair, and the celebration was on! Carl Yastrzemski was as satisfied with this victory as he had been with any in his career. He had produced three hits including the decisive home run. He was certain that they would win the next day and he was sure that he would play a major role.

Yaz did indeed play a major role the following day. When Sunday's game was over, he had achieved an incredible record over the 12 final, crucial games. Here are the highlights of his 12-game rampage:

Carl Yastrzemski: September 18-October 1, 1967							
G	AB	Runs	Hits	HR	RBI	BA	SA
12	44	14	23	5	16	.523	.955

Yaz had gone twenty-three for forty-four for an unbelievable batting average of .523. He had driven in sixteen runs in the twelve games, scored fourteen and banged out five home runs. But even those awesome numbers don't begin to tell the story. Hit after hit had been a critical one and homer after homer had been a game-winner. Most baseball observers call it the greatest exhibition of clutch hitting in baseball history.

Yaz went on to star in the World Series that followed. He had ten hits in the seven game series and batted .400. His two homers in the second game carried the day for Boston. When you combine the last twelve games and the Series, Yaz was thirty-three for sixty-nine for an out-of-this-world batting average under pressure of .478.

Yaz came within one vote (one writer inexplicably voted for utility player Caesar Tovar of the Twins who batted .267 for the 1967 season) of a unanimous selection as the Most Valuable Player of the American League. He was selected by *Sports Illustrated* as the "1967 Sportsman of the Year" at year-end. And he achieved baseball's Triple Crown, leading the American League in batting (.326), runs batted in (121), and home runs (44). In all the baseball seasons that followed, no player had been able to match his Triple Crown feat until Miguel Cabrera did so in 2012, 45 years later. Yaz also led the league in hits (189), runs (112) total bases (360), and slugging percentage, not to mention on-base percentage. His On-Base plus Slugging (OPS) was 1.040.

The next year, 1968, Yaz won his third batting title with a .301 mark. This was, for sure, the Year of the Pitcher, and Yaz was the only batter in the league to crack .300, 11 points ahead of runner-up Danny Cater. Only four batters hit .285 or above. And when compared with the American League overall batting average, his .301 average was the equivalent of Bill Terry's .401 for the New York Giants in 1930. But his home run total fell to 23 from 44 and his RBI total fell to 74 from 121. Yaz played through injuries and he was targeted by opposing teams from Opening Day on, but there was some rumbling from fans that he was a one-season wonder.

Between 1965 and 1979, Yaz was named to 15 consecutive All-Star teams. The game he remembers best is the 1970 All-Star Game held in Riverfront Stadium in Cincinnati. Yaz had four hits, to go along with a run scored and an RBI to earn him MVP honors that year, even though his AL team lost to the NL in 12 innings. He and Ted Williams [1946] are the only two American Leaguers with four hits in an All-Star Game.

Yaz with Jean Yawkey.

When I asked him about this record Yaz, never one to focus on personal statistics, responded, "I never knew that before. To tell you the truth, I was so sick of losing to the National League that I didn't pay much attention to that stuff."

It is often written that Yaz had a "career year" in 1967, but never again approached that standard. It should be noted that in 1970 he led the American League in runs scored, on-base percentage, total bases, and slugging percentage; and he lost the batting title by just .0004 to Alex Johnson. When coupled with his all-time high of 23 stolen bases, you have a year that would have been a career year for almost any other player. In fact, you can make a strong case that the only things missing for Yaz in 1970, was the strong Red Sox supporting cast he had in 1967. There was no Dick Williams to stir things up, no Cy Young pitcher to win the must games, and no super-sub to save the day, so Yaz's outstanding season went relatively unnoticed.

In February 1971, Carl Yastrzemski signed a three-year contract that was reported to pay him $500,000 over the three seasons. At that time his contract was the largest in baseball history. Over the next several seasons Yaz settled into something of a routine. He became a .280-type hitter who would hit fifteen or so homers and knock in 80-85 runs. He gradually came to spend more time at first base than left field. In many ways, he was happier with his relatively low profile out of the spotlight. Yaz never thought of himself as a superstar. He certainly didn't have a superstar's dimensions at 5' 11" and 175 pounds. He came from a hard-working background and he thought of himself to be an above-average, blue-collar ballplayer.

Boston fans had a bit of a love-hate relationship with Carl Yastrzemski. They loved him for 1967 and they loved the fact that he was in the lineup day after day. They hated the fact that he couldn't get the team to duplicate 1967 single-handedly. And they hated the fact that he was not Ted Williams. Ted was larger than life but Yaz was closer to "every-fan." Yaz was largely indifferent to the fans' wishes; he just wanted to be Carl Yastrzemski.

The year 1972 was a frustrating one. The season started late, due to struggles between players and owners. Teams agreed to simply play out the schedule without worrying about whether one team played more games than another. There was no chance of a playoff tie. The Tigers had a record of 84-69 going into the October 2 game, and the Red Sox were a marginally-better 84-68. Whichever team won two of the three games would win the pennant. The Tigers took a 1-0 lead in the first game, but Yaz doubled in the top of the third to tie it, and the Red Sox would have scored at least one more run (with Yaz safe at third with a triple) except that Luis Aparicio stumbled after rounding third and retreated to the bag where he met up with the oncoming Carl, who was called out. This was a pivotal play and the Red Sox lost the pennant by a half-game.

Carl and the fans had a reconciliation of sorts in 1975. By then he was thirty-six, and after fifteen years in town, he qualified as an institution. Besides, the gold dust twins of Fred Lynn and Jim Rice were in the spotlight and Carl could do his workmanlike job without being the center of attention. Yaz actually had a subpar year in 1975, batting just .269 with 14 homers and 60 RBI, but his play throughout the postseason reminded fans that he had always been at his best in clutch situations throughout his career. His stellar play in the field and at bat carried over to the American League Championship Series against Oakland (he was 5-for-11, with a home run and two RBI) to the World Series against the Cincinnati Reds. Although the Red Sox lost to the Reds in seven games in one of the greatest World Series ever played, Yaz had scored 11 runs and batted .350 during the ten postseason games. As in 1967, the Red Sox fell just short.

Carl Yastrzemski played eight more years for the Boston Red Sox. He was used largely as a designated hitter and his average settled down in the range of .270. He could still hit for power on occasion and as his 23rd season came to a close, he had clouted sixteen home runs in only 131 games. From 1976 to 1983, Carl Yastrzemski made the American League All-Star team six times. On July 14, 1977, he notched his 2,655th hit, moving past Ted Williams as the all-time Red Sox base hit leader. In 1979, he became the first American Leaguer to accumulate both 400 homers (he reached the plateau on July 24) and 3,000 lifetime hits (his September 12 single off New York's Jim Beattie was #3,000). Back on June 16, he'd banged out his 1,000th extra base hit.

On October 1, 1983, the next-to-the-last game of the season, 33,491 of the Fenway Faithful gathered to pay tribute to Carl Yastrzemski. The pre-game ceremony lasted for about an hour, and then came Yaz's turn to speak. After 23 years of never flinching in a pressure situation, Yaz broke down and cried when he stepped to the microphone. Once he regained his composure, he asked for a moment of silence for his mother and for former Red Sox owner Tom Yawkey. After thanking his family and everyone connected with the Red Sox, he finished with the words, "New England, I love you."

Carl Yastrzemski had played in 3,308 major-league ballgames—the record until Pete Rose topped it the next year—and played for 23 years for one team: the Boston Red Sox.

A few months after Carl retired, his son Carl Jr. was drafted by the Atlanta Braves in the third round of the January 1984 draft. Known as "Mike," the younger Yastrzemski played five years of minor-league ball, making it all the way to a couple of years of Triple A, but not to the majors. He came back to work in Massachusetts, but died of a heart attack in September 2004 at the age of 43.

Mike's son, Mike, Jr., grew up in the greater Boston area, graduated from St. John's Prep in Danvers, MA, and then matriculated at Vanderbilt University. After an excellent career at Vanderbilt, he was drafted in the 13th round of the 2013 draft by the Baltimore Orioles. As of this writing in 2016, he has progressed nicely through the Orioles minor league system over three seasons.

In January of 1989, in his first year of eligibility, Carl Yastrzemski was elected to Baseball's Hall of Fame. His vote total that year was among the highest recorded in the history of the Hall of Fame. On August 6, 1989, the Red Sox retired his uniform number and it still hangs today on the right-field facade, overlooking Fenway's outfield.

The baseball careers of Ted Williams and Carl Yastrzemski are inexorably linked. Their paths crossed directly for the last time when they were introduced before the 1999 All-Star Game at Fenway Park as two of the 100 greatest baseball players of the 20th century. The crowd reaction when Yaz was introduced shook the ballpark to its ancient foundations. The response of the crowd when Ted was driven from the far reaches of center field to a spot near the pitchers' mound nearly equaled the decibel count of the jet fly-by following the National Anthem. At the home opener in 2005, Carl Yastrzemski and Johnny Pesky joined to raise the 2004 World Championship banner that flew over Fenway throughout the 2005 season.

Over the years I have interviewed 22 members of the 1967 Red Sox, and most of his more prominent teammates from his 23 seasons with the ball club. They have all told me that Yaz worked as hard as any teammate they ever had. Russ Gibson of the 1967 Red Sox captured the overall assessment of Yastrzemski's teammates when he said, "We all knew that Yaz was headed to the Hall of Fame. His game was just at a whole different level than the rest of us. But he never asked or expected to be treated any differently and nobody outworked him. We all loved him as a teammate," Gibby emphasized.

In his biography, *Yaz*, Carl Yastrzemski talks about what 1967 meant to him: "You can't kill what we had and what we did just because we lost one game in October. It remains a part of people to this day. They call it the Impossible Dream or the Miracle of Fenway. For me it always went beyond a slogan. It wrapped me up forever with New England. No matter what, I would always be a part of them, the fans, the team, the city. It became our permanent connection to each other, like a family tie. And nothing could ever break that. Not to a Yastrzemski."

Carl Michael Yastrzemski: the man we affectionately call Yaz.

Chapter 12

Jose Santiago: From the Bullpen to Center Stage

Boston Red Sox vs. Minnesota Twins, Saturday, September 30, 1967

Jose Santiago, a twenty-seven-year-old right handed native of Juana Diaz, Puerto Rico, was the surprise starting pitcher for the "win or go home" next-to-last game of the 1967 Boston Red Sox regular season. Santiago was pitching in his 50th game of the season but he was making only his 12th start for the Impossible Dream Red Sox team. In fact, it was only his 47th start in the big leagues, and clearly he was pitching in the game of his life. But Jose had been pitching in the Puerto Rican Winter League since he was age 20, and by age 22 he was the San Juan Senadores best pitcher. His seven years of experience in the Puerto Rican Winter League came at a time when every team had a large number of big league regulars on their roster, and games were played before large, enthusiastic crowds. Jose Santiago was confident that he was the right choice to start this all-important game and that he would pitch well.

Saturday September 30, was a beautiful early fall day in Boston, following a heavy rain the night before. By game time at 2:05 EDT, the temperature had reached the low 70's, and with full sun over Fenway Park, it was unseasonably warm. It was a near perfect day for the most important game to date in the Impossible Dream Red Sox season. The Twins had a one-game lead over the Red Sox and the Detroit Tigers, and everyone at Fenway Park knew the Red Sox had to win to stay alive in the American League pennant race.

Jose Santiago had been named as the starting pitcher for the big game and it was the most important game of his career to date. Almost 50 years later I asked Jose if he was nervous when he took the mound against the Twins in the first inning, and he replied, "I was more excited than I was nervous. It was the biggest game I had ever pitched to that point. I was certainly anxious, but nervous, not really."

Santiago was in his second season with the Red Sox. Boston had acquired Jose from the Kansas City Athletics before the 1966 season. He had started 28 games for the 1966 Red Sox and managed to win 12 games for the ninth place team. He had nine wins by the All-Star game, but he came up with a dead arm and he was only able to make two starts in September.

The Red Sox asked him not to pitch in the Puerto Rican Winter League that offseason so he would be fresh for spring training in 1967. But in January Red Sox assistant general manager Haywood Sullivan told reporters, "Jose did what we asked him to but local fans were so upset that he wasn't pitching that they threw rocks at his house and generally caused a terrible disturbance. We had to give him permission to go ahead and pitch." Asked all these years later if it really happened that way, Jose just smiles.

At the end of spring training in 1967, he had been told that he would spend the season in the Red Sox bullpen. "Sal Maglie [Red Sox pitching coach] told me 'Jose, you are only a seven inning pitcher, so we are going to move you to the bullpen.' I have to laugh because today if a pitcher lasts seven innings he gets a standing ovation," Jose chuckled. "But at the time I told Maglie, 'If it will help the team, of course I'll do it.'"

Jose still remembered what a big adjustment it was to be exiled to the bullpen. "I had primarily been a starter my whole career," he emphasized. "I didn't even know how to warm up properly as a reliever. As a reliever you have to be ready after maybe 12-15 pitches sometimes." It was the solidarity of the bullpen crew that ultimately helped Santiago to adjust to his new role. "John Wyatt, who had been my teammate in Kansas City, and Don McMahon, before he was traded, both taught me how to prepare and how to warm up to be ready to go in as a reliever. They really helped me out of a tough spot."

Through mid-August, Santiago had pitched in 36 games for the Red Sox, 30 in relief, and six as a spot starter. On August 19, Dick Williams gave him a start against the California Angels, and Santiago lasted only 4 2/3 innings, giving up six runs in a game Boston ultimately won 12-11. But the very next day, in the second game of a doubleheader, after the Red Sox had come back from an 8-0 deficit to take a 9-8 lead, Jose pitched two scoreless innings to get back into Dick Williams's good graces.

He got a start three days later against the Washington Senators, and he pitched seven strong innings, holding the Solons to just two hits and two runs. He followed that outstanding outing with two strong starts against the Chicago White Sox. But then he was put back in the bullpen where he made six effective relief appearances in important games down the stretch. A crucial, complete game win in a spot start against the Orioles on September 22, led Dick Williams to select Santiago for the start in the season's crucial 161st game.

Red Sox fans, which included just about everyone in Boston and New England for that matter, just couldn't get enough information about their heroes. The September 30th morning edition of *The Boston Globe* included an article by Will McDonough headlined "Wife Coaches Santiago: She's His Right Arm," based on an interview with Jose where he explains that his lovely wife Edna knew nothing about baseball when they were married but she had made herself a "near expert." He went on to tell McDonough that after a nice dinner on Friday night the Santiago's would sit at their kitchen table and go over the Twin's lineup. "She'll ask me things like 'How are you going to pitch Oliva.'" Jose went on to say, "I always make sure her seat is behind home plate where I can see her. Sometimes she will notice little things and give me a signal."

Jose Santiago pitched in 50 games for the 1967 Red Sox.

Jose Santiago insists that the Red Sox clubhouse was very loose before the Saturday afternoon game. Carl Yastrzemski and Harmon Killebrew of the Twins were tied for the lead in American League home runs with 43 each, and Jose remembered that he walked across the clubhouse and said, "I'm going to tell you something Yaz. I promise you Killebrew isn't going to hit one out of the park off me today. He laughed and promised he would hit a home run for me."

Fenway Park had a distinct World Series feeling on Saturday with the overflowing crowd, the bunting ringing the field boxes, and the number of politicians preening in the box seats between home plate and the Red Sox dugout. There were about 125 additional sports writers on hand, and many of them were seated out in sections one and two of the right field grandstand. According to Red Sox announcer Ken Coleman, "Multiple Western Union teletype machines were set up all over the grandstand roof behind the main press box." About ten minutes before the first pitch, Vice President Hubert H. Humphrey and Massachusetts Senator Ted Kennedy emerged from the Red Sox dugout and took their seats in the front row directly behind the Red Sox on-deck circle. Vice President Humphrey was there to root on the Twins from his home state of Minnesota, and Senator Kennedy was carrying on the family tradition of rooting for the Red Sox. Ted was the grandson of John "Honey Fitz" Fitzgerald, who had been the Mayor of Boston and the leader of the "Royal Rooters," the colorful organization that supported the Red Sox from their inception in 1901, through their last World Championship in 1918.

The Red Sox reported a paid attendance of 32,909, and hundreds of thousands of fans watched the telecast featuring announcers Ken Coleman, Ned Martin, and former Red Sox pitcher Mel Parnell. It is hard to believe fifty years later, but the last two games of the season were not scheduled to be televised because when the schedule was set no one expected the Red Sox to be contending for anything. When this omission came to light, Boston's Channel-5 was flooded with phone calls from irate Red Sox fans. But Channel-5 held off announcing that the two games had been added to their schedule until one week before the big weekend. Happily, the Chanel-5 telecast has been preserved in video format and it is the oldest baseball telecast in color known to exist.

It is clear in viewing the telecast for the first time in many years that the Red Sox may have been loose in the clubhouse before the game, but it still takes them a half-inning to dial down their tension. On the first play of the game, Twins shortstop Zoilo Versalles lines a single directly at Yaz in leftfield and he boots it. The ball bounces off Yaz's chest and rolls away. Yaz immediately retrieves it so there is no harm, but the next hitter, second baseman Caesar Tovar fouls a ball that catcher Russ Gibson loses sight of, and it bounces harmlessly behind home plate. Tovar flies out to Reggie Smith in center field, so again, there is no harm. But Jose Santiago is working too quickly and he walks Harmon Killebrew. The next batter, Tony Oliva lines a single into center scoring Versalles, and even before every fan in the overflow crowd has taken a seat in Fenway Park the Twins are up 1-0.

Dick Williams wasn't fooling around in this critical game. Before Versalles even touches home plate with the first run, Williams had Gary Bell up and throwing in the Red Sox bullpen. The next hitter, right fielder Bob Allison, slashes a grounder between third and shortstop for a single. The Red Sox are saved by Harmon Killebrew's lack of speed and Carl Yastrzemski's strong arm in left field. Killebrew wisely holds up at third base to load the bases. Dick Williams bolts out of the dugout immediately and makes a bee-line for Santiago. Williams wasn't going to stand on the protocol of sending pitching coach Maglie out to the mound first, not after taking his team this far.

All these years later Santiago didn't remember exactly what Dick Williams said to him on the mound in the first inning. "He asked if I felt okay and was I going to be able to get out of it. I told him I was fine. I think he wanted to give me a break and maybe slow me down." The next batter was the dangerous Rod Carew who came into the game hitting .293. Carew swung at Santiago's first pitch and sent a hard line drive directly into the glove of Jerry Adair who is playing third base. Twins center fielder Ted Uhlaender came to the plate with two outs and the bases still filled with Twins. Santiago went to 3-1 against him, causing the crowd to buzz, but Uhlaender grounded to Mike Andrews at second base who tossed the ball to first baseman George Scott for an easy out that ends the inning. The Red Sox are down by one run but it could have been much worse.

Jose R. Santiago-Alfonso was born in Juana Diaz, Puerto Rico, on August 15, 1940. Juana Diaz is located about ten miles northeast of Ponce, near south-central Puerto Rico. Juana Diaz was a city with a population of about 35,000 when Jose was a youngster, and it was known for its sugar cane and marble.

His father, Alejandro Santiago, loved baseball and he had been a pretty good third baseman growing up according to Jose. "He and my mother, Merida Alfonso, ran a small grocery store for the sugar cane workers. We didn't have a lot of money but my dad bought some bats and balls, enough equipment that the kids in the neighborhood could play. We played against other kids from Juana Diaz," he remembered. "We loved it. I mostly played center field."

The Red Sox were facing Twins lefthander Jim Kaat who was trying for his eighth straight win in September. Of his seven wins six of them were complete games and the seventh was eight full innings. Kaat was not an overpowering pitcher and he fit the classic definition of a "stylish southpaw." He excelled at changing speeds, big breaking balls, and pinpoint location. He had faced the Red Sox three times in 1967 with one win in a 2-1 decision over Red Sox ace Jim Lonborg, and two no-decisions.

Mike Andrews led off for the Red Sox and he quickly got the crowd back into it with a sharp single into center field, just beyond the range of shortstop Versalles. But Jerry Adair grounded directly to Carew at second for a tailor-made double play. That brought Carl Yastrzemski to the plate with two outs and the bases empty. Yaz had been hitting about .500 over the previous ten games so you could sense that everyone in Fenway Park expected him to get a hit. He didn't disappoint, stinging a line drive down the line in right, heading for the corner. But the field is definitely soggy, and it slowed the ball down, causing Yaz to hold up at first base. Cleanup hitter Ken Harrelson followed Yaz but he disappointed the crowd by striking out on a big Jim Kaat roundhouse curveball.

"I felt more comfortable in the second inning," Santiago remembered. His memory is on target as he got the first batter, catcher Jerry Zimmerman, to pop out to George Scott at first base just a step onto the outfield grass. Zimmerman was followed by pitcher Kaat, who wasn't much of a threat. He grounded to Andrews at second for an easy second out. This rolled the Twins over to the top of the order to Zoilo Versalles who had singled to left field just one inning before. This time Jose kept the ball down and Versalles grounded to shortstop Rico Petrocelli for the third out. Santiago needed an easy, quick inning and that is exactly what he got. "My stuff was good from the beginning but I was working too quickly and I was wild high in the first inning," he admitted.

"I wanted to continue to play center field," Jose remembered looking back to his youth, "because I wanted to play every day. I fooled around pitching a little, but all I had was a strong arm—no breaking stuff." He continued to play in the field through high school, but when his father saw him pitch one day he convinced Jose that he had a better future in baseball as a pitcher. "When I went to Catholic University in Ponce, the coaches, Carlos Negron and Gonzalez Pato made me into a pitcher. I owe them a lot. And Cefo Conde, who had pitched in the Negro Leagues, was a big help also. Cefo was Sandy Alomar, Sr.'s uncle, and Sandy has been my lifelong friend."

In the last of the second inning, George Scott, who was hitting exactly .300 when he came to the plate, got things going with a single up the middle into center field. But Petrocelli flied out softly to Oliva in right field, Reggie Smith struck out swinging on a tantalizing Kaat curveball, and catcher Gibson took a called third strike to end the inning.

Caesar Tovar popped harmlessly to George Scott, who barely had to move from his position at first base, to open the Twins' third inning. But hammerin' Harmon Killebrew swung so hard at a 1-0 Santiago fastball that he dropped down on one knee after sending a deep fly ball towards the wall in left field. For a moment it looked like Jose had broken his promise to Yaz to hold Killebrew homerless, but the drive hit halfway up to the top of the wall, and Harmon had to settle for a double. Santiago got Oliva to strike out swinging after a long at-bat, and he sent Bob Allison down on strikes as well, ending the threat.

At the tender age of 17, Jose came as close to being a member of the New York Giants as you can be without having your name in their record book. "My friend told me that scouts were holding a tryout in Juana Diaz. I knew my father wanted me to finish college but I snuck away from the store and went to the tryout." Legendary New York Giant scout Alex Pompez liked what he saw and he wanted to sign young Santiago and he was willing to offer a $25,000 bonus.

Pompez convinced Alejandro Santiago that Jose would do well professionally and that there was a good chance that he would make the big leagues. Alejandro signed the contract for Jose and Pompez agreed that the $25,000 would be paid when Jose reported to spring training. Jose reported to spring training and did well but no money appeared. When Alejandro called the Giants they assured him that the money was coming and Jose reported to Class D ball where he was scheduled to pitch on Opening Night. When the money still didn't arrive, Alejandro sent his son a plane ticket and Jose flew back to Puerto Rico and returned to Catholic University!

The Red Sox half of third started quite routinely as Jim Kaat picked up his fourth strikeout with Jose Santiago as his victim. But as soon as Santiago was retired Kaat motioned for catcher Zimmerman to come to the mound and after they talked, plate umpire Jim Honochick gave Kaat permission to throw a few test pitches. After throwing five practice pitches Kaat said he was ready to go. Kaat threw two balls to Mike Andrews and then motioned to the Twins dugout to let them know he couldn't go on. It turned out that Kaat had injured a ligament in his pitching elbow. "Every time I threw it was like hitting your funny bone. The elbow vibrated,"

How glad were the Red Sox to see Jim Kaat out of the game? Russ Gibson told me years later, "I don't think we could have beaten him. He had absolutely pinpoint control that day. Everything was on the black and his curve was unhittable." Dalton Jones echoed Gibson's comments. "Man we were glad to see him go!" Dalton said years later.

The Twins brought in 31-year-old right-handed pitcher Jim Perry to replace Kaat, and Perry was given all the time he needed to warm up. Perry had gone 8-7 that season in 11 starts and 26 relief appearances. One of those starts had been a complete game, 10-3 win over the Red Sox on July 29 at Fenway Park. .

Considering the circumstances Perry pitched extremely well in the third inning. After Andrews walked he went to 2-2 on Adair, and then forced Jerry to hit a soft roller to shortstop Versalles. Zoilo charged the ball but his only play was to first. Now Perry had to face the hottest hitter on the planet, Carl Yastrzemski, with the tying run on second base. Yaz ran the count to 3-2 and then, proving he was merely mortal, he struck out on a Perry fastball.

Santiago got the ever-dangerous Rod Carew to hit a lazy groundball to George Scott on his first pitch of the fourth inning and Jose barely beat Carew to the first base bag to take Scott's throw for the first out. Then Ted Uhlaender hit a deep fly ball to the warning track in front of the Red Sox bullpen. Ken Harrelson appeared to catch the ball but it clanged off his glove while Uhlaender raced to third base. Santiago was in another tough spot with a runner at third and one out, but with the infield in to the edge of the grass, he reached back and struck out Jerry Zimmerman for the second out. When pitcher Perry flied to Reggie Smith in front of the center-field wall, Santiago and the Red Sox had dodged another bullet.

Shortly after returning to Catholic University, Kansas City A's scout Felix Delgado began following Santiago and he quickly realized that Jose had big league potential. After watching him pitch an outstanding game against the University of San Juan, Delgado arranged to sit down with Jose and his father. Delgado offered a $15,000 bonus payable immediately, and Jose Santiago signed a contract with Kansas City Athletics in 1959.

Jose Santiago began his professional baseball career in the United States as an 18-year old in Grand Island, Nebraska, and after 15 games there he was moved up to Olean, New York. Asked if it was an adjustment, Jose laughed and said, "Grand Island and Olean were a long way from Puerto Rico. But I had picked up English in high school and I adjusted pretty well," he recalled.

Santiago spent seven years in the Kansas City system, winning 15 games at Albuquerque, NM, in 1960, and 12 games at Portland, OR, at Triple-A. He made his major league debut for the Athletics in 1963, pitching a scoreless inning against the Yankees in Kansas City. "I enjoyed my time with the A's. I got along really well with Charlie Finley (former Athletics owner), and I met my wife Edna there. I also got to know Sully (former Red Sox minority owner Haywood Sullivan) very well."

Jose's progress to the big leagues had been slowed by a badly sprained ankle and an appendectomy. But when he became available after the 1965 season, the Red Sox quickly grabbed him on the advice of Haywood Sullivan, who had moved to the front office in Boston.

Jim Perry had very little trouble with the Red Sox 4-5-6 hitters in the last of the fourth. Ken Harrelson struck out, George Scott grounded harmlessly to Carew at second base, and Rico Petrocelli hit a weak foul popup that Harmon Killebrew caught in the first base coach's box.

Santiago was just as effective against the Twins top of the order in the fifth inning. He began by striking out Zoilo Versalles on a fastball and then he got Tovar to bounce routinely to Jerry Adair for the second out. Jose pitched carefully to Killebrew and fell behind 3-0. But he froze Killebrew with a 3-2, side-arm curveball and Harmon was called out on strikes.

"We weren't a very good team in 1966," Jose admitted referring to his Red Sox club that lost 90 games and finished one-half game above the cellar-dwelling New York Yankees. "But we started to play better in the second half. And my wife Edna and I loved the city and the fans from the beginning. Our oldest son, Alex, was just a baby when we moved there in 1966. We had a nice apartment in Brookline, not too far from Fenway.

"In 1966 we had guys like Lonborg, and Scotty (first baseman George), and Joe Foy who were starting to come into their own. And guys like Yaz, Rico and Tony C were team leaders by then. We played very well in the second half of the season, but hardly anybody noticed because we were so terrible in the first half!" Jose laughed in remembrance. "And then we got a look at guys like Mike Andrews and Reggie

Smith who came up in September and we knew they would help us in 1967."

Jim Perry, who was 21-9 lifetime against the Red Sox to this point, prepared to face Reggie Smith, who had turned around to bat lefty against the right-handed veteran. Rookie Smith, who had originally signed with the Twins as an 18-year-old prospect had come on strong in the second half of the 1967 season. Smith slapped Perry's fourth pitch towards left center and when the ball hit about half way up the Green Monster he hustled into second base with a stand-up double.

Catcher Gibson was scheduled up next, but manager Williams, pulling out all the stops, sent up Boston's best pinch hitter, Dalton Jones, to bat for him. Dalton's job was to hit the ball to the right side to at least advance Smith to third base and Jones hit a hard ground ball directly at second baseman Carew. At the last minute Jones' grounder took a bad hop, handcuffing Carew, and Dalton hustled down the line for a base hit that moved Smith to third. Now it was Perry's turn to bear down and he struck out pitcher Santiago and lead-off hitter Andrews.

With two outs and runners on first and third, Jerry Adair hit a blooper beyond Carew at second and in front of Uhlaender who was charging in from center field. Adair's flare into shallow center field scored Smith with the tying run and advanced Jones to third. Then Carl Yastrzemski did what he seemed to do in every game: he singled to drive in Dalton Jones with the go-ahead run. Perry got Ken Harrelson to pop out to Caesar Tovar and the fifth inning ended with Boston leading 2-1.

The Red Sox lead was short-lived as the Twins touched Santiago for one run in the top of the sixth to tie the game at two apiece. The inning began quietly enough with Tony Oliva fouling out to Jerry Adair. Bob Allison walked but Jose struck out Rod Carew for the second out. Then Ted Uhlaender drove a ground ball just out of Rico Petrocelli's reach and the Twins had runners on first and second. Williams had Gary Bell warming up (again!) along with Sparky Lyle and the skipper made another visit to Santiago. "He just wanted to know if I was getting tired," Jose remembered. "I told him I was fine."

Twins manager Cal Ermer sent Rich Reese up to pinch hit for catcher Zimmerman, and Reese obliged by grounding another hit just to Rico Petrocelli's right, allowing Allison to score the tying run from second base. Ermer went to his bench again and sent up Frank Kostro to hit for Jim Perry. When Santiago walked Kostro to load the bases, Red Sox fans feared the worst. But Jose reached back once more and came in with a terrific sidearm curve getting Versalles to lift an easy pop up to Jerry Adair. The Red Sox were out of the inning with just one run scored. Looking back Jose said, "That pitch I threw to Versalles was my best pitch of the game." The Twins brought veteran right-handed reliever Ron Kline in to replace Jim Perry in the Sox half of the sixth inning. George Scott was the first batter Kline faced, had come into the game batting .300, which was a vast improvement over his .245 rookie average in 1966. His home run total had dropped from 27 the season before to 18, and he hadn't homered since August 19, but the tradeoff was well worth it.

Legendary Red Sox announcer Ned Martin had just finished telling viewers how Scott's production had benefited from his loss of seven pounds when Kline threw his first pitch. Scott jumped all over it and sent a missile screaming in the direction of straightaway center field. Within seconds his rocket had landed about ten rows deep among the jubilant fans in dead-center field. The Boomer had picked a near perfect moment to break his homerless streak.

Kline retired Petrocelli with a fly ball to short right field and then he got Reggie Smith on a line drive to fairly deep center field. Finally he retired Jose Tartabull, who had come in to replace Ken Harrelson in right field on a called third strike.

When Jose Santiago took the mound to start the seventh inning Red Sox fans knew that he would be on a very short leash. He had held a strong Twins' offense to just two runs in six innings, which is probably the best Dick Williams had hoped for before the game, and he had wiggled out of jams in the first, fourth and sixth innings. Along the way he had given up seven hits and four walks to go with the Twins' two runs. And how did Jose feel, "I was tired,' he recalled, "but I still had good stuff. I was getting them out and I still hoped to go all the way."

It was very obvious that Santiago still had some gas in his tank as he mowed the Twins down in the top of the seventh inning. Facing three of the Twins most dangerous hitters—Caesar Tovar, Killebrew, and Tony Olivia—he set Minnesota down 1-2-3.

With 32,000+ Red Sox fans on their feet for the seventh inning stretch, the general agreement was that this was one heck of a ball-game—and that the Red Sox just might live to play another day! With Carl Yastrzemski ready to bat if one runner reached in the seventh, there was every reason for optimism. And they must have willed some more good Sox luck since dame fortune was about to smile on them again.

Dick Williams showed a lot of faith in Jose Santiago by sending him up to bat to lead off the Red Sox half of the seventh inning. "I had told Dick [Williams] that I still felt good. And I was a pretty good-hitting pitcher," Jose insisted. He was greeted by an extended standing ovation that lasted until he was set in the batter's box. Jose swung at Kline's first pitch and grounded sharply towards shortstop but Versalles handled it easily and there was one away. The next batter was Andrews who offered at Kline's third pitch, tried to check his swing, but ended up with a swinging bunt in the direction of third base. Kline was off the mound quickly to field the ball but Andrews was even quicker down the line and he beat Kline's high throw to Killebrew at first base

Jerry Adair stepped to the plate at 1-3 for the afternoon and he fouled off the first three pitches he saw. With the count 0-2, Adair hit a one-hopper directly back at Kline that had double play written all over it. Kline grabbed the ball cleanly, wheeled around, and threw a perfect strike to Zoilo Versalles covering second for the first out. But wait: Versalles dropped the ball before he even had control of it!

Just like that the Red Sox had runners on first and second with only one out and Carl Yastrzemski coming to the plate. Kline had faced three batters and nobody had hit a ball beyond the pitcher's mound, but Twins manager Cal Ermer played the percentages and signaled the left-handed Jim Merritt in from the bullpen to face Boston's—and the planet's—hottest hitter. Pitching carefully, reliever Merritt ran the count to 3-1. When the count went to 3-1, Yaz was sitting on Merritt's fastball. Yaz got his wish and took a big swing.

Here's Ken Coleman's call on the Red Sox TV network, underlining that back in the day announcers were willing to let the picture tell the story: "Deep to right field, [dramatic pause until the ball drops into the Twins' bullpen, and then] number 44!" Carl had done it again with a three-run homer at the most crucial moment.

That achievement symbolizes Yaz's season as well as any single moment. Most fans believed that Yaz would homer in that at-bat. Yaz believed he would do it. In fact, he acknowledged that during the last two weeks of the season he was trying to hit a home run in almost every at-bat. Most fans and players hope for a home run. On that turn at bat, on that day, in that special year, everyone **knew** that Yaz would hit a home run.

Years later Carl remembered the crowd's reaction to his home run. "It may have been the most memorable home run and ovation of my big league career." And you could almost **feel** the jubilant, standing-room-only crowd relax a little bit with the Red Sox in the lead 6-2. Merritt then retired Elson Howard on a fly ball to Bob Allison in left field, and George Scott on a ground ball to shortstop, but the damage had been done.

The crowd stood and cheered for Carl Yastrzemski as he headed to his position in left field, and the volume increased as Jose Santiago made his way to the mound. Asked about his pitch count at that point, Jose replied, "What's a pitch count?" and laughed. "Nobody talked about pitch counts in those days. They handed you the ball and you went out and did your best to go all nine innings." Jose walked Bob Allison on five pitches and Dick Williams headed for the mound. "He asked me if I was tired and I had to tell him, 'yes.' I wanted to keep going but it was time to get someone fresh in," Jose admitted. Williams motioned Gary Bell in from the bullpen and Jose Santiago walked off to a tremendous standing ovation. "That cheering from the crowd, with everyone standing, is one of my greatest moments in baseball. Even now, just telling you about and thinking about it, I get the chills."

Bell got Rod Carew to fly out to Jose Tartabull in medium right field for the first out. It was obvious that Tartabull was bothered by the sun and Dick Williams raced out to Mike Andrews at second base, apparently asking him to help out Jose and Reggie Smith on any fly balls hit out to the sun fields. Three pitches later, Ted Uhlaender hits a vicious one-hopper that appeared to bounce off of Andrews' shin. Mike recovered quickly and threw to Petrocelli at short to barely force Allison at second base. The obsequious Williams then raced to the mound to give Bell some advice on how to pitch to Gary's former roommate on the Indians, catcher Russ Nixon. Nixon proceeded to slap a line drive to left field and Yaz turned tail to make a nice running catch for the third out of the Twins' half of the eighth inning.

Jim Merritt continued on the mound for the Twins in the Red Sox half of the eighth inning, and he began by walking Rico Petrocelli. Reggie Smith faced Merritt next and he hit a ground ball to Versalles that forced Rico at second, but Smith used his speed to beat Tovar's throw to first. The weak-hitting Jose Tartabull was next and he hit a fly that Tony Oliva finally tracked down in front of the Twins bullpen. Reggie Smith tagged up and reached second base in time to put himself in scoring position. But pitcher Bell grounded out harmlessly to Carew at second base and it was on to the ninth inning. The Red Sox were three outs away from staying alive in the pennant race.

The late afternoon sun had given way to clouds and the lights at Fenway Park were turned on before the top of the ninth inning. There was double-barreled action in the Red bullpen with right-hander John Wyatt joined by nineteen-year-old leftie Ken Brett. Brett had made his major league debut three days earlier, pitching two innings against the Cleveland Indians. Twins part-time third baseman Rich Rollins pinch hit for Jim Merritt and he worked the count to 3-2 against Bell. Rollins then hit a sharp grounder to Jerry Adair at third who threw Rollins out for the first out. Shortstop Versalles, who was 1-4, was the next hitter. Versalles had singled and scored the Twins' initial run in the first inning but he was hitless in his last three trips to the plate. Zoilo swung at a 2-2 Bell fastball and lofted a fly ball into short center field where Reggie Smith caught it with ease. Caesar Tovar, who was the Twins' last hope, looped a fly ball down the leftfield line that landed fair just beyond the reach of Carl Yastrzemski. Tovar pulled into second base with a stand-up double.

The next hitter was the ever-dangerous Harmon Killebrew who had walked, doubled against the left-field wall, and struck out the last two times up against Santiago. Wyatt and Brett were warm and had stopped to watch the drama unfold. When the count went to 2-2 on Killebrew, Dick Williams, who was calling the pitches from the Red Sox dugout in the ninth inning, ran out to the mound to offer Bell some tips on pitching to Killebrew. Despite Gary Bell's best efforts, Williams' tips on how to pitch Killebrew, and the manager's pitch calling, Hammering Harmon turned on a 2-2 Bell fastball and drove it high and deep in the direction of the Green Monster. Killebrew's titanic blast cleared the 37-foot wall, cleared the 23-foot screen atop the wall, and was last seen heading in the direction of the Massachusetts Turnpike. The Twins had cut the Red Sox lead to a manageable two runs, and Harmon had tied Yaz for the American League lead in home runs with 44.

Dick Williams decided to let Gary Bell face one more hitter. Tony Oliva, who had driven in the first Twins run with a single in the first inning, stepped in against Bell. Gary threw him an outside fastball and the left-handed hitting Oliva scorched a line drive in the direction of the hole between third base and shortstop. But Jerry Adair had positioned himself perfectly and he snagged Olivia's ferocious line drive for the final out. The ball was hit so hard and grabbed so quickly by Adair that it took a second for the players and crowd to realize what had happened. When they finally processed that the game was over the home crowd let out a roar.

The Red Sox had won the most important game at Fenway Park since their playoff game against the Cleveland Indians for the American League pennant on October 4, 1948. Jose Santiago had surpassed all expectations by holding the Twins to two runs over seven innings to win the most important game of his career. And Carl Yastrzemski had come through once more, driving in four runs, including the winning runs with two singles and a home run.

Jose Santiago told the assembled reporters, "I called down to Puerto Rico last night and told them, 'Have faith in your boy. I'm going to do it tomorrow!' I guess I did," he shouted. Then he walked across the clubhouse to Carl Yastrzemski and planted a kiss right on the slugger's cheek. "You're too much baby," Jose hollered.

On the final day of the season all Jose could do was sit and watch game 162. "In some ways that was harder," Jose remembered. His other memory is talking to Sunday's starter Jim Lonborg who said, "You know Jose, if we win it today you are going to start Game One of the World Series." Santiago recalled that he hadn't given it a thought until then and he put it out of his mind. Jose clearly remembered the celebration on the field and in the locker room after the Red Sox 5-3 victory. "The fans were so excited we didn't think we would get off the field. And we were pretty happy in the clubhouse afterwards. The celebrating really started after we found out the Tigers lost the second game [of their doubleheader] and we were going to the World Series. And Lonnie [Lonborg] was right. Dick Williams came over and told me that I was going to start the World Series opener." September 30, 1967, had been Jose's most important game. But on October 4, 1967, Game One of the World Series would replace it.

Several memories of Game One of the 1967 World Series stood out for Jose Santiago. "I called my parents right after the final game of the regular season and told them I was flying them up for Game One. And I remember how excited the whole island of Puerto Rico was to have a countryman start Game One. It wasn't until later, but I learned I was the first native of Latin America to start the World Series opener. And of course I remember that we lost. I pitched pretty well [limiting the Cardinals to two runs over seven innings] and I hit a home run off Bob Gibson, but we still lost. I still see Bob Gibson a lot and he always says, 'Jose, I love you but I hate you too. I love you like a brother but I hate you for hitting that home run. Do you know how embarrassed I am when people ask me how I could give up a home run to **you**?'"

The Cardinals' 2-1 lead turned out to be the final score, but Jim Lonborg came back the following day with a brilliant one-hitter to even the Series. Game Three in St. Louis produced a 5-2 victory for the Cardinals, and Jose Santiago prepared for a rematch with Bob Gibson in Game Four. "I told my wife, Edna, before Game Four that my arm was dead,

I still hadn't recovered from the first game. But I thought that maybe when I get out there it will be okay." But it wasn't okay, and Santiago didn't make it out of the first inning in a game the Red Sox eventually lost 6-0. That was Jose's last appearance in the World Series.

In 1968, Jose Santiago got off to the best start of his major league career. By late June he had run his record to 9-4, and he had seven complete games to his credit. Dick Williams selected him for a well-deserved spot on the American League All-Star roster.

But then Santiago came up with the first real sore arm of his career. After skipping a couple of starts, Jose agreed to try a start against the Twins in Minneapolis. "I was going along pretty good for a couple of innings. Then I got two strikes on Tony Oliva and I tried to put him away with a slider. I felt something snap in my arm. I had injured my elbow and they had to take me out of the game. I never was the same pitcher again."

Santiago was out for the balance of the season. He split his time between Boston and the Red Sox Triple-A club in Louisville over the next two seasons, but his arm never returned to big league form. "One thing I will always remember," Jose said with emphasis, "is that the Red Sox treated me with as much respect when I was a sore-armed pitcher as when I was an All Star. Dick O'Connell, who was the general manager at the time, was wonderful to me. And the Yawkey's were very special people."

Santiago continued to pitch winter ball in Puerto Rico through the mid-70s. "I still knew how to pitch, but I knew I wasn't at big league form." After Jose hung up his glove for the last time, he continued his long association with the Puerto Rico Winter League. He was a pitching coach, a manager, and he served as the General Manager of the San Juan Senadores. He also established, and for many years operated, a baseball school: "Academia Beisbol Palillo Santiago." For years now he has been a household fixture on TV and radio for the Puerto Rican Winter League. Over almost 60 years Jose Santiago has been for the Puerto Rican Winter League what Johnny Pesky was for the Red Sox.

Jose and his wife Edna celebrated their 50th wedding anniversary in 2014. They have four grown boys Alex, Arnold, Albert and Anthony, and they dote on their two beautiful granddaughters. In 2015, Jose and Edna were visiting Arnold, his wife, and their two granddaughters in Salem, MA, when Jose developed serious chest pains. He was rushed to Mass General Hospital where he had heart surgery and where he was hospitalized for one week. "The doctors and all the health care folks at MGH saved my life," Jose says emphatically. "I can't say enough good things about them."

When I first got to know Jose Santiago many years ago he said, "Herb, I am a national hero in Puerto Rico." He said it in his deep baritone voice with a wink at the end, so I assumed it was another example of his great sense of humor. Then in 1997 I went to visit him in Puerto Rico and he took me to a press conference for the upcoming Puerto Rican Winter League All-Star game. The press conference was filled with media people, All-Stars like Juan Gonzalez of the Texas Rangers, and former stars like Vic Power of the Cleveland Indians and Ruben Gomez of the Giants. But everybody wanted to say hello to Jose. He was like the Pied Piper.

Later my wife, Janet Salsman, and I went with Jose to a Winter League game in Caguas, PR. As soon as Jose was spotted in the box seats, a steady stream of youngsters began heading down to get his autograph. Jose of course obliged all of them and had a kind word for each of them. But after about three innings it was clear that Jose would not get a moments peace and so we called it a night.

It turns out that Jose is indeed a national hero in Puerto Rico!

Chapter 13

The Quiet Intensity of "Gentleman Jim" Lonborg

Boston Red Sox vs. Minnesota Twins, Sunday, October 1, 1967

Jim Lonborg, a lanky, twenty-five-year-old California native pitched the most important game of his young career in this vintage matchup with the Twins at Fenway Park. The drama as to who would prevail for the American League pennant had been played out throughout September. It had been a four-team race until Thursday night when the Chicago White Sox effectively eliminated themselves with a doubleheader loss to the lowly Kansas City A's. Coming down to the last day of the season, the Detroit Tigers with 90 wins could ensure a tie and force a playoff by sweeping the pesky California Angels in their doubleheader that day. The winner of the Red Sox-Twins contest, with each team tied with 91 wins, was assured of at least a tie and would emerge as the outright winner if the Tigers stumbled in either game. Lonborg, a native of San Luis Obispo, California, and a pre-med graduate of Stanford University, was the undisputed ace of the Red Sox staff with twenty-one wins already to his credit. However, the big right-hander entered the game winless against the powerful Twins, a team that had always given him trouble. Lonborg couldn't have known it as the sun came up over Boston Harbor that morning, but he was about to achieve the most important victory of a distinguished career that would span fifteen seasons in the major leagues.

Saturday's contest against the Minnesota Twins featured unseasonably warm temperatures and bright sunshine for most of the game. But overnight a touch of fall crept into New England, and October 1, 1967, broke with a crispness more associated with football than this day's premier event. Lonborg thought it would be a good day for pitchers as he walked to Fenway Park for his big game. The air was crisp but mild and the sun was warming but not too bright from a pitcher's point of view. Lonborg remembers that "it wasn't a perfect day on the mound; but it was a nice cool fall day."

Lonborg was well rested for the day's epic contest. Pitching on only two day's rest on Wednesday, Jim had lasted just two innings before taking an early shower in a 6-0 loss to the Cleveland Indians. When the Indians arrived in Boston on Tuesday for the two game series, the Red Sox held a 13-3 season's edge over the Tribe, but Cleveland proved to be a "spoiler" taking both games from the home team. In his typical forthright candid manner, Lonborg recalled, "I didn't do well against the Indians on Wednesday." With his usual three full days of rest, he felt strong—but not too strong, he hoped.

Jim Lonborg had gone 0-3 against the Twins in 1967 and he was 0-6 lifetime against Minnesota. Lonborg had looked for an edge in preparing for the big game and he thought he had found it by spending Saturday night in Ken Harrelson's room in the Sheraton Boston. In Lonborg's words, "I was a bachelor at the time and I had an apartment at the Charles River complex in town but I didn't think it was a good idea to stay there that night because of all of the excitement going on with my single roommates. I knew I needed a good night's sleep."

Lonborg's thinking went like this: he had a better road record—a sparkling 13-4 versus 8-5 at home—during the season so by treating it as an away game, he would give himself an edge. He followed the routine right through to ordering his regular pregame breakfast from room service. Lonborg reflected that "I just thought it would be different if I treated it as if I was on a road trip . . . having room service meals . . . coming out of the hotel and walking to the park. . ."

It wasn't that Lonnie was superstitious as much as he was analytical and competitive. He considered every angle of every important issue in order to gain the maximum leverage. That was partly his nature and partly due to his academic training at Stanford. In any event, it helped to make him the successful pitcher he had become.

Lonborg was really pumped when he awoke Sunday morning. "We had so much going for us in terms of energy. We had a sense of momentum. It almost felt like we couldn't be denied. When you think about it, we were so lucky really to even have a chance of still winning the pennant on Sunday," he marveled. "We were losing Saturday's game against the Twins until the last of the fifth when we got two runs. Jim Kaat had blown out his elbow and eventually we unloaded on them."

The final game at Fenway Park in recent years had been traditionally witnessed by relatives and close friends of the players plus a few optimistic fans who had purchased their tickets in the euphoria of the previous April. In fact, on the last day of the 1966 season, Red Sox announcer Ned Martin had opened his radio broadcast by saying, "Hello...hello... is there anybody out there?" But this fateful day was perhaps the most exciting of any season-ending game in Red Sox history. A win in the last game of the 1948 season had brought the Red Sox to their one-game playoff loss to the Cleveland Indians, and a win in the last game of the 1949 season would have given Boston the American League pennant, but the Yankees beat them 5-3 at the Stadium on October 2, 1949. There was every reason to hope for a happier ending to the last game of 1967.

Fenway Park's capacity was listed at slightly in excess of 33,000, but on this Sunday the attendance was announced at 35,770, and there had to have been at least 37,000 souls crammed into every nook, cranny and hiding place in the venerable park. It was reported that thousands of Red Sox fans had been turned away from the ticket window prior to the game because the maximum capacity had been reached. The sellout crowd brought attendance for the season at Fenway Park to 1,727,832 fans, up from 811,172 in 1966. The 1967 attendance set a new record for the Boston Red Sox, surpassing the old record of 1,596,650 set in 1949.

At game-time, 2:05 EDT, the air temperature was 62 degrees, there was a 10 MPH wind blowing from third base out towards right field, it was mostly cloudy, and the lights had been turned on at Fenway Park to ensure perfect conditions. On Saturday the VIP box next to the Red Sox dugout had been occupied by Senator Ted Kennedy and Vice President Hubert Humphrey, but in a show of non-partisanship on Sunday

Jim Lonborg shows his Cy Young Award form.

the seats were occupied by Massachusetts Republican Senator Ed Brooke and MLB Commissioner William Eckert.

The game was televised in Boston on local Channel-5, but according to urban legend the video of game 162 was taped over by a video of Bozo the Clown. NBC was covering the game as their game of the week with their "first team" of Curt Gowdy, Pee Wee Reese, and Sandy Koufax. The

NBC video has been lost as well, but fortunately their audio survives and it is quite descriptive. As a large, national network, NBC had instant replay available and for several plays this allowed the announcers to add to their original descriptions. NBC was also televising the first game of the Tigers-Angels doubleheader to other cities, and from time-to-time NBC's Tony Kubek would give viewers an update on that game.

In many ways, Jim Lonborg and Dick Williams represented the odd couple. Lonborg was thoughtful and well-spoken; Williams was acerbic and outspoken. Lonborg could find his way around *Scientific America*; Williams read *Male Magazine*. But Lonborg knew that Williams had made him into a better pitcher. Even if you hated the S.O.B., you had to realize that he goaded you into showing him that you were better than he thought you were. "Looking back I remember how angry he used to make me. I would be furious and I would say to myself, 'I'll show that son-of-a-gun!' It seems obvious when I repeat that out loud now but it wasn't until years later that I realized that was exactly the response he was hoping for!"

While the Red Sox were assuming the mantle of the "Impossible Dream" team, a nickname that took hold in June after it was used in a *Boston Globe* headline, Lonborg was more akin to another Broadway hit. That same season, "A Man for All Seasons" was enjoying a successful run based on the life of the Sir Thomas Moore. Lonborg was close to a Renaissance Man. He had entered Stanford University—the Harvard of the west, or Harvard is the Stanford of the east as some would have it— on an academic scholarship. His first love at that time was medicine.

Jim Lonborg was born on April 16, 1942, in Santa Maria, CA. The son of a professor at California Polytechnic Institute, he had grown up in a loving environment which emphasized the whole person. At age 10, Lonborg played Little League baseball in San Luis Obispo, CA, for the Kiwanis Red Sox. "When we won our championship our coach, Stub Sweeney wrote to the Red Sox and the team sent along individual pictures from the 1952 Red Sox and I got pitcher Mel Parnell. I still have that picture, so maybe I was meant to pitch for the Red Sox," Jim smiled. At 6' 5" Lonborg was better known for his basketball achievements at San Luis Obispo High, but he was the best pitcher on the baseball team. "I wasn't the best player on the team though," he acknowledged. "Our shortstop Mel Queen, who was my best friend growing up, signed with the Reds for around $90,000, right out of high school. He later married my sister Celia and he did play in the majors for eight years."

Jim was good enough on the hardwood that Stanford scouted him in high school, and he played on their freshman basketball team. Jim tried out for the freshman baseball team where he really came into his own. Lonborg's upper body had begun to fill out and his skill on the mound developed along with his physical growth. The Baltimore Orioles were the first team to recognize his potential and they guided him to summer baseball programs after his sophomore and junior years. "I hadn't really thought about professional baseball until I had a good year in the fast college league in South Dakota," Jim said. "I was playing with guys like Jim Palmer and Merv Rettemund, and I was holding my own." The Red Sox offered Jim an $18,000 bonus to sign. "I was certainly loyal to the Orioles but they had just given Jim Palmer [future Baltimore Oriole starting pitcher and member of the Baseball Hall of Fame] a $100,000 bonus to sign, so they couldn't match the Red Sox offer and I signed with Boston."

History was being made on October 1, 1967, since it was the first time in American League history that three teams were in contention to win the pennant on the last day of the regular season. There was a lot at stake and as Lonborg made his way to the mound that day, he knew he was ready. He had told his teammates the day before "this is the first **big** game of my life. This one really matters." He had meant it and he really wanted this one.

Looking back Lonborg didn't feel as if he had really gotten into his rhythm right away. When he had been **on** that year—and he had been **on** a lot—his fastball moved in on a right hand hitter, his curve ball broke right at the left hand hitters and his sharp slider gave them both fits. In the early going, he wasn't quite loose and the ball didn't go **exactly** where he wanted it to.

His teammates were tight as well. The first inning started well enough. Jim got Zoilo Versalles to fly out harmlessly to Yaz in shallow left, and then he induced Caesar Tovar, who was playing in his American League record-setting 164th game of the season, to ground out routinely from Petrocelli at shortstop over to George Scott at first base. Then Lonborg had walked the dangerous Harmon Killebrew on four pitches.

Before the series even started, Williams and the Red Sox had decided that they weren't going to let Killebrew beat them even if they had to walk him four times each game. Lonborg remembers, "We weren't ever going to let Harmon hurt us with one swing of the bat.....we figured that even if we walked him, it would take two or three major hits to get him around the bases." Following the walk to Killebrew, Tony Oliva's line drive hit halfway up the left-field wall. Reggie Smith picked the ball up quickly and fired it towards home plate. Killebrew appeared to hold up at third base but Twins' third

Lonborg looks in for the sign.

base coach Billy Martin waved him home. George Scott came across the diamond, cut off Smith's throw, and then threw the relay ten feet over catcher Gibson's head.

You could almost feel the bubble burst collectively for 35,770 fans. Twenty-one years of waiting for a pennant can quickly make even the most partisan fan into a pessimist. Then big Bob Allison flied out routinely to Yaz in left field, ending the inning and limiting the damage.

After signing with the Red Sox in 1963, Jim Lonborg returned to Stanford and finished the first semester of his senior year. He reported to spring training in March 1964, and he was assigned to the Red Sox Class A team at Winston Salem, NC. After eight impressive starts and six wins the Red Sox front office promoted him all the way to their Triple A club in Seattle, WA. His teammates in Seattle included Joe Foy, Russ Gibson, and Rico Petrocelli. Jim made 22 starts for Seattle and pitched well enough to be invited to the Red Sox spring training camp in Scottsdale, AZ, in 1965.

Jim Lonborg had a great spring training camp with the Red Sox in 1965. In fact, he was so impressive in camp that he was promoted to the big league club. After just one season in professional baseball, he was about to get his first look at Fenway Park.

Jim Lonborg's first trip to Fenway Park is indelibly etched in his memory. "After spring training we came to Boston to get ready for Opening Day. We stayed at the Kenmore Hotel and since I had never been to Boston, I had to ask the doorman for directions to Fenway Park," Jim chuckled. "As I approached the park it didn't look anything like any ballpark I had ever seen before," he recalled. "I was from California and I had been to Dodger Stadium and Candlestick Park, which were newer parks, so Fenway looked very different to me.

"When I walked up the ramp from the concourse behind first base, the first thing I could see was the top of the Green Monster," he remembered. "And as you continue up the ramp the wall gets bigger and bigger. It's quite an imposing sight, especially for a pitcher. The first thing I did when I got onto the field was to pace off the distance down the line to see exactly how far the wall was from home plate!"

Dean Chance was the starting pitcher for Minnesota and he was no slouch. He brought a 20-13 record into the game, and his lifetime record against Boston was 16-8. He had beaten the Red Sox four times already in 1967, with two of these victories coming against Jim Lonborg.

Chance handled the top of the Red Sox lineup with ease—except for Carl Yastrzemski of course—in the top of the first. Leadoff hitter Jerry Adair, who had moved over to second base to replace Mike Andrews, grounded deep into the hole at shortstop, but the slick-fielding Versalles got to the ball and caught Adair at first with a strong throw. Dalton Jones, who had taken Adair's spot at third base, was the next hitter. Dalton hit a hard line drive in the direction of second base but Rod Carew made a leaping grab for the second out. Yaz hit a scorching one-hopper toward the mound but Chance couldn't handle it as it bounced off his glove. Yaz hustled down the line for a single and the first Red Sox base runner. Then Hawk Harrelson hit an easy grounder to Carew and Chance had retired the Red Sox without a ball leaving the infield.

Jim Lonborg set the Twins down in order in the top of the second inning. Ted Uhlaender led off the inning and he flied to Yaz who hardly had to move a step in left field. Rod Carew was next to the plate and the second baseman was celebrating his 22nd birthday on that day. There was no celebrating in the second inning for Carew as he made the second out on an easy grounder to George Scott at first base. The next hitter was catcher Jerry Zimmerman. The weak-hitting catcher hit an easy grounder to Rico Petrocelli at shortstop and the inning was over.

Jim Lonborg was promoted to Boston for the 1965 season along with shortstop Petrocelli, and pitchers Dave Morehead and Jerry Stephenson. All four rookies were in their early-20's, and Lonborg was the oldest at 23, but he also had the least professional baseball experience among the four. The 1965 Red Sox were not a very good ball club. The team lost 100 games, the first time that had happened since the terrible 1932 Red Sox team that went 43-111. And the team finished ninth in the American League, the lowest level in the standings in Red Sox history.

Jim Lonborg got off to a great start in his big league debut, limiting the Baltimore Orioles to two hits in six sharp innings. Although he took the loss, *The Boston Globe* wrote, "The Red Sox lost a game Friday night against the Orioles but found a pitcher." The Boston reporters were pleased to have someone interesting to write about on the 1965 Red Sox and Jim became a media favorite. Drawing on his pre-med course at Stanford he soon became, "Dr. Jim," and once they got used to his thoughtful demeanor he became, "Gentleman Jim," a nickname that fit him then and still fits him today.

In mid-May he pitched a complete game shutout against the Yankees at the Stadium, winning 3-0, and at the end of May, he was 4-2, with a sparkling ERA of 2.48. Looking back at his early big league success, Jim said, "I was the new guy and nobody had seen me pitch before. It took a couple of turns around the league before they developed a book on you." At the end of June his ERA was still under 3.00, but the league did catch up with him in the second half, and he ended up 9-17, with an ERA of 4.47. "I was learning how to pitch while competing at the big league level. I hadn't pitched over 100 innings until 1964 in the minors, so I was taking my lumps, and learning from the experience," he acknowledged.

Dean Chance didn't have a lot of trouble with the Red Sox in the second inning either. George Scott hit a pop-up to Harmon Killebrew to open the inning and then Rico Petrocelli hit a hard groundball right up the middle into center field for a single and his first hit of the weekend. But Reggie Smith struck out on a Chance curveball and catcher Russ Gibson flied out to the right-field corner to end the inning.

Disaster struck the Red Sox for a second time in top of the third inning. Lonborg started off the inning by striking out his counterpart Chance for the first out. Back at the top of the Twins order Versalles hit a popup into foul ground in left field that Petrocelli made a nice running catch of for the second out. Then Lonnie walked Tovar to bring up Killebrew with a runner on first and two down. Jim elected to pitch to Killebrew and the slugger hit a sharp line drive base hit into left field. Yaz employed his classic kamikaze outfield style in pursuit of Killebrew's single but this time it backfired on him. The ball went under his glove and eluded his pursuit long enough for the speedy Tovar to score all the way from first base.

The crowd grew even quieter. Two errors and two unearned runs gave even the most optimistic Red Sox fan pause. And maybe worst of all the invincible Yastrzemski had proven that he was only human. Perhaps the magic had evaporated. As the autumn shadows inched their way across the playing field, it was almost as if the curtain was starting to set on this improbable dream.

Jim Lonborg remembers this as perhaps the darkest point of the game. Five errors against the White Sox in the second game of the season was one thing, but two errors in the first three innings of the most important game of the season was quite another. Lonborg then walked Tony Oliva intentionally since Killebrew had advanced to second on the Yastrzemski error. It was a good decision since Lonborg struck out Bob Allison to end the inning.

Now Lonborg was feeling a lot better about his pitching rhythm. The Red Sox were down two runs but the Twins weren't hitting him hard, and both runs were unearned. Jim was leading off the Red Sox third and he was hoping to get on base to get something going. Get on base is exactly what he did as his bloop hit dropped in front of Oliva in right field. But leadoff hitter Jerry Adair hit into his second double play of the weekend, Versalles to Carew to Killebrew. Dalton Jones hit a hard ground ball towards second base, but Rod Carew scooped it up for a nice play to end the inning.

Jim Lonborg sailed through the Twins' top half of the fourth inning. He got center fielder Ted Uhlaender to fly out to Reggie Smith. Then Carew hit a sharp grounder to Petrocelli's left but Rico made a nice grab and his throw beat Rod to first. Catcher Zimmerman hit an easy grounder to Rico and just like that the Twins were down 1-2-3.

Jim Lonborg showed a lot of improvement over his 1966 season, and so did the Boston Red Sox. The team started slowly and on the fourth of July they were a dismal 29-51, but from that point forward they went 43-39. Jim Lonborg pitched in 45 games, splitting his appearances between starting and relieving, and he got off to a slow start as well. On the fourth of July his record was 4-7 and his ERA 4.98, but for the balance of the season he was 6-3 and he lowered his ERA by one run to finish at 3.86. "Players like Rico and me were starting to feel comfortable at the big league level," Jim said. "And rookies George Scott and Joe Foy added a lot, especially on defense."

Did it bother him to play in front of an average of 25,000 empty seats at Fenway in 1966? "Not really, because we knew the fans that were there were avid fans that knew the game. And when we started to play better in the second half attendance picked up. It's funny because most people didn't notice that we were staring to play better," Jim remarked. "But our diehard fans noticed and responded by turning out to watch us."

The Red Sox fourth started out on a hopeful note as Carl Yastrzemski—who else? –lined a ball to near the top of the left-field wall and beat Bob Allison's throw to second for a double. Ken Harrelson did his best to move Yaz over to third base with a fly ball but it wasn't deep enough and Carl held. Then George Scott scalded a line drive that went straight at Chance who caught it in the webbing of his glove. Yaz had taken off as soon as Scott connected and Chance threw to Versalles to double him off second base.

Lonborg drew Dean Chance as the Twins' leadoff hitter in the fifth inning and NBC's Pee Wee Reese described him as "the worst hitter in the world." Down 0-2, Chance decided to try to bunt and fouled it off for strike three, lowering his batting average to .032. The next batter, shortstop Versalles, was something of a mystery man. In 1965, he led the Twins to the World Series while leading the American League in doubles, triples, runs scored, and total bases, winning the MVP Award in a near-unanimous vote. When he stepped to the plate in the fifth inning he was batting exactly .200. Zoilo's misery continued as he topped a grounder to Petrocelli who retired him easily. Caesar Tovar hit an easy grounder to Dalton Jones at third base and the Twins were down in order once again.

Chance sailed through the fifth as well. Rico swung at the first pitch and he popped feebly to Uhlaender in shallow center. Then Chance jammed Reggie Smith and he fouled out to Tovar over near the third base stands. Curt Gowdy observed, "Yesterday the Red Sox fans were so keyed up and vocal that you could barely hear yourself think. But right now this place is like a morgue." At this point Dick Williams got right-handed pitcher Lee Stange up and throwing in the Red Sox bullpen. If the next hitter, catcher Gibson, got on base, it seemed quite possible that Williams would pinch hit for Lonborg. But Gibby struck out and Lonborg headed back to the mound for the top of the sixth inning.

Harmon Killebrew led off the sixth inning for Minnesota. Lonborg wasn't taking any chances with Killebrew and he walked him on four straight pitches. The next hitter, Tony Oliva had been on base twice, once on his double to score Killebrew and then again in the third inning when he was intentionally walked by the Red Sox. Lonborg got Oliva to a 3-2 count and then struck him out with a curveball. Bob Alison, who was 0-2, was next and Lonborg struck him out looking on a fastball. The inning ended when Ted Uhlaender hit a routine fly to Hawk Harrelson in right field.

Although Lonborg came off the mound trailing 2-0 in the middle of the sixth inning, he still hadn't given up an earned run. Even better, he had really found his rhythm now. His three pitches were all moving and he was able to locate them just where he wanted them. His strike out total had reached five, and he felt that he was setting the pace.

At that point, Lonnie had logged a fraction over 270 innings in 1967. The fact that he was as strong as he was at this point in the last game of the regular season was no accident. Right after the end of the 1966 season, he had gone to Venezuela to pitch Winter Ball for a couple of months. His expressed purpose was to work on his curve ball in tough spots like

2-1 and 3-2. And it had worked. From South America he went directly to the ski slopes where he spent two months working on his conditioning. When Lonborg reported to Winter Haven in February of that year, he was in the best shape of his life. That rigorous program was serving him well on that afternoon of October 1, 1967.

Lonborg was due to lead off the last of the sixth. At that point, Chance looked almost unhittable. He had given up only four hits and no walks. The silence of the crowd was almost eerie. They were disappearing in the lengthening shadows along with the Red Sox' chances. The mood of the fans seemed to be "well, Lonborg is leading off so there's one automatic out—are we ever going to get a run off this guy?"

I asked Dalton Jones if the Red Sox bench was "down" at this point in the game. And he responded, "No, not all. Nobody expected anything from us that year and we had made it to this point. And we got there by coming from behind time and again. Did we recognize how serious it was getting? Absolutely. Were we worried that we couldn't come back? Not for a second."

Jim Lonborg was proud of his skills as a hitter. Most American League pitchers were before the introduction of the designated hitter. But the reality was that he was bringing a .134 average to the plate. Lonborg recalled with some pride, "I could hit Chance. He had this funky windup where he would turn around and you wouldn't see his head. I won a few games that year with my bat. I won my twentieth game by hitting a triple off Yankee pitcher Catfish Hunter. First I faked a bunt, then I swung away and hit the ball over the right fielder's head."

Ever the thinking man, Lonborg considered his options as he studied the field from the on-deck circle. His calculation of all of the combinations and permutations paid off. By the time he reached the plate to face Dean Chance, he had determined that Cesar Tovar was a shade too deep at third base. The perfect symmetry of a bunt just might be the solution to the problem.

Lonborg could fly before his conditioning mishap (read: ski injury) and fly down the first base line he did after he had perfectly calibrated the flight of the ball and the angle of the bat. Third baseman Tovar did not grasp the principles of empirical research nor did he grasp the sphere dropped down by Lonborg. Instead he studied it like some prehistoric relic and looked for the hole it might have emerged from so he could crawl into it.

Lonborg's brilliant play inspired the crowd and seemed to breathe new life into his teammates. In a matter of seconds Fenway Park went from a morgue to a mad-house. One minute fans seated behind the plate could hear Pee Wee Reese doing the play-by-play on NBC and the next minute Pee Wee couldn't be heard by TV viewers at home over the roar of the crowd. The roar continued as Jerry Adair, who was 0-2, stepped in. Adair was first pitch swinging and he hit a sharp grounder right up the middle into center field as Lonborg advanced to second base. Dalton Jones had hit the ball hard twice but he had nothing to show for it. That changed quickly as he slapped a ground ball between Killebrew and Carew and into right field to load the bases.

If you see the 1967 Red Sox as high drama brought to life, you knew you would see Carl Yastrzemski step to the plate at some point with the bases loaded and the game on the line. And every Red Sox fan knew he would get the needed hit in this spot. In this year—his year.

If you thought he would hit a grand slam homer, you didn't know Yaz. He said after the game, "I wasn't going to try for a home run . . . he gave me a pitch I could have hit out of the park, but I hit it for a single." Yaz was such an extreme competitor that he wouldn't chance glory at the risk of a rally-killing pop-up or a double play grounder. His single into center scored Lonborg and Adair to tie the game.

Hawk Harrelson came up with Yaz on first and Jones on third. Chance nearly sawed his bat in half with a 3-2 slider, but Hank managed a ground ball to Zoilo Versalles at short. Then the inexplicable happened. Versalles threw home to try for a play on Jones who was nearly stepping on home plate when Zoilo released his throw. Runners on first and third, no one out and the Red Sox up 3-2. The Twins seemed to be coming apart at the seams!

Twins' manager Cal Ermer had seen enough and he brought veteran relief pitcher Al Worthington in to face George Scott. Worthington kept the comedy of errors going by throwing his first pitch to the backstop as Yaz moved up to third base and Jose Tartabull, who had come in to run for Harrelson, took second. Worthington worked the count to 1-2 on Scott, and then tried to get George to swing at a pitch in the dirt. But the ball got by catcher Zimmerman, rolled to the backstop, as Yaz scored from third with the fourth run and Tartabull advanced to third.

After a Scott strikeout and a Petrocelli walk, Reggie Smith hit a ground ball directly at Harmon Killebrew at first. Grown men and women don't believe in gremlins but one seemed to be loose in this inning. Killebrew bungled what should have been a routine play. The "Killer" played it like a hockey goalie and while he didn't get credit for a "save," the Red Sox got credit for another run as Tartabull raced in from third base. The Red Sox were up 5-2. Worthington finally retired the next two hitters, including Lonborg, to bring the inning to a merciful end for the Twins.

In the normal course of events, a 5-2 lead after six innings with a strong pitcher on the mound would appear safe. But 1967 was anything but normal. Besides, this was a team without the precedent of victory. Twenty-one years is a long, long time between pennants.

The Red Sox had something special going for them as they attempted to hold a 5-2 lead over the last three innings of this, their most important game: Jim Lonborg. Lonborg is as charming and thoughtful a man as you will ever meet. But he is also about as intense an individual as you will ever meet. A dental school professor recalled that "He was as dedicated and conscientious as any student I ever had. It was as if he applied the perfectionism of pitching to the study of dentistry."

Jim Lonborg is an extremely competitive individual. As he faced the prospect of retiring nine more Twins, he applied every ounce of his considerable concentration. In 1965 and 1966, Lonnie had compiled a mediocre record of 19-27. Some of it was his inexperience, and some of it was due to poor support from a lackluster team. But a large part of it was his failure to move the hitters off the plate by throwing inside with seriousness of purpose. To establish the inside quarter of the plate as his territory. To reclaim the outside quarter of the plate for his curve ball.

The Red Sox had counseled him on this subject. Sal Maglie, the Red Sox pitching coach, had continually urged him to employ the "brush back" pitch. Maglie had been so proficient at the art during his days with the Brooklyn Dodgers and later with the New York Giants that he was known as "the barber." And Dick Williams had used his sharp needle on Lonnie on more than one occasion. Williams really knew how to get under a guy's skin.

But most important of all, Lonborg had decided to get tough. He is a gentleman by nature but he is driven to excel and he would never be happy with mediocrity at anything. He had worked hard at establishing his new image right from opening day. He had begun marking the inside of his glove to record every "hit." When he took the mound at the top of the seventh against the Twins, his glove reflected nineteen "scores." Jim told me, "The battle between the pitcher and the hitter is all about who owns the inside of the plate. As a pitcher I have to have the inside, and if the hitter leans over to take it away from me, I have to move him back and reclaim it." He added, "I never felt that I hit anyone—they just failed to get out of the way!"

Lonnie breezed through the Twins' order in the seventh without a scare. He now was 271 innings into the season but he seemed to be getting stronger as the game wore on. The first batter, Rod Carew was 0-2 on his 22nd birthday and after he hit an easy grounder to George Scott at first he was 0-3. Next the Twins sent up Russ Nixon to pinch hit for catcher Zimmerman. Nixon had played six seasons for the Red Sox and he had a little pop. But in this at-bat he could only manage a pop-up that Yaz corralled in short left field. Frank Kostro pinch hit for pitcher Worthington but he hit a lazy fly to Jose Tartabull to end the inning. In the last four innings Lonnie had held the Twins hitless and he had only given up one walk. Six more outs, he thought as he walked to the dugout. Get me some more runs!

But the Red Sox squandered their opportunity to pad their lead in the seventh. Jerry Adair led things off against new pitcher Jim Roland with a screaming line drive that went off of shortstop Versalles' glove to give the Red Sox a base runner. Dalton Jones followed with a nearly identical line drive that bounced off second baseman Carew's glove to bring Yaz to the plate with two runners aboard. Of course Yaz got a hit—a line drive to right field to load the bases. That was it for Roland as Jim "Mudcat" Grant came in from the bullpen. Grant got Jose Tartabull to hit a hard ground ball to Harmon Killebrew at first base. Killebrew threw home to force Adair and catcher Nixon's throw back to first just nipped Tartabull. When George Scott struck out a big chance had gone by the board.

Lonborg walked to the mound to start the eighth inning with a three-run lead. These Twins, it turned out, were not inclined to go gently into the rapidly advancing night. Happily for Lonborg, the Red Sox defense would rise to the occasion and save the day. Rich Reese led off with a pinch-hit single in place of the beleaguered Zoilo Versalles. Cesar Tovar followed with a one-hop shot right at second baseman Adair. Adair fielded it cleanly, brush-tagged Reese and threw quickly to Scott at first for the double play. Two down and no one on! Adair took a spike wound for his trouble and was replaced by Mike Andrews at second. That double play would turn out to be one of the key plays of the game.

And then the Twins erupted again. Killebrew and Oliva put together back-to-back singles to keep the inning alive. This created Yaz's chance to return to center stage. Bob Allison hit a smash into the dreaded corner beside the left field wall. It scored Killebrew and it had double written all over it. But in his trademark style, Yaz aggressively cut it off and came up firing to second. The throw was right on the money and Allison was an easy out to end the Twins threat and the inning. Allison had apparently assumed that Yaz would not throw behind the lead runner and thought the double would be automatic.

For Jim Lonborg this was the first point he felt that victory was assured. "As a pitcher when you go in seconds from a situation with runners on first and third . . . the potential winning run at the plate . . . to a situation where you're out of the inning . . . at that point I was certain that we would win. We had made the big play all year and you felt that if we had to do it one more time we would. Yaz's play made the difference."

The mix of excitement and anxiety was palpable in Fenway Park. Jim Lonborg had more control over the outcome than anyone else in the ballpark. With help from the defense he could hold the Twins to fewer than two runs and the game was won. All Red Sox fans could do was root and hope. Elston Howard, who had replaced catcher Gibson in the sixth inning dropped a line drive into right field to give Boston a base runner. When Jim Lonborg who had two of Boston's twelve hits, stepped to the plate, the crowd gave him a prolonged standing ovation, but Lonnie grounded to short and the inning ended when Howard was forced at second base.

And just like that, the end was in sight. After two hours and fifteen minutes of suspense, all of a sudden the Red Sox were three outs away from at least a share of the American League pennant. The crowd knew that the Tigers had defeated the California Angels 6-4 in the first game of their doubleheader, keeping Detroit's hope for a first-place tie alive, but the fans at Fenway Park were totally focused on the outcome before them. A low murmur could be heard throughout the ballpark. It was if half the fans turned to their companions and said, "You know, I think this is really going to happen!" And half of the crowd replied, "There is a lot that could go wrong." Jim Lonborg was four years old when Boston lost the 1946 World Series, and he grew up in California so he had a clean slate. He was completely confident that he could find the strength in his strong right arm to nail down the victory.

But there was one more gremlin to deal with. At the last moment, a Ted Uhlaender ground ball hit something and caught shortstop Petrocelli right below the right eye. Rico shook it off: this was no time to miss an opportunity for immortality. Rod Carew's grounder to Andrews at second produced an exact duplicate of the Adair double play in the previous inning. Andrews took a rolling block from Uhlaender but was bailed out by Scott's scoop save at first. Two down . . . one out to go! Everything seemed to be coming up lucky two's for the Red Sox in the late innings. Two wild pitches by the second Twins' pitcher in the sixth inning, with the second one scoring what proved to be the winning run. And now two identical double plays in two back-to-back innings.

The left-handed swinging Russ Nixon was due up next but for reasons known only to him, manager Ermer sent up right-handed pinch hitter Rich Rollins for Nixon. Rollins represented the only barrier to the Red Sox' first share in the pennant since their tie with the Cleveland Indians in 1948. Lonborg looked in, went into his big windup and came inside with a pitch that nearly sawed Rollins' bat in two.

Lonborg recalls, "I remember that my last pitch of the game was a fastball to Rollins. At that time I was just throwing fastballs, one after another. I was really pumped up and I was in my groove. I didn't have to go with much of anything else. We had runs to work with. It wasn't a matter then of having to trick somebody at the plate. It was just a matter of going straight in at the hitter."

For sheer drama, the sky-high popup that Rollins hit towards Petrocelli at short can only be compared to one other batted ball: the fly ball that Roy Hobbs hit off the light tower in "The Natural." In reality, Rollins's ball was a looping pop-up but to Red Sox fans it seemed to go up forever. As it reached the peak of its arc, it seemed to have become suspended for a split second. For that split second Red Sox fans throughout New England—the nation really—held their collective breaths. They almost seemed to be saying in unison "this can't be happening; this is only a dream and I'll wake up in a second." Rico Petrocelli told me later, "That may have been the easiest play I had to make all year. But while I was waiting for it to come down, I was saying, 'Please Lord, let me catch this ball!'" Then the ball began its downward descent, gaining in acceleration just like a roller coaster. Suddenly, it was in Petrocelli's glove and time stood still for another split second. An alert cameraman near the Red Sox dugout captured this scene with one single frame of film. It shows Lonborg poised to celebrate on the mound . . . Rico grasping the ball as if it were his first born . . . Yaz beginning his dash in from left field . . . and . . . most importantly, over Yaz's shoulder the iconic scoreboard reading "Boston 5, Minnesota 3." For this single frame, all was right with the world. It was like everybody's first Christmas. The girl of your dreams really did love you. And then the celebration began.

Lonborg remembers it as the happiest moment in his baseball career. Pure unadulterated joy and celebration. Players and fans together: an unthinkable scene in the current day. Mike Andrews and Rico Petrocelli hoisted Jim upon their shoulders and the trio was carried around the field by the surging crowd. It was uplifting at first for the winning pitcher but it soon became downright scary and he had to be rescued by the police.

"The first person I saw rushing toward me was Scotty. And then Gibby was there and Dick and all the guys. Then very quickly as I looked around there were all these strange faces, but they were happy faces. Everybody was yelling, jumping around and enjoying the moment to the utmost. Some of the players were smart enough to run for the clubhouse straight off, but I was enjoying the occasion. I guess I was more personally involved than anyone else."

Rico Petrocelli saw the mob scene that was developing and he made tracks for the Red Sox dugout and safety. "I could see what was going to happen: bedlam! But I still had the ball I caught for the final out and I put it in Lonnie's locker." Carl Yastrzemski told me he took a different route. "I could see what was developing so I ran for center field, lifted the old garage-like door out there, and walked under the stands to the clubhouse. That whole time walking all the way around to the clubhouse I never saw a single fan!"

As the crowd on the field swelled with each passing moment, Lonborg began to have second thoughts about his decision not to run for cover. "When we started moving in the middle of the crowd initially, I thought we were moving toward the dugout. That's exactly where I wanted to go. Next thing I looked up and we were headed for the right field foul pole. Now some of the faces don't look familiar at all. In the middle of this chaos I looked around and spotted a fraternity brother from Stanford that I hadn't seen in years. My shoelaces disappeared, my sweat shirt was being torn off, and my hat was long gone. Finally, Boston's finest came out and rescued me from those happy but wild fans."

Pandemonium reigned in the Red Sox clubhouse. The obligatory shaving cream was everywhere and every visitor had a beer in his hand. The champagne would come later. Tom Yawkey made a dramatic entrance and tearfully embraced winning pitcher Lonborg.

After about thirty minutes, the celebration wound down so that everyone could listen to the second game of the Tigers-Angels doubleheader. With their first game victory the Tigers needed to win their second game to force a one game playoff on Monday. Williams had already decided that Lee Stange would go for the Red Sox.

The Tigers took an early 3-1 lead. As the game droned on, the Angels started to come on and the Tigers began to fade. "Go get 'em, Rig," Yaz encouraged California manager Billy Rigney. Finally, the waiting was over. The Tigers had lost 8-5 and the Red Sox were the undisputed champions of the American League for the first time in twenty-one years. Williams had kept his promise that they would win more than they would lose and he brought home a 100-1 longshot.

Lonborg remembers October 1, 1967, as the highlight of his major league career. "When you combine what we went through to get there, the obstacles we overcame and the drama of the setting . . . nothing can compare."

Lonnie went on to cover himself with more glory in the World Series against the Cardinals. He pitched a one-hitter in game two and a three-hitter in game five. After his first two World Series games his ERA for three of the most important games in Red Sox history stood at a sparkling 0.67. While he ran out of gas in Game Seven, pitching on only two days' rest, Lonborg was the hands down choice for the Cy Young award in the American League. *The Sporting News* also selected him as Pitcher of the Year and the Boston baseball writers named him Most Valuable Pitcher.

The following Christmas Lonborg suffered an injury that would have great impact on his major league career. While his training regimen of skiing had stood him in such good stead for the '67 season, it nearly finished him that Christmas as he suffered torn ligaments in his left knee on the slopes.

Lonborg struggled to regain his Cy Young form in 1968, 1969 and 1970. He even accepted a demotion to the Triple-A farm club in Louisville at one point to try to pitch himself into shape. He had changed his motion to compensate for his leg and it hurt his arm in the process. He managed only a total of seventeen victories over the 1968-70 seasons.

When Lonborg showed signs of promise in 1971 with ten victories, the Red Sox quickly shipped him off to Milwaukee. It was a disappointment to Jim. "I was newly married and thought of Boston as my home. But the Milwaukee club was a class operation." After fourteen wins with Milwaukee in 1972, he found himself traded again. This time he was traded to the Philadelphia Phillies in the National League. "I was fortunate. The Phillies were also a very fine organization. Very much like the Red Sox in many ways."

Red Sox fans may not be fully aware of it but Lonborg enjoyed a number of successful seasons in Philadelphia. In fact, he won seven

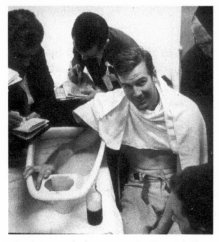

Lonborg soaks his arm and talks with the media.

more games in a Philadelphia uniform (seventy-five wins) than in a Red Sox uniform (sixty-eight wins). His high point with the Phillies was an 18-10 record in 1976. He had learned to pitch with his head—the same scientific approach that had led to his successful bunt to lead off the sixth inning on October 1, 1967—even though some of his arm strength had deserted him.

The Phillies released him in June of 1979. But Lonborg felt he still had some baseball left in him. He had gone to a lot of effort to get into shape for the season and he hooked up with the Town Team in Scituate, Massachusetts. "I enjoyed it but those guys came right of their pickup trucks swinging at the first pitch they saw. I spent all those years learning how to set hitters up and they never gave me a chance!"

Lonborg transferred his earlier interest in medicine to dentistry. He enrolled in the Tufts Dental School in Boston and drew on his baseball earnings to carry his family through four years of schooling. He applied the same intensity that made him a successful pitcher to his new field, and more than held his own against fellow students freshly out of school.

Jim Lonborg has gradually cut back on his time but his dental practice in Hanover, MA, continues to thrive. He lives in his long-time home in nearby Scituate with his lovely wife Rosemary. The Lonborg's six children are all grown and Jim and Rosemary dote on their nine grandchildren.

One last anecdote remains to be told. It tells a lot about the kind of year that 1967 was. It tells a lot about the Red Sox ball club. And it tells a lot about Jim Lonborg. Lonborg was perhaps the last player to leave the clubhouse. Hours had passed since the game had ended and the quiet of Fenway was disturbed only by the sounds of the post-celebration cleanup. Only one other man remained in Fenway Park.

Lonborg made his journey to the top of Fenway. He found his way to the office of the man who **was** the Boston Red Sox: Thomas Austin Yawkey. He found Mr. Yawkey sitting in solitary reflection in his office. Lonborg had barely escaped from the fans with his life, but thanks to Rico Petrocelli he had ended up with the game ball. He walked over to Yawkey, handed him the ball and said, "if anyone deserves this, you do."

Dreams do come true.

Chapter 14

The Fight and Fire
of Dick Williams

Boston Red Sox vs. St. Louis Cardinals, World Series Game 7,
Thursday, October 12, 1967

As the sun rose on Columbus Day, 1967, Dick Williams faced the most important game of his brief managerial career. In spring training the brash Williams had said, "We'll win more than we lose." Not even the cocky Williams had dared to dream that this would mean twenty-two more wins than losses, clinching the pennant by one game on the last day of the season, and coming within one game of the first Red Sox World Championship in almost fifty years. Williams had the ace of his staff, Jim Lonborg, ready to go to the mound in this winner-take-all Game Seven. Unfortunately, because of the way the schedule was set-up, "Gentleman Jim" was going on only two days of rest. He was also pitching his fourth "must-win" game in just twelve days. Williams knew he was taking a gamble by starting the overworked mainstay of his staff. But Williams had come within one game of a championship by going with his hunches all year. The thirty-eight-year-old native of St. Louis had started the season with an one-year contract and a three-year lease on the furniture in his rented apartment. Williams had put together thirteen years in the big leagues through cunning and gut instincts and he had complete confidence in his intuition. "Red" Schoendienst would go with his "horse," future Hall-of-Famer, Bob Gibson, who had three day's rest. Williams would counter with the guts and competitive spirit of Lonborg. Just let Lonborg get through five or six innings with minimal damage and the rookie manager knew he would think of something. Besides, there really was no one else.

In some ways the 1967 World Series was anti-climactic for the Boston Red Sox. Their impossible dream had already come true on October 1 when they clinched the American League pennant. No one had ever expected them to be playing for the World Championship. Plus, the World Series is also a week and a half of parties and celebration.

The Red Sox entered the Annual Classic as 3-1 underdogs to the National League Champion St. Louis Cardinals. And well they should have been. The Cardinals, led by wily manager Red Schoendienst, had finished ten games atop the strong National League.

Schoendienst was Dick Williams' superior in several respects. He had just finished his third full year at the helm of the Cardinals and he was six years older than Williams. Red had played nineteen years in the big leagues including three World Series. He was a starter at second base for most of those years and his batting average nearly always hovered around .300. Schoendienst began and ended his career with St. Louis; he had a brief stop in New York with the Giants and a longer successful stint with the Milwaukee Braves.

Schoendienst also knew how to deal with adversity. In 1959 he had been stricken with tuberculosis and endured months of hospitalization. At age thirty-six, his big league career appeared to be over. But Red refused to give up and achieved a miraculous comeback with the Braves in 1960. Traded to the Cardinals in 1961, Schoendienst batted .300 that season and .301 the next as a part-time second baseman and oft-used pinch hitter. Yes, Red could handle a tough spot.

The Cardinals were led by MVP first baseman, Orlando Cepeda. The "Baby Bull's" numbers: a .325 batting average, twenty-five home runs and 111 runs batted in, were nearly Yaz-like stats. Cepeda fielded flawlessly at first base, and Red Sox fans shuddered at the prospect of his right handed power and Fenway's friendly left-field wall.

The rest of the Cardinal infield was well-balanced. Julian Javier was a steady glove and a solid .280 hitter with speed and power. Dal Maxvill at short had a weak stick (.228) but he made up for it with his slick fielding. St. Louis native, Mike Shannon, was in his sixth season with the Cards and he had made a nice transition from the outfield to third base in 1967.

The St. Louis outfield was their jewel. It featured a future Hall-of-Famer, a home run record-setter, and one star that would become the scourge of the baseball owners. The latter was Curt Flood, who would later pioneer in challenging the players' rights to free-agency.

Labor relations were far from Flood's mind in 1967, and he put together a career year. Curt batted .335 and anchored the Cardinal outfield in center field. Left field was patrolled by Lou Brock, one of the great base stealers in major league history. All Brock did in 1967 was to lead the league in at-bats (698), runs scored (113), and stolen bases (52). Schoendienst hoped that Brock's base running antics would prove a distraction to Red Sox pitchers.

Right field was home for the enigmatic Roger Maris. Roger had astonished the baseball world by smashing 61 home runs in 1961 to break Babe Ruth's record of 60 set in 1927. What is even more astonishing is that Roger was basically a solid, if unspectacular, ballplayer who caught fire for two years, 1961, and the year before when he edged teammate Mickey Mantle for AL MVP honors. The next year his home run output dropped to thirty-three, and Maris would never approach even that level again. Roger performed credibly for St. Louis in the field and batted a respectable .261 with nine home runs.

The St. Louis pitching staff featured four starters all with earned run averages below 3.00. Bob Gibson was the anchor. Gibson had been hit in the leg by a Roberto Clemente line-drive in mid-July fracturing his right fibula bone. He missed seven weeks of the season but returned in early September in top form. Another future Hall-of-Famer,

Steve "Lefty" Carlton chipped in with a 14-9 record. Nelson Briles had his own career year with a 14-5 record, and Dick Hughes had a record of 16-6 and an ERA of 2.67. Joel Hoerner and Ron Willis provided depth in the bullpen.

On paper, the St. Louis Cardinals were clearly much stronger than the Boston Red Sox. If the series went the maximum of seven games, four of the games would be played in Fenway Park and three of the games

Dick Williams at Spring Training.

at Busch Stadium in St. Louis. And none of the games would be played on paper.

Nineteen sixty-seven was the next-to-last year that each league's representative to the World Series was determined solely by the results of the full regular season. The Championship Series playoffs were introduced in 1969, the Division Series playoffs added four more teams in 1995, and now with two wild card teams in both leagues, there is a one-game play-in leading to the League Division Series. Winning the playoffs to get to the Series is like a victory in a 5-K race. Winning the pennant over the regular season is like winning a marathon. It was with the joy and fatigue of the long distance runner that the Red Sox began the 1967 World Series.

Dick Williams spent his last two years in the major leagues as a utility player for the 1963-64 Boston Red Sox. When he took over as the rookie manager of the Boston Red Sox in 1967, he knew that he had to get rid of the country club atmosphere. The most famous Williams in club history, Ted, left camp muttering about the folly of pitchers playing volleyball on a baseball diamond.

Looking back on the last week of the best pennant race in major league baseball history, Williams told me, "I remember with just a couple of games left, the White Sox were playing Kansas City in a doubleheader. The only way I could follow the games was to sit in my car and listen. I went out to my car with a six-pack of beer. When the second game ended, my six-pack was gone and so were the White Sox. Kansas City took both games."

Reflecting on his mind-set on the eve of the World Series, Williams said, "I felt that we would make a good showing in 1967. But I never, not even in my wildest dreams, imagined that we would win the American League pennant."

GAME ONE

Wednesday, October 4
Fenway Park

Red Sox fans celebrated in Kenmore Square and throughout the city of Boston after the Red Sox victory over the Twins Sunday afternoon and the celebrations accelerated after the Tigers lost game two of their doubleheader to make Boston the American League pennant winners. On Monday evening an estimated 10,000 fans descended on the Fenway Park ticket offices to buy the 26,000 remaining bleacher and standing room tickets for the four potential home World Series games. Every ticket was gone in less than two hours. Massachusetts Governor John Volpe joined in the festivities, hoisting an eight foot Red Sox banner to fly below the stars and stripes at the State House. The Red Sox clubhouse was home to hundreds of telegrams including good wishes from acerbic White Sox manager Eddie Stanky, and congratulations to Carl Yastrzemski from the student body at Notre Dame, which Yaz had attended as a freshman.

The Series opener was played before a capacity crowd at Fenway on a sparkling fall day. The crowd responded all day as if they were just happy to be there: as if winning was too much to hope for. Perhaps they didn't know how to behave at a World Series game after twenty-one years of waiting. The Red Sox played pretty much the same way.

In defense of the Red Sox, St. Louis starter, Bob Gibson, was flat-out overwhelming. Gibson had only pitched in 175 innings that year and he was in mid-season form. He "put on a clinic" on the mound.

Williams started Jose Santiago who was simply the best pitcher available. Jose had come on strong in the second half of the season and finished with a record of 12-4. Just four days after pitching the most important game of his life in the defeat of the Twins in game 161, Jose was called upon to start Game One of the World Series. "It was my biggest thrill in baseball," Jose told me, looking back at the opener of the 1967 World Series. "My son Alex had been born a couple of years before, and that was the biggest thrill of my *life*. But in all my years in baseball" he said looking back on 20 years in professional baseball, "getting to pitch in front of these great fans in the World Series opener, that is my favorite baseball memory."

The Cards drew first blood in the top of the third. Roger Maris knocked in Lou Brock to begin this series which would be his last moment in the spotlight. Roger would go on to bat .385 and knock in seven runs in the seven-game series.

The Red Sox got on the board in the bottom of the third through an unexpected source. Much to the surprise of the assembled multitude, especially Mr. Robert Gibson, Jose Santiago homered into the left-field net. Since Jose had only one other home run during his eight-year big league career, we can only assume that Gibson had suffered a momentary lapse in concentration.

Santiago fought through seven innings like a middleweight fighter. He gave up ten hits and three walks. But he persevered until Messrs. Brock and Maris repeated their earlier feat to put the Cards up for good, 2-1 in the seventh inning.

The Red Sox appeared relieved that they had acquitted themselves well in the opener. Looking back on Game one of the World Series, Russ Gibson told me, "We won the pennant on Sunday and we were playing in the World Series on Wednesday. We had been celebrating for three days of course, but the big thing was that we never had any chance to get used to the idea of being in the World Series. Our chances had still been in doubt 72 hours earlier!" Tomorrow would be another day and Game Two starter Dick Hughes was no Bob Gibson.

GAME TWO

Thursday, October 5
Fenway Park

Dick Hughes was no Bob Gibson but Jim Lonborg went Gibson one better. If Gibson was overwhelming in game one, Lonborg was just plan unhittable. Well, almost unhittable. Lonborg set the Cards down like ten pins over the first four innings. In the last of the fourth, lightning struck again. Carl Yastrzemski took Dick Hughes downtown for a two-run home run and the Fenway crowd finally came alive.

Lonborg continued unhittable nursing a 2-0 lead into the last of the seventh. Yaz then struck one more time to put the game on ice with a three-run homer. The lingering suspense was whether or not Lonborg could preserve his no-hitter. This dream was shattered when Julian Javier cleanly doubled into left center with two out in the eighth inning. After the Javier double the sellout crowd at Fenway rose as one to give Lonborg an extended ovation. Jim retired the final four St. Louis batters with ease and finished with a one-hit, 5-0 victory. It was arguably the most dominant Red Sox pitching performance in World Series history.

Looking back on his Game Two masterpiece, Jim Lonborg told me that it was a conversation with Dodgers' pitcher, and future Hall-of-Fame member, Sandy Koufax that stands out for him. "I was talking with Sandy, who was with the NBC-TV crew, before my start in Game Two," he remembered. "He asked me about my pre-game warm-up routine and I told him I worked on each of my pitches and generally just tried to get loose. He suggested warming up by running through the Cardinal's batting order and focusing on how I would pitch to each of their hitters. It worked so well that day that I used his approach for the rest of my career."

And Russ Gibson remembered a very different climate in the Red Sox clubhouse before Game Two. "We might have been a little bit in awe before the series opener, but the next day our attitude was 'Let's get it together and win this thing.'"

"Nobody thought we had a chance against the Cardinals," Dalton Jones remembered, "but no one had given us a chance all season so we were used to it. In fact, being the underdog helped us because we had learned we could overcome anything."

ON TO ST. LOUIS

As the series moved on to St. Louis for Games Three, Four and Five, Dick Williams was going home. Dick Williams was born in St. Louis, Missouri, on May 7, 1929. As a youngster he played all sports, but baseball was always his first love. "We lived close to old Sportsman's Park where the Cardinals and the Browns [now the Baltimore Orioles] played. They both had Knothole Gang clubs that let kids in for free. You were supposed to be at least ten years old, but every year from the time I was seven I would grab my older brother Ellery's pass and act like I was ten. I used to leave school at 3:15, and get to the ballpark about the second inning."

The country was in the midst of the Depression when Williams was a young fan, so buying a baseball bat was out of the question. One of Williams' favorite baseball memories is the day that former St. Louis Cardinal star outfielder Pepper Martin gave him a broken bat. "I ran all the way home, and then I started worrying how my parents would feel about it. But my dad found some tape and helped me reconstruct my bat. Years later, I met Pepper Martin and thanked him for the bat."

The Williams family moved to Southern California when Dick was a teenager. After starring in baseball and football at Pasadena Junior College, he signed a minor league contract with the Brooklyn Dodgers in 1947. A highly-regarded prospect, Williams made it to the big leagues in 1951. The Dodgers of that era were a powerhouse, winning six pennants between 1947 and 1956.

"That team had been very successful and they were very close. No one made an effort to make me feel welcome as a rookie--no one except Jackie Robinson, that is," Williams recalled. "Maybe he realized how tough it is to fit in. Whatever it was, he went out of his way to make me feel welcome and I will always remember that."

The following season, shortly after Williams had won the starting leftfielder's job, disaster struck. Diving for a routine fly ball, Williams wound up with a three-way shoulder separation. Following that injury, he went from being a highly-prized prospect to a well-traveled big league jack-of-all-trades. "In the next 11 years, I was traded six times, spent time with five different organizations, and played four different positions. And I had to become a smarter player. When I was sitting on the bench I would study our manager—and even the other manager—to see which moves they made in different situations. I spent a lot of time studying strategy and human nature. That injury put me on track to become a manager."

Williams spent his last two major league seasons as a part-time player with the Boston Red Sox. "The place was a country club. Players showed up when they felt like it and took extra work when it didn't interfere with a card game," Williams recalled. At the end of the 1964 season, then Red Sox Farm Director Neal Mahoney offered Williams a spot as a player/coach for the Red Sox Triple A farm team in Seattle. When the Seattle franchise was moved to Toronto prior to the 1965 season, Williams was named to manage the club.

"It was really tough financially. As a minor league manager I didn't get paid very much." Dick remembered. "My wife [Norma] sent our son Ricky to spend the summer with me after school ended and the two of us had to live in the clubhouse because I couldn't afford an apartment. The two of us ate peanut butter and jelly sandwiches all summer," he laughed. But Dick Williams' return to the major leagues and Fenway Park was only two years in the future.

GAME THREE

Saturday, October 7
Busch Stadium II

Williams was going home and the series was tied. But even Dick Williams couldn't will Gary Bell into going beyond the second inning of Game Three. Gary just did not have it and left for a pinch hitter after giving up three runs in his brief stint. "I stunk," was Gary's memory of his Game Three performance. George Thomas pinch hit for Bell in the top of the third inning, and Dick Williams went with another Gary—Gary Waslewski—in the last of the third hoping Waz would keep the game close.

Gary Waslewski had spent most of the season with Toronto but he had pitched for the Red Sox between mid-June and late July, and then again from mid-September. He had pitched in 12 games for Boston, eight of them as a starter, achieving a record of 2-2. He had been added to the World Series roster when injured pitcher Darrell Brandon was dropped from the roster. Waslewski faced the Cardinals' top of the order in the last of the third inning and set them down in order. In the fourth inning he struck out Orlando Cepeda, and retired Tim McCarver and Mike Shannon on ground balls for another 1-2-3 inning. In the fifth inning he retired all three batters in order, running his string to nine consecutive outs.

Mike Andrews pinch hit for Waslewski to open the sixth inning and he singled to center to get things started. Jose Tartabull sacrificed Andrews to second and when Dalton Jones singled Mike home to make it 3-1, there was some hope. But Brock and Maris combined again against Waslewski's replacement Lee Stange in the bottom of the inning to make in 4-1. The teams traded runs and the Cards ultimately prevailed 5-2 behind Nellie Briles' seven-hitter.

Williams was distressed by the lack of fire in his team. During the third game Nelson Briles had nailed Yaz in the leg with a pitch that was clearly in retaliation for his two homers in Game Two. After the game, Williams told reporters, "The St. Louis Cardinals are as bush as the name of the beer company that owns them." Never let it be said that Williams would miss any opportunity to motivate his team. After Williams calmed down a little he took Waslewski aside to compliment him on his three innings of work and to promise he would see action again in the series.

GAME FOUR

Sunday, October 8
Busch Stadium II

Game Four appeared to be another "must win" game for the Red Sox. The last thing they wanted to do was go down three games to one. But go down 3-1 they did as Williams' incendiary remarks failed to strike the desired sparks. Bob Gibson was even better in Game Four than he had been in the opener.

He scattered five hits and walked only one in nine complete shut-out innings.

Jose Santiago finally ran out of gas. He had made nine appearances in September for Red Sox, including three starts. In addition, in the past nine days he had made the two most important starts of his career and pitched extremely well in both of them. Jose started for the Red Sox and never got out of the first inning. Jose gave up six hits and four runs: all of them earned. In a curious move, Williams relieved Santiago with Gary Bell who had been shelled out as the starter the day before.

Bell didn't embarrass himself this time but reliever Jerry Stephenson gave up two runs in the bottom of the third and it was all over but the shouting. The way Gibson was pitching, a six-run lead was as sure a thing as a Democratic Mayor in Boston. The two teams went through the formality of playing innings four through nine but the game was not as close as the final score of 6-0 suggested.

It was the general consensus that the Red Sox flirtation with destiny was finally over. They appeared to be overmatched against the Cardinals. The club seemed to have peaked in Game Two and most of the so-called experts thought they would simply show up for Game Five.

GAME FIVE

Monday, October 9
Busch Stadium II

Anyone who thought that the Red Sox would simply go through the motions in Game Five just didn't know Jim Lonborg. Or Carl Yastrzemski. Or Dick Williams for that matter. This team wasn't through yet by a long-shot.

In the diary that he kept all season, first base coach Bobby Doerr noted "Now we're down three games to one, and everyone realizes that we can't lose again. But we've come back all year and I think we will again." All Lonborg did was throw his third superb game in nine days.

All three games were money games: had-to-win games. And all three games were tightly contested from beginning to end.

Steve Carlton started for the Cards and pitched well. The only run that Carlton allowed came on a single by Joe Foy, an error and a single by Ken Harrelson in the third.

Jim Lonborg, however, had pitched even better. Through eight innings he had held St. Louis scoreless on just two hits.

The Red Sox eked out two all-important runs in the top of the ninth. St. Louis manager, Red Schoendienst, elected to walk Rico Petrocelli to load the bases to get to Ellie Howard. The cagey veteran dropped a single down the line into right field to bring in two runs.

Roger Maris homered off Lonborg in the ninth to end Jim's series scoreless streak at seventeen and two-third innings but nothing could detract from his achievements. In two key games, Jim had held the mighty Cards to only four hits and just one run. Here is his pitching line in the three most important games for the Red Sox in 1967:

	G	IP	H	ER	K	BB	ERA
Jim Lonborg	3	27	11	2	13	5	0.67

That is a strong pitching line in any context. As a pitching line in the three most important games of the season, it is Sandy Koufax-like, or of even greater relevance, Bob Gibson-like!

BACK TO BOSTON

Dick Williams selected his starter for the crucial sixth game of the series based on two factors: principle and hunch. Williams had a few choices available to him. Lee Stange had started twenty-four games during the regular season and had a strong ERA of 2.77. But Williams thought he took too long between pitches and caused the fielders to lose their concentration.

GAME SIX

Wednesday, October 11
Fenway Park

Williams startled most of the baseball world by naming little-used Gary Waslewski to start Game Six. Waslewski had only appeared in twelve games with the Red Sox for a total of forty-two innings during the regular season. He was the most surprising choice to start a critical postseason game for the Red Sox since Joe McCarthy picked Denny Galehouse to start the 1948 playoff game against Cleveland. And all long-time Red Sox fans know how that turned out! Williams made his decision partly because he had promised Waslewski a big pitching role after a great relief outing in Game Three. Dick Williams never went back on his word. Williams also made his choice based on the hunch that Waslewski would rise to the occasion. As it turned out, Williams had rolled another seven.

Baseball writers, both local and national, were delighted with Williams' unorthodox choice of a pitcher. The off-day for travel between games five and six is always a challenge for World Series news, but now the media had their story-line. Most stories stuck to the theme of Waslewski as the least experienced starting pitcher in World Series' history. Nationally-syndicated columnist Red Smith compared the Red Sox chances to "Mission Impossible," the top-rated TV show at the time.

Gary felt good about his chances in Game Six. "I had handled the Cardinals in Game Three and I couldn't see any reason I couldn't handle them again." Was he nervous? "Not really. I was excited of course, but Dick said he only need six innings from me and I felt I could do that," Gary remembered 50 years later. "And I had gotten a taste of the World Series in St. Louis with 55,000 Cardinal fans screaming at me.

"If I was nervous it was for my wife Nancy. She was eight months pregnant and she didn't need all this excitement. For me it was almost like any other ballgame. Go to the ballpark, answer reporters' questions—with a bigger crowd of course!" Gary got off to a great start, striking out Lou Brock, and retiring the Cardinals in order in the first inning. In the second inning it was three Cardinals up and three Cardinals down, while Rico Petrocelli put the Red Sox ahead 1-0 with a home run in the bottom of the second. Waslewski gave up two Cardinal runs in the top of the third as speedster Lou Brock set the pace with an RBI single, a stolen base and a run scored to put St. Louis up 2-1. But Boston struck back in the fourth with home runs from Yaz, Rico, and Reggie Smith, giving Boston a 4-2 lead.

Gary held the Cards scoreless in the fifth, but after walking two and retiring one in the sixth inning he was clearly out of gas. Dick Williams came to the mound to call in John Wyatt and the crowd gave Waslewski a tremendous ovation. The Cardinals fought back, scoring two runs in the seventh inning on a Lou Brock home run to tie the game at four apiece.

Dalton Jones pinch hit for pitcher John Wyatt with one out in the seventh inning and the score tied 4-4. Asked how much pressure he felt with the game and season on the line, Dalton told me, "I was very aware of the score and situation," he remembered, "but I didn't feel any great pressure. You feel pressure when you are on a losing team but not on a winning team because you are confident that one of the guys behind you will pick you up," he emphasized. "I felt a lot of pressure the two years before when we lost 190 games, because I felt that if I didn't do it there wasn't anyone behind me to get it done."

Pressure or no pressure, Dalton Jones, who has more pinch hit base hits than any player in Red Sox history, came through with a line-drive single to right field. Dalton came all the way around to score what proved to be the winning run on a Joe Foy double to left-field. Singles by Mike Andrews, Carl Yastrzemski, and Reggie Smith produced insurance runs and the Red Sox took an 8-4 lead into the eighth inning. Gary Bell caused some anxiety for the capacity crowd in the last two innings but he hung in there ensure the win.

When Dick Williams was asked about Waslewski after the game he said, "I thought he was marvelous. I just wish he got credit for the win." Gary's comment was, "When I heard the crowd cheering for me I thought, 'I wished I had pitched better.'"

The Boston Red Sox, who had begun the season as 100-1 long-shots to win the American League pennant, were one win away from winning the World Championship and fulfilling their Impossible Dream.

GAME SEVEN

Thursday, October 12
Fenway Park

Columbus Day is a major holiday in Boston. All of the schools and businesses are closed. There is a parade in the city and smaller celebrations throughout greater Boston.

This holiday spirit added to the festiveness of the occasion. Every fan in New England waited expectantly as game-time neared. Fenway was crammed to the rafters with 35,188 spectators.

This did not include the mass of fans sitting on the base of the billboard far beyond the center field bleachers.

Most of the Red Sox' hopes were pinned on the tired right arm of James Reynold Lonborg. Not counting winter ball or spring training games, at that point Jim had thrown 291 innings of baseball. That translates into perhaps 4,000 pitches. First-year Red Sox manager Dick Williams had added "newspaper columnist" to his resume during the World Series. The headline over his article in the *Boston Record-American* that morning read: "**LONBORG AND CHAMPAGNE.**"

Jim Lonborg, who was pitching on only two days of rest, laughed when I asked him if he enjoyed Dick Williams's journalism. "I know the Cardinal players enjoyed that headline. They had it plastered all over the walls of their clubhouse before the game. Not that they needed any more motivation."

Lonborg's opposing pitcher, Cardinals' starter Bob Gibson had been immense in the series so far. He had beaten the Red Sox in the Series opener 2-1, limiting Boston batters to six hits while striking out 10. In Game Four, he was even more dominating, tossing a five-hit shutout as the Cards romped 6-0, bringing the Cards within one game of a World Series Championship. And Gibson had his regular three days of rest between Game Four and the deciding game.

If anything, Lonborg had been even better than Gibson. In Game Two he had held the Cardinals hitless through seven innings Boston's ace finished with a one-hitter and a 5-0 Red Sox victory. In Game Five, with Boston facing elimination, Gentleman Jim threw a three-hit complete game to keep his team's hopes alive. His achievement of limiting the Cardinals to only four hits over two complete games established a World Series record at the time.

Jim Lonborg managed to hold the Cardinals at bay during the first two innings of Game Seven. "I felt pretty good warming up," Lonborg remembered.

"I had pitched on two days rest several times that year. I felt a little tired, but in a big game like that you are more interested in pitching command than power."

In the top of the third inning, weak-hitting Cardinals shortstop Dal Maxvill led off with a triple off the centerfield wall. Lonborg retired the next two batters, but a single by Curt Flood, and a wild pitch, allowed the Cardinals to take a 2-0 lead. He retired the Cards 1-2-3 in the fourth inning, but Lonborg recalls that he was laboring.

"I think the Maxvill triple was the tip-off that I didn't have my best stuff. We had hoped to score some early runs so I wouldn't have to be quite so fine. But Gibson just overpowered us."

Red Sox fans greeted Bob Gibson with a generous round of applause when he came to the plate in the fifth inning. Gibson rewarded the classy crowd with a shot off the left field wall to the right of the flag pole which caromed into the center field bleacher seats. All true Red Sox fans recognize that pinball shot as a Fenway Park home run.

While Gibson had used power to put his signature on the series, Lou Brock then used speed to ensure that his accomplishments would live on in legend. Brock worked Lonborg for a walk. Then he stole second. Then he stole third. Then he tagged up and scored on Maris' line shot to Ken Harrelson in right. It seems poetic justice that Gibson's athleticism and Brock's speed would seal the verdict for St. Louis. Red Schoendiest's hope that Brock's base running would be a critical difference had come to pass.

Red Sox partisans grew very quiet as the game reached its halfway point. As bona fide Red Sox fans, they had arrived hoping for the best and prepared for the worst. The worst seemed to be transpiring before their very eyes. But this Red Sox team had pulled off more escape acts than Houdini. They hadn't earned the label the "Cardiac Kids" for nothing. They had one last gasp left in the repertoire.

George Scott led off the fifth against Gibson: raw power against raw power. Scott had been disappointing in the series. When he stepped into the batter's box he was just five for twenty-three with only one extra-base hit. But Scott was always a long ball threat and he caught every bit of a Gibson fastball driving it into the deepest part of Fenway. The ball bounced around in the right center field triangle 420 feet from home plate and Scott was hell-bent for third. When Julian Javier's errant relay throw landed in the Cardinal's dugout, Scott came on to score the Red Sox' first run of the game. Gibson cranked it up a notch and he got out of the inning without further damage. But the Red Sox

were now within a grand slam home run of victory and hope burned eternal.

The game, the series and the season turned on the decisions made by Dick Williams over the next ten minutes. The Red Sox season had officially began 230 days earlier on February 25, 1967. Over that time, Dick Williams had made thousands of decisions. Many of his decisions were gutsy; and some of his decisions were courageous. This time he failed to make a decision. He simply let Jim Lonborg walk out to the mound to begin the sixth inning.

Lonborg recalled later, "Dick (Williams) was thinking about taking me out in the sixth but I wanted to pitch. That's the funny thing about the pitcher's role; you always want to go on." The mark of a great pitcher is that he always believes he can get the next hitter out. The mark of a great manager is knowing when to take the ball from a great pitcher.

Bobby Doerr's seventh game journal entry: "I have to believe if Jim had three day's rest, we might have won it. He's been outstanding in his last three games, but today he just didn't 'snap' the ball the way he was in his two previous starts in the series."

Williams' indecision came back to haunt him in the Cardinal's sixth. Tim McCarver doubled off the tiring Lonborg. Joe Foy failed to handle a Mike Shannon one-hopper and two were on with no outs and the pesky Julian Javier coming to the plate. Dick Williams went to the mound to confer with Lonborg.

Williams had one more opportunity to make a tough decision in 1967. Jose Santiago was ready in the right field bullpen.

Williams elected to leave the pressure on Lonborg's broad shoulders and returned to the Red Sox dugout. The only sound audible throughout New England over the next several minutes was the sound of Javier's bat sending Lonborg's 1-2 pitch soaring into the left field net for a 7-1 Cards lead. Lonborg somehow finished the inning through sheer courage. Then he walked off the mound with tears streaming down his face.

The Red Sox refused to go quietly. Petrocelli doubled in the eighth inning, moved to third on a Gibson wild pitch and scored on a ground out. But a 7-2 lead would be too much to overcome. As the Cardinals tried to pad their lead in the top of the ninth inning it was obvious to even the most loyal Red Sox fan that the clock was ticking down on the most amazing Red Sox season of all-time. Recognizing that the end of the year was near, a cluster of fans along the third baseline started to applaud the team. Dalton Jones, playing third base, was one of the first Red Sox players to hear the fans. "At first I didn't know what was going on but when I figured it out I couldn't help misting up." The applause quickly spread throughout the grandstand. And before long every one of the 35,188 fans that filled Fenway Park were on their feet saluting the Impossible Dream Team.

The crowd had one last memorable hurrah left. When Carl Yastrzemski came to bat in the ninth inning, the sellout crowd gave him one of the greatest ovations ever heard in Fenway Park. But Bob Gibson was not to be denied his moment on this Columbus Day. He took the final bow with his celebrating teammates. He had won his third victory of the series with a three hit, ten-strikeout, 7-2 win.

Could the Red Sox have won if Williams had lifted Lonborg after five innings? Maybe. Four different Red Sox relievers had combined to shut down the Cardinals over the last three innings. After the game, Gibson acknowledged that he was "dead tired" and couldn't have pitched another inning.

Does Jim Lonborg ever wonder how the seventh game would have turned out if he had been pitching on three days of rest? "People ask me that all the time. And I always remind them that Bob Gibson would have had one more day of rest as well." Gentleman Jim remembered that the Red Sox locker room was tomb-like after the 7-2, Game 7 defeat. Asked how long it took the Red Sox players to get over their heartbreaking loss, Lonborg responded, "Pretty quickly we realized that we had given it everything we had. It was a very special year."

Red Sox catcher Russ Gibson's memory was similar to Lonborg's. "We were devastated when we lost Game Seven. After all, we had come within one game of becoming World Champions," he emphasized. "But as we talked among ourselves we started to realize what we had accomplished. No one thought we had a chance to win the pennant let alone the World Series. Then we started to leave the World Series loss behind us and enjoy our great year,"

In *No More Mr. Nice Guy*, Williams recalled his thoughts on the eve of his subsequent 1972 World Series appearance with the Oakland A's. He remembered, "Yes, I was happy about making it to my second World Series in five years as a manager. But no, I didn't want to go through another 1967 Series, where I'd suffered not only the pain of losing but the far worse pain of wondering whether I'd done enough. In 1967, I was as awed as the players, and perhaps sometimes I managed like it."

Is this Dick Williams' way of saying that he erred by leaving Jim Lonborg in too long? If so, it is pretty oblique for a guy who happily recounts his confrontations with Yaz in 1967 and who holds nothing back in his recollections of the late Tony Conigliaro. The headline in the next day's *Boston Globe* over Carl Yastrzemski's byline read, "We'll Be Tough For 5-10 Years." Carl went on to say, "...we're going to be pennant contenders over the next five to ten years." Carl Yastrzemski and the Red Sox would next appear in a World Series in 1975.

This is the last entry in Bobby Doerr's 1967 diary: "There were some tears in the clubhouse afterwards, but there was also a lot of pride and good feeling. This had been a truly amazing year. I'm sure that what happened this year will stay with us and the fans a long, long time."

Sweet dreams. It has.